D0206056

Counseling Refugees

**Recent Titles in
Contributions in Psychology**

Counseling Refugees

A Psychosocial Approach to Innovative Multicultural Interventions

Fred Bemak,
Rita Chi-Ying Chung,
and Paul B. Pedersen

Contributions in Psychology, Number 40

GREENWOOD PRESS
Westport, Connecticut • London

Library of Congress Cataloging-in-Publication Data

Bemak, Fred.
 Counseling refugees: a psychosocial approach to innovative multicultural interventions /
 Fred Bemak, Rita Chi-Ying Chung, and Paul B. Pedersen.
  p. cm. — (Contributions in psychology, ISSN 0736–2714; no. 40)
  Includes bibliographical references and index.
  ISBN 0–313–31268–0 (alk. paper)
   1. Cross-cultural counseling. 2. Cultural psychiatry. 3. Cross-cultural counseling—
 Case studies. 4. Cultural psychiatry—Case studies. I. Chung, Rita Chi-Ying. II. Pedersen,
 Paul, 1936– III. Title. IV. Series.
BF637.C6 B347 2003
158′.3′08691–dc21   2002017104

British Library Cataloguing in Publication Data is available.

Copyright © 2003 by Fred Bemak, Rita Chi-Ying Chung, and Paul B. Pedersen

All rights reserved. No portion of this book may be
reproduced, by any process or technique, without
the express written consent of the publisher.

Library of Congress Catalog Card Number: 2002017104
ISBN: 0–313–31268–0
ISSN: 0736–2714

First published in 2003

Greenwood Press, 88 Post Road West, Westport, CT 06881
An imprint of Greenwood Publishing Group, Inc.
www.greenwood.com

Printed in the United States of America

The paper used in this book complies with the
Permanent Paper Standard issued by the National
Information Standards Organization (Z39.48–1984).

10 9 8 7 6 5 4 3 2 1

Contents

Acknowledgments

This book is dedicated to the collective memory of my grandparents and great grandparents, and the untold millions of other refugees and immigrants who struggled, and continue struggling, to make their way across the world to find a better life and fulfill their dreams. I would also like to thank my parents, Walter and Ruth Bemak, who carried their legacies into my family and helped bring my dreams alive. To my daughters, Amber Bemak and Lani Bemak, who will carry the torch of the future in bettering our world and to my wife, Rita Chi-Ying Chung, who without her inspiration, support and collegiality I wouldn't be who I am today.

Fred Bemak

I would like to thank the following people who have been instrumental in life. First to my parents Chung Tai Hing (Jack) and Young Lai Yung (Daphne), who have installed in me courage, strength, tenacity, and endurance. They also taught me my cultural roots and heritage that enabled me to develop a strong cultural identity and sense of belonging and to be proud of my ethnicity regardless of life's challenges. To my younger brother Colin, who was at all times supportive and understanding. To older brother Michael, who was my role model for success in life. To my older sister Elizabeth and my younger sister Annie, who taught me to look inwards and grow from my faults and weaknesses. To my husband and partner Fred Bemak, who assisted me in developing who I am by supporting me as I integrate and negotiate Eastern and Western values. He taught me to appreciate all aspects of live, encouraged my sense of humor, appreciated and celebrated my humble achievements, and was always there during life's challenges. And lastly to Frank Walkey and the late Eru Pomare who had faith in my abilities.

Rita Chung

I would like to acknowledge the staff of the Unaccompanied Refugee and Entrant Minors program in New York State who taught me a great deal about refugee and entrant minor youth.

Paul Pedersen

Chapter 1

Introduction

As we enter the 21st century, refugee migration continues to grow due to issues ranging from ongoing political conflicts to natural disasters (United Nations, 1995). Since World War II various policies have resulted in genocide and the destruction of the cultural fabric of families, clans, and communities in various regions of the world including Africa, Asia, Latin America, and Europe. Refugees affected by war are no longer innocent bystanders caught accidentally in the cross fire; they are targets of a deliberate strategy to terrorize and displace civilian populations (Widgren, 1988). Most groups affected by war tend to be from the poorest social classes, often in rural and small towns (Boothby, 1994). Therefore, refugee migrations in the latter part of the 20th century have been characterized by exposure to serious life-threatening traumatic events (Bemak & Chung, 2002).

Current estimates project that there are 26 million refugees throughout the world (Balian, 1997). As the refugee population increases, there are major social, economic, and political issues that raise growing concern about psychosocial adjustment, acculturation, and adaptability. Although mental health professionals have examined some areas of clinical interventions with refugees, this book is the first to define a model of psychotherapy for refugees, presenting a description of the model and its application through a series of case studies specific to this population. The book is unique in that it focuses on major contemporary issues regarding the mental health of refugees as they attempt to adjust to new cultures and presents a new model of psychotherapy specifically designed for these populations within this context. Furthermore, the book addresses the refugee situation from global perspectives and provides a representative discussion on challenges encountered by refugees in Africa, Europe, the Pacific Rim, and the United States. From a global perspective the book will highlight relevant issues in the refugee experience that are critical for effective and culturally sensitive therapeutic interventions with this population. Although some of the constructs are similar to those of other cross-cultural counseling situations, the cultural dynamics as well as the sociopolitical and historical backgrounds of various refugee groups present unique characteristics that are traceable to respective cultures of origin and cultures of resettlement. These differences must be clearly understood and incorporated into therapeutic relationships at the multiple levels of individual, family, group, and community.

The book is divided into three parts: Part I, Chapters 2–5, presents an overview of the refugee population, premigration experiences, the influence of culture on mental health, barriers to assessing mainstream mental health services, and postmigration psychosocial adjustment issues. Although a majority of the literature in this section is based on studies in the United States, the issues presented are generalizable and specific to refugees regardless of their resettlement country. Chapter 2 provides an overview of the refugee population, including global demographics, who they are, the changing refugee population and subsequent impact on the definition of a refugee, and what unique issues are associated with refugees. The chapter will also provide a brief historical overview of the 1951 Geneva Convention on the Status of Refugees and a discussion on the limitations of the convention's definition of refugee status, as well as current policies and governmental resistance that impact refugee resettlement. The chapter will also discuss premigration and refugee camp experiences, as well as discuss the effects of these experiences on psychological distress. Chapter 2 also provides an overview of the different refugee groups that are at risk for developing serious psychological problems and emphasizes the important interplay and effects of premigration experiences on postmigration psychosocial adjustment. Chapter 3 examines the interrelationship between culture and mental health, including a discussion on cultural influences on the conceptualization, manifestation, and symptom expression of mental illness. Since cultural belief systems impact the utilization of mental health services, this chapter will also explore the use of traditional indigenous versus mainstream Western healing methodologies. The utilization of bicultural and bilingual mental health workers will also be presented. Chapter 4 discusses the postmigration adaptation issues encountered by refugees in the resettlement country beginning with a discussion on acculturation, followed by a discussion on psychosocial adjustment and adaptation issues such as language, education and employment, changing family dynamics, refugee children and school, racism, and other societal barriers. This chapter ends with a discussion on resettlement policies and the implication for refugee mental health. Chapter 5 presents the Multi-Level Model (MLM) of psychotherapy specifically designed for refugee populations giving an in-depth description of the different levels and implementation of the model. All of the references cited in Part I appear after Chapter 5.

Part II, Chapters 6–24, presents 18 diverse case studies to illustrate the application of the MLM. To assist the reader in applying the MLM, each case study is divided into five sections: (a) a description of the situation, (b) critical incident, (c) sequence of events, (d) key clinical questions, and (e) the application of the Multi-Level Model of psychotherapy. Different refugee groups are presented to illustrate the applicability of the model for the refugee population. Although the case studies are based in the United States, it is the experience of the authors that similar situations occur in other resettlement countries, and therefore both the model and the case study examples are relevant to refugees globally.

It should be noted that the case studies are not to be used as stereotyping specific refugee groups but rather to illustrate the diverse application of the MLM with different refugee populations. It is important to acknowledge and understand intergroup and intragroup differences within and between refugee groups. For example, it has been found that there are intergroup differences within the Southeast Asian refugee population with variations in the predictors and level of distress among Vietnamese, Cambodian, and Lao refugees (Chung & Kagawa-Singer, 1993; Chung & Bemak, 2002). Furthermore, gender differences were also found between and within each of the Southeast Asian refugee groups (Chung & Bemak, 2002; Chung, Kagawa-Singer, & Bemak, 1998). Therefore the reader is cautioned not to stereotype refugees in specific ethnic or cultural categories but to be aware of intergroup differences and differences in the intersect of gender by ethnicity. The case studies, however, do provide a generalized description of the refugee situation and applicability of the MLM.

Part III, Chapters 25–30, presents a representative global perspective on refugees written by mental health experts working in Africa, Europe, and the Pacific Rim. Chapter 25, by Edvard Hauff, discusses the refugee situation in Norway, looking at the numbers of refugees as well as the similarities and differences encountered by different refugee groups that cause differences in adjustment. Refugee adjustment and adaptation is discussed within the unique Norwegian cultural and sociopolitical context and includes an overview of refugees' access to mental health services in Norway and an analysis of opportunities for refugees to find meaningful activities in the new country.

Chapter 26 presents the Swedish perspective on refugee adjustment, resettlement, acculturation, and mental health. To provide a framework of understanding refugee resettlement in the Swedish context, the chapter begins with a discussion on aspects of Swedish multicultural society and a brief overview of migration patterns. Solvig Ekblad provides a discussion on culturally specific mental health interventions in Sweden, taking into account governmental policies, health and medical care issues, mental health utilization of the refugee populations, and community, family, children, and gender issues.

Chapter 27 discusses the situation with southern Sudanese refugees living in northern Uganda. In this chapter Nancy Baron describes the process of the southern Sudanese refugees moving from transit camps into settlement sites, describing the focus on the refugees to become self-reliant and better adjusted in the new country. The chapter discusses the challenges in implementing this process and similar backgrounds yet inherent cultural differences between the Sudanese and the Ugandans. Nancy Baron describes the challenges for refugees in Uganda, discussing issues such as the overriding feeling of threat experienced by Ugandans living in areas where they are outnumbered by refugees, unique challenges of resettlement faced by southern Sudanese refugees when they are forced to be self-reliant after years of unstable dependency and learned helplessness, and the ongoing activity from Ugandan rebels who periodically raid refugee camps and settlement sites to acquire food and abduct youth and women. Finally, the chapter discusses the changing psychosocial problems of these long-term refugees and the efforts to implement sustainable community-based psychosocial and mental health interventions.

Chapter 28 presents cultural problems encountered by Western counselors working with Ethiopian refugees. Lewis Aptekar skillfully discusses cultural challenges in working with Ethiopian refugees in Ethiopia. The chapter provides examples of how traditional Western counseling techniques are not culturally appropriate and therefore ineffective for this population. The chapter also discusses issues facing the professional mental health practitioner, exploring how the counselor's individual need to be a helper promotes an "innocence" that may, in the long term, be detrimental to the client. Aptekar highlights the need for Western counselors to be aware, understand, acknowledge, and accept traditional indigenous healing methods and the integration of Western and traditional healing methodologies.

Chapter 29 provides a New Zealand perspective on refugee mental health. The chapter begins with a historical perspective on the refugee resettlement in New Zealand and describes current refugee resettlement policy. Alan Chapman presents current mental health services, service delivery models, and issues encountered in the delivery of effective services for the refugee population.

Given the recent events of September 11, 2001, with the attack on the United States, Fred Bemak and Rita Chi-Ying Chung examine the current and previous plight of Afghan refugees (Chapter 30). They provide an overview of the historical and present events that have precipitated refugee migration as well as a discussion of the religious, sociocultural, and gender issues that relate to psychological well-being. Included in this chapter is an examination of cultural and religious healing practices that impact the Afghan refugees' mental health.

Chapter 31 concludes the book and summarizes the issues and challenges encountered by refugees in resettlement countries. The chapter highlights the need to examine the refugee situation from a global perspective. The final chapter underscores the need for mental health professionals to employ culturally responsive treatment methods as discussed in the MLM in order to be effective with this population. The MLM also emphasizes the changing role of the mental health professional that includes taking a leadership role and being an advocate and change agent, that are essential in working toward social justice.

Part I

Refugee Population: Overview of Refugee Population, Premigration Experiences and Psychological Distress, Culture and Mental Health, Barriers to Mental Health, Acculturation, and Postmigration and Psychosocial Adjustment Issues

Chapter 2

Overview of Refugee Population and Premigration Experiences

OVERVIEW OF REFUGEE POPULATION

It has been estimated that there are close to 70–150 million displaced persons in the world today as a result of ongoing political instability, regional and national conflicts, war, genocide, social and economic upheaval, poverty, natural disasters, deportation, and population increase (United Nations, 1995). Displaced persons are classified as "refugees" if they travel within the borders of their own countries or travel to other impoverished countries. According to the United Nations (UN) 1951 Geneva Convention definition, the term *refugee* applies to "any person who . . . owing to a well-founded fear of being persecuted for reasons of race, religion, nationality, membership in a particular social group or political opinion, is outside the country of his nationality, and is unable or, owing to such fear, is unwilling to avail himself of the protection of that country" (UN, 1995). This definition therefore includes displaced people who are in refugee camps in hope of resettlement.

International refugees are classified as those who have resettled in established nations. In 1976 it was estimated that there were 2.7 million international refugees throughout the world: by 1982 this number had increased to 10.3 million; and by 1997 there were estimates of more than 26 million international refugees (Balian, 1997), although numbers may actually be much higher since they are based on recognition by government agencies or the United Nations

High Commission on Refugees (UNHCR). Official classification as a refugee is sometimes difficult, as illustrated in 1997 when only 35% of those who applied for refugee status in asylum countries were recognized, rejecting 65% of the applicant claims (UNHCR, 1998).

At the end of World War II refugee migration was due mainly to the destruction in Europe and the political, religious, and ideological conflicts in China and India (Marsella, Bornemann, Ekblad, & Orley, 1994). Since World War II there has been a steady flow of refugees to industrialized nations in North America, Europe, Australia, and New Zealand. Today the immigration problem has expanded because of the worldwide local and regional conflicts and natural disasters. For example, it is estimated that the wars in the former Yugoslavia have produced more than 2.5 million refugees, and within the Horn of Africa region alone it is estimated that at any given time, more than 1 million refugees are facing the threat of starvation (Marsella et al., 1994). Amnesty International USA stated that the problems of the world's displaced persons are not likely to improve as human rights violations around the world continue to grow (Healey, 1993). Most wars are now within, and not between, countries, especially in Africa, but also in the Balkans, Chechnya, Sri Lanka, and Afghanistan. Civil wars have pitted civilian militias against government armies. Rebel groups have forcibly recruited civilians to fight, and the populations of whole villages or towns have sometimes become hostages of one side or the other. It has been estimated that there are currently 35 armed conflicts going on around the world (*The Economist*, 2001). Some of these wars are the aftermath of geopolitical fallout after the Cold War and thus may abate. In contrast, others are the product of collapsing states, heightened ethnic tensions, and violence driven by economic goals (such as diamond extraction in Sierra Leone and battles for oil in Angola), while some are simply the result of large-scale banditry (*The Economist*, 2001). Most recently, the September 11 terrorist attacks in the United States have prompted a call by the United States to world governments to collaborate in a global eradication of terrorism. To date, this has resulted in a joint effort by the United States, the United Kingdom, and Australia in the retaliation of the events of September 11 by bombing Afghanistan and by numerous detentions and arrests of suspected terrorists worldwide. The retaliations have produced a dramatic increase in the number of Afghan refugees, with estimates of 1.5–2 million refugees, and therefore resulting in the UNHCR designating this group with emergency status (Pomfret, 2001). The large numbers of Afghan refugees who have been abruptly dislodged from their homes and communities, and have experienced the horrors of war, starvation, and death, are yet another example of the desperate need to provide assistance to refugee populations that goes beyond attending to basic needs of food, clothing, and shelter.

Despite the reasons for international migration, whether due to war, conflict, violence, or natural disasters, the outcome of these events produces the same results of poverty, starvation, disease, brutality, and psychological degradation. Most of the world's international refugees are located in Africa, Asia, the Middle

East, Southeast Asia, Central America, eastern Europe, and Russia. A majority of the refugees in the world today are women, children, and handicapped people who often lack the mental and physical resources to survive under harsh conditions (Marsella et al., 1994). In fact, UNHCR's assisted refugee population consists of an equal distribution of women and men of all ages; however, refugees who apply for asylum status in industrialized countries are predominantly male (UNHCR, 1998).

To truly understand the situation of refugees, it is important to comprehend the distinction between refugees and immigrants, or "forced" versus "free" migration. According to Murphy (1977) refugees are forced to leave their country of origin, based on the 1951 Geneva Convention on the Status of Refugees (U.N. Convention Relating to the Status of Refugees, 1951, 31 [1]), which provided protective guidelines and protocol for refugee migration. Refugees are therefore distinguished from other migrants, such as immigrants, sojourners, or guest workers, primarily by the involuntary nature of their departure that results in displacement by events outside of their control, such as war and political turmoil. These circumstances make it no longer viable to remain in their home countries and lead their customary way of life. Consequently, the determination of the refugee status is based on involuntary and sudden movement.

The result of this abrupt departure is that refugees are not prepared psychologically or pragmatically for the rapid movement and transitions. They are faced with uncertainty, chaos, personal danger, and complete disruption of normal life-sustaining processes. Loss of reference groups such as family and community, culture, and country may mean, for the individual, loss and disruption of occupation, status, identity, and role definition. In addition, many were victims of torture, rape, brutality, and other human atrocities before, during, and after their escape from their home country and overwhelmed by uncertainty, despair, and desperation. For many refugees, reaching refugee camps symbolizes hope for psychological and physical safety and the beginning of a semblance of order and meaning in their lives. Unfortunately, the refugee camps are oftentimes riddled with problems of overcrowding, poor nutrition, unsanitary conditions, poor medical care, and continued violence that contribute to a perpetuation of earlier psychological problems.

UN 1951 GENEVA CONVENTION ON THE STATUS OF REFUGEES

Despite growing numbers of refugees, many countries are increasingly reluctant to resettle them. There has been some international protest and resistance to the convention, arguing that the 50-year-old Geneva Convention is outdated and irrelevant. The result of the reluctance to adopt or support the convention has, in some instances, resulted in individual governments more rigidly interpreting the 1951 UN Convention governing the determination of refugee status (Jupp, 1994; UNHCR, 2001). To fully understand governmental reactions toward refugees, and hence refugee policies, a discussion of the history of the 1951 convention, as well as a critique, will be presented.

Throughout history people have fled numerous communities to avoid persecution. Simultaneously as people escaped from these communities, a tradition of offering asylum evolved to offer a safe haven and provide basic needs. It was not until the early 20th century that nations began to develop an international conscience regarding the assistance of refugees. The first refugee High Commission of the League of Nations, the precursor of the United Nations, was appointed in 1921. The United Nations Relief and Rehabilitation Agency (UNRRA) assisted 7 million people during and after World War II, and the International Refugee Organization (IRO) created in 1946 resettled more than 1 million displaced Europeans around the world and helped 73,000 civilians to return to their former homes (UNHCR, 2001). Subsequently, international laws governing the plight of refugees were established. The 1933 League of Nations' Convention Relating to the International Status of Refugees and the 1938 Convention Concerning the Status of Refugees provided limited protection for displaced peoples. The 1933 convention introduced the notion that signatory states were obligated not to expel authorized refugees from their territories and to avoid "no-admittance (of refugees) at the frontier" (UNHCR, 2001, p. 8).

Several years after the end of World War II there were still hundreds of thousands of refugees wandering aimlessly across Europe or squatting in makeshift camps (UNHCR, 2001). The lack of success and legal protection of the early refugee organizations prompted a global discussion on the status of refugees. Twenty-six countries participated in discussions about the state of refugees in the world. Although the countries were mainly Western or liberal in orientation, other countries such as Iraq, Egypt, and Colombia also participated, (UNHCR, 2001). The meetings were limited to mainly refugees in Europe and to events occurring before January 1, 1951. A major controversial debate was over who could be considered a refugee. Some countries favored a general description that included all future refugees. Other countries wanted to limit the definition to existing refugees. The outcome of the discussion was the 1951 Geneva Convention providing a general definition for refugee status that included a "well-founded fear of persecution" and was limited to those who had become refugees as a result of events occurring before January 1, 1951 (UNHCR, 2001, p. 8).

Another important provision of the convention that was strongly debated was the obligation by governments not to expel or return (refouler) an asylum seeker to a territory where the refugee faced persecution. The debate was over whether nonrefoulement applied to persons who had not yet entered a country and, therefore, whether governments were under any obligation to allow large numbers of persons claiming refugee status to cross their frontiers (UNHCR, 2001). Although the principle of nonrefoulement is now generally recognized, it still presents controversy. An example is the 1993 decision in which the U.S. Supreme Court concluded that immigration officials did not strictly contravene the convention when they seized and repatriated boatloads of Haitian asylum seekers in waters outside U.S. territory.

Despite strong and heated debates, in December 1952 Denmark became the first country to ratify the convention. After five additional countries—Norway, Belgium, Luxembourg, the Federal Republic of Germany, and Australia—had also consented, the convention officially came into force on April 22, 1954. The convention was not only a global instrument that provided a general definition of the term *refugee* and *refugee rights*, but it clearly stated the obligations of refugees toward host countries. To avoid the situation in which refugees might exploit and not conform to the laws of the resettlement country, the convention stipulated those who would not be covered by its provisions in its "exclusion clause" (e.g., people who commit war crimes). Table 2.1 provides a list of countries, as of May 2001, participating in the 1951 Geneva Convention.

Table 2.1
Participants to the 1951 Convention and/or the 1967 Protocol Relating to the Status of Refugees (at 1st May)

Albania	China	Greece
Algeria	Colombia	Guatemala
Angola	Congo	Guinea
Antigua and Barbuda	Costa Rica	Guinea-Bissau
Argentina	Côte d'Ivoire	Haiti
Armenia	Croatia	Holy See
Australia	Cyprus	Honduras
Austria	Czech Republic	Hungary
Azerbaijan	Democratic Republic	Iceland
Bahamas	of the Congo	Iran (Islamic Republic of)
Belgium	Denmark	Ireland
Belize	Djibouti	Israel
Benin	Dominica	Italy
Bolivia	Dominican Republic	Jamaica
Bosnia and	Ecuador	Japan
Herzegovina	Egypt	Kazakhstan
Botswana	El Salvador	Kenya
Brazil	Equatorial Guinea	Korea (Republic of)
Bulgaria	Estonia	Kyrgyzstan
Burkina Faso	Ethiopia	Latvia
Burundi	Fiji	Lesotho
Cambodia	Finland	Liberia
Cameroon	France	Liechtenstein
Canada	Gabon	Lithuania
Cape Verde	Gambia	Luxembourg
Central African Republic	Georgia	Macedonia (former
Chad	Germany	Yugoslav Republic of)
Chile	Ghana	Madagascar

(continued)

Table 2.1 (*continued*)

Malawi	Romania	Tajikstan
Mali	Russian Federation	Tanzania
Malta	Rwanda	(United Republic of)
Mauritania	Saint Vincent and	Togo
Mexico	the Grenadines	Trinidad and Tobago
Monaco	Samoa	Tunisia
Morocco	Sao Tome	Turkey
Mozambique	and Principe	Turkmenistan
Namibia	Senegal	Tuvalu
Netherlands	Seychelles	Uganda
New Zealand	Sierra Leone	United Kingdom
Nicaragua	Slovakia	United States of America
Niger	Slovenia	Uruguay
Nigeria	Solomon Islands	Venezuela
Norway	Somalia	Yemen
Panama	South Africa	Yugoslavia
Papua New Guinea	Spain	Zambia
Paraguay	Sudan	Zimbabwe
Peru	Suriname	
Philippines	Swaziland	
Poland	Sweden	
Portugal	Switzerland	

Source: UNHCR, 2001.

   The UNHCR was established in 1950 and the foundation of its work was to carry out the mission of the 1951 convention. It was anticipated that the "refugee crisis" could be cleared up quickly within a 3-year time period, harboring the expectation that UNHRC would be disbanded afterwards. However, 50 years later the world continues to face global instability, resulting in the convention still having significance and the continuation of UNHCR, which has assisted an estimated 50 million people in rebuilding their lives (UNHCR, 2001). Although there have been changes to the convention, with continued global crises, from Europe in the 1950s, Africa in the 1960s, followed by continuing problems in Africa, Asia, Europe, and Latin America, and current post-September 11 problems in Afghanistan and other related countries, it has been argued that these current crises have outgrown parts of the original document and the 1967 Protocol to the convention, which eliminated the time constraints and geographical restrictions.

   For instance, as the number of people seeking safe refuge increased to 27 million in 1995 and as new categories of exiles, such as the internally displaced people were created, the Geneva Convention is outdated and irrelevant to the current needs and issues. Crises such as those in Kosovo provide another example of sudden dramatic numbers of refugees seeking safe haven. In addition, intercontinental and international travel has become far easier, creating a growing business in human trafficking of illegal immigrants seeking asylum. Governments, especially in Europe, have reported that they are overwhelmed with this situation (UNHCR, 2001). Furthermore, it is noteworthy that the original 1951 convention delegates were all males and never considered gender-based persecution as becoming a major problem.

Given the growing refugee situation, the limitations of the convention, and xenophobia in resettlement countries, some countries that welcomed refugees during earlier times or had accepted large groups for political as well as humanitarian considerations began to close their doors. This resulted in perceptions that certain formerly responsive countries were significantly less open to refugee resettlement, so that terms such as "fortress Europe" was coined (UNHCR, 2001). Inevitably, the convention came under closer scrutiny leaving issues open to interpretation. This was evident with such terms as *persecution*, which was not defined by the Geneva Convention, leaving the definition open to more rigid interpretations. Given a consensual agreement about the definition of persecution, some countries argue that the nature of persecution has changed over the past 50 years and that people who flee civil war, generalized violence, or a range of human rights abuses in their home countries, and who usually do so in large numbers, are not fleeing persecution per se. In contrast, the UNHCR argued that according to the convention, war and violence have been used increasingly as instruments of persecution. For example, conflicts in the former Yugoslavia, the Great Lakes region of Africa, and Kosovo produced violence that was deliberately used to persecute specific communities, whereby ethnic or religious "cleansing" was the ultimate goal of those conflicts.

The controversy continues to be over the "agents of persecution." In 1951 it was generally assumed to be states. Now, refugees more often flee areas were there is no functioning government, where they are victims of shadowy organizations, rebel movements, or local militia. Some countries insist that actions by these "nonstate agents" cannot be considered "persecution" under the convention. However, UNHCR believes that the source of the persecution is less a factor in determining refugee status than whether mistreatment stems from one of the grounds stipulated in the convention. In 2000 the European Court of Human Rights reaffirmed that persecution by nonstate agents is still persecution, and therefore returning asylum seekers to situations in which they could face persecution violates the European Convention of Human Rights. Some governments argued that the convention only applies to individuals and does not apply to large groups of people seeking asylum in a country en masse, which is increasingly the case (UNHCR, 2001).

Unfortunately, this debate remains highly controversial and presents a complex legal challenge as illustrated in the hijacked Afghan airliner that was planned in London's Stansted airport in 2000. This incident reached international attention. In the beginning the British media greeted the Afghan passengers as innocents escaping Taliban rulers. However, the rising xenophobia in Britain quickly turned the welcome into condemnation so that even women and children were denounced by some newspapers as frauds and "bogus" asylum seekers. The hijackers claimed that they had escaped Afghanistan only one step ahead of the Taliban, who had already tortured some of their group. The British government insisted the Afghans could not remain in the United Kingdom and should be returned home at the earliest possible time without exception. Under the "exclusion clause" in the 1951 convention, persons involved in hijacking normally could be denied refugee status. UNHCR, however, insisted that, despite growing pressure from governments worried about increased terrorism, even seemingly clear-cut exclusion situations must be treated with the utmost delicacy, an approach vindicated by the hijack drama.

GENDER VIOLENCE AND REFUGEE STATUS

The 1951 convention neglected to include gender issues on its list of grounds for refugee status. To date there has been little thought given to the forms of persecution that might only affect women despite the growing recognition that gender-related violence under certain circumstances falls within the refugee definition. Although it was recognized that women may be refugees in their own right, they have had difficulty asserting these claims (UNHCR, 2001). For example, it is a common occurrence that husbands play a dominant role in interviews, causing wives to be more silent and unable to share their personal stories. In fact, women may often hide or avoid the topic of rape or sexual violations from everyone, including husbands and family members for fear of being stigmatized and ostracized. This code of silence is further exacerbated by insensitivity to gender differences in the interview process where men are frequently the interviewers and other family members are present during the interviews.

Issues around gender have been long-standing. Gender-based persecution was first identified in the 1980s during the first UN Decade for Women. In 1984, the European Parliament passed what was then a revolutionary declaration, asking states to consider women who transgress religious or societal norms as a "particular social group" for the purpose of determining refugee status. Some critics viewed this as Western impingement on cultural traditions of non-Western societies. Others felt it was too broad and argued that persecution needed to be personal and specific. In 1985, UNHCR's Executive Committee adopted its first Conclusion on Refugee Women and International Protection, and in 1988 UNHCR organized its first Consultation on Refugee Women.

In the 1990s the human rights violation of women gained visibility and international recognition. By 1991, UNHCR issued its "Guidelines on the Protection of Refugee Women" (UNHCR, 2001). In 1993 Canada's Immigration and Refugee Board published groundbreaking guidelines on "Women Refugee Claimants Fearing Gender-Related Persecution" (UNHCR, 2001). The United States, Australia, and the United Kingdom followed with their own guidelines. Today many countries are increasingly hesitant to deny claims from women using the "cultural relativism" argument, that is, the violations of women's rights are private incidents specific to a particular religion or culture. However, a few countries, led by Germany, maintain the argument that for individuals to be recognized as refugees, the persecution feared must be perpetrated by the state or by an agent of the state. Nevertheless, UNHCR and the majority of asylum countries insist that what is important is not who perpetrates the harm, but whether the state is willing and able to protect the victim. Related to this is the controversial issue that questions whether there must be malicious intent to harm the victim. This is extremely important in view of traditional practices such as female genital mutilations, where it is certainly not the intent of the perpetrators to harm girls, even though it is widely accepted that the practice results in serious damage.

Women are targeted for persecution for a number of other reasons. They may face maltreatment because of their own opinions as well as the opinions of their husbands. Women can face discriminatory treatment compared to their male counterparts because of religious norms, such as dress, education, employment, and travel. This is particularly evident in fundamentalist Islamic countries, where women's dress or prohibition to attend schools may be socially institutionalized or even become law. Categorizing women as having "membership in a particular group" has created controversy. Though it has been agreed that some women may be considered part of a "particular social group" for the purpose of refugee status determination, the debate is focused on the broadness of the definition. This issue relates specifically to women who are victims of domestic abuse, which is the leading cause of injury to women worldwide (UNHCR, 2001), yet is not directly correlated with determining refugee status. The U.S. Attorney General, Janet Reno, had to deal with this complex issue before leaving office in January 2001. She subsequently ordered the Board of Immigration Appeals to review a 1999 decision to deny asylum to a severely battered Guatemalan woman who had sought protection in the United States from abuse by her former husband.

A historic development occurred in Rome, in July 1998, with the adoption of the Statute of the International Criminal Court. The court provided a broad definition of gender-related acts, such as rape, sexual slavery, enforced prostitution, forced pregnancy, and enforced sterilization. In February 2001, the International Criminal Court for the former Yugoslavia handed down its first convictions of Bosnian Serb officers for rape as a crime against humanity. Even so, 50 years after the adoption of the 1951 Geneva Convention there are still five grounds for recognizing someone as a refugee that generally do not include situations such as the ruling against the Bosnian Serb officers. Although it has been suggested that gender should be included as the sixth ground, to date this has not been done. The argument against including this sixth ground has been the contention that there is a global recognition of gender-related issues so that case law from around the world already provides ample evidence that gender-related claims can be handled within the framework of the existing convention.

GLOBAL PERSPECTIVES OF REFUGEES

The United Kingdom has been taking the lead in arguing to reform the Geneva Convention. The recommendations by the United Kingdom are not aimed at changing the inherent values of the original convention but on how the convention functions and operates (UNHCR, 2001). Concurrently, there have been ongoing discussions in the United Kingdom about who should be classified as a refugee. In the past the United Kingdom has redefined refugee status so that individuals must be victims of war but excludes those suffering from economic hardship due to war, national and state conflicts, and natural disasters, which constitutes the plight of many contemporary refugees. This strict definition has serious implications for who can enter the United Kingdom as a refugee, and therefore, given that status, receive resettlement benefits. A ramification of this type of restricted definition, as mentioned previously, is the neglect and rejection of refugee status for victims of war atrocities such as women and girls who were repeatedly raped during armed conflict in their home countries. However, contrary to global trends, a case in 1999 prompted Great Britain's House of Lords to determine that women could be considered "a particular social group" when persecuted because of behaviors or attitudes at odds with prevalent social policy (UNHCR, 2001).

In contrast, Japan, which has less than one percent of a foreign population, has avoided debates by maintaining a closed-door policy (Watanabe, 1994). Australia is another example, with national disagreements about the numbers and types of immigrants and refugees who should be allowed to enter the country. This is a reaction to previous policy by which Australia had an acceptance rate of two to three times the number of immigrants in proportion to its population as compared to Europe (Coleman, 1995). Furthermore, Australia formerly had an "all White" immigration policy, which has recently been under review for reinstatement because of the conflicts between immigrants and refugees and the members of the resettlement country.

These examples represent major global tensions between refugees and resettlement countries, sometimes escalating into reactionary dialog, platforms, and policies by conservative governments advocating highly restrictive policies. This is especially true since countries are often backlogged and restricted by foreign policy when they consider admitting more refugees. For example, it was estimated that in 1991 in the United States, 11,000 asylum cases were decided, but a backlog of 216,000 remained (*Harvard Law Reports*, 1992, cited in Marsella et al., 1994). In fact, in 1992 only 37% of refugee applications were accepted in the United States, Narrow and rigid definitions of refugee status may accentuate their vulnerability and cause retraumatization as they are subjected to stringent regulations and difficulties trying to enter, or entering, developed or Western countries for resettlement (Baker, 1992; Cox & Amelsvoort, 1994). The stress of migration is heightened as a result of dealing with officials. In the United States, it was found that officials who determined whether applicants had "a well-founded fear of persecution" were insensitive and poorly prepared (Marsella, et al., 1994). The combination of these issues and domestic problems in resettlement countries has led to more restrictive policies. Interestingly, it has been suggested that the United States, is more receptive to applicants from "enemy" countries compared to applicants from "friendly" countries, regardless of torture, beatings, rape, or death threats (*Harvard Law Reports*, 1992, cited in Marsella et al., 1994). This may be generalizable to other resettlement countries.

The continuing international debates regarding refugees are timely, given the 36 current ongoing international conflicts and 140 countries presently involved in the resettlement of refugees. Within the current status of geopolitical conflict and ongoing natural disasters, it is anticipated that there will be a continuation of refugee displacement as they emigrate to other countries. Despite national and international debates over refugee status and policies, governments in developed countries cannot ignore the growing number of refugees. Given the expected increasing numbers of refugees in Western countries such as the United States, which already has an almost 10% immigrant and refugee population (Balian, 1997), developed countries will be forced to continue to reexamine policy and practice related to this population. For example, Ruud Lubbers, recently appointed as high commissioner, warned that "many prosperous countries with strong economies complain about the large number of asylum seekers, but offer too little to prevent refugee crises, like investing in conflict prevention, return, reintegration." In reference to Europe, he stated that "it is a real problem that Europeans try to lessen obligations to refugees . . . In any case, no wall will be high enough to prevent people from coming" (UNHCR, 2001, p. 7).

PREMIGRATION EXPERIENCES
AND PSYCHOLOGICAL DISTRESS

Although refugees come from a large variety of countries with dramatically different cultural backgrounds, values, customs, beliefs, social practices, and religions, they share common pre- and postmigration experiences. The commonality originates with the usual hasty and involuntary departure from one's home (Berrol, 1995), resulting in shared premigration experiences including genocide, being exposed to war atrocities and other traumatic and stressful life events, experiencing and witnessing torture and killing, being forced to commit atrocities, being incarcerated and placed in reeducation camps, starvation, rape and sexual abuse, physical beatings, and personal injury. These horrific experiences are underscored by forced or involuntary migration, the escape, and refugee camp experiences. The hasty departure from one's home country and the precariousness of the flight itself frequently cause profound loss and separation of family, identity, and culture, a downgrade in socioeconomic status and employment, language problems, dramatic shifts in social, familial, and gender roles, and acculturation problems in the new country. Critical to postmigration adjustment is coming to terms with premigration issues, which will be discussed in Chapter 4.

Studies on the premigration experiences of refugees are well documented and clearly point to the relationship between refugee status and mental health problems. Due to the extent and exposure to trauma prior to migration, it is not surprising to find that premigration trauma is a major predictor of psychological problems (Bemak & Greenberg, 1994; Chung & Bemak, 2002; Chung & Kagawa-Singer, 1993; Hinton, Tiet, Tran, & Chesney,1997; Mollica et al., 1998; Nicolson, 1997). The major psychological problems exhibited by refugees as an outcome of premigration trauma are depression, anxiety, posttraumatic stress disorder (PTSD), somatization, and suicide (e.g., Ajdukovic & Ajdukovic, 1993: Beiser, 1987; Bemak & Chung, 1998, 1999; Bottinelli, 1990; Carlson & Rosser-Hogan, 1991; Cervantes, Salgado, & Padilla, 1988; Chung & Kagawa-Singer, 1993; Dadfar, 1994; El-Sarraj, Tawahina, & Heine, 1994; Farias, 1991; Fawzi et al., 1997; Hinton et al., 1997; Jenkins, 1991; Karadaghi, 1994; Kinzie, Frederickson, Ben, Fleck, & Karls, 1984; Kozaric-Korvacic, Folnegovic-Smalc, Skringjaric, Szajnberg, & Marusic, 1995; Lin & Masuda, 1983; Mollica et al., 1998; O'Brien, 1994; Westermeyer, 1986). In addition to the mental health problems refugees also have serious health concerns given the conditions of the escape and refugee camps. Health problems that seem to be prevalent with refugees include tuberculosis, scabies, malaria, skin lesions, measles, malnutrition, dental problems, venereal diseases, cholera, diarrhea, meningitis, hepatitis, human immunodeficiency virus/acquired immunodeficiency syndrome (HIV/AIDS), leprosy, intestinal parasites, anemia, and hearing loss (Catanzaro & Moser, 1982; Clinton-Davis & Fassil, 1992). In addition, some refugees report neurologic disorders, head injury, and a host of physical disorders (Mollica & Jalbert, 1989; Mollica, Laveller, & Khuon, 1985, Muecke, 1992). A large percentage of refugee women have undergone abortions as a result of high incidence of rape and sexual abuse. Both women and men have experienced sexual dysfunction and mutilation of their genitalia (Mollica & Jalbert, 1989).

The majority of the epidemiological studies investigating refugees and migrants have found that rates of psychopathology for these populations to be significantly higher than the general population (Garcia-Peltoniemi, 1991; Kinzie, 1993; Weisaeth & Eitinger, 1993). For example, Marsella, Friedman, and Spain (1993) found greater rates of depression, anxiety, and PTSD among refugees. The occurrence of PTSD among the clinical refugee population is estimated to be 50% or higher, and depressive disorders range from 42 to 89% (e.g., Hauff & Vaglum, 1995; Mollica, Wyshak, & Lavelle, 1987; Ramsay, Gorst-Unsworth, & Turner, 1993; Van Velsen, Gorst-Unsworth, & Turner, 1996). Bemak and Greenberg (1994) found higher rates of depression among Southeast Asian refugees, and Dube's (1968) earlier study indicated higher rates of psychiatric disorders among Punjabi refugees. Different studies have found depression ranging from 15 to 80% in the refugee community (e.g., Carlson & Rosser-Hogan, 1991; Pernice & Brook, 1994; Westermeyer, 1986).

Premigration trauma therefore contributes to the psychosocial maladjustment along with problems related to resettlement and adjustment. Studies have found that there may be a delay in the onset of PTSD years after the initial trauma (Sack, Him, & Dickason, 1999) and that premigration trauma tends to wane with time as other postmigration variables, such as employment and housing, assume more importance (Hinton et al., 1997; Rumbaut, 1989). Nevertheless, it has been clearly established that premigration trauma has a long-standing negative impact on mental health after resettlement and underscores the influential interaction between premigration experiences and postmigation psychosocial adjustment (e.g., Chung & Kagawa-Singer, 1993; Hauff & Valgum, 1995; Hinton et al., 1997).

AT-RISK SUBGROUPS

Specific subgroups within the refugee population have been identified as being at high risk for developing mental health disorders. These subgroups include the following:

Older Refugees

Refugees who are older have been found to have a higher risk for mental health problems (Buchwald, Manson, Ginges, Keanne, & Kinzie, 1993; Kinzie et al., 1990; Matusuoka, 1993; Weine et al., 1995). They enter the resettlement country at an older age with longer histories of living in their home countries and more pronounced cultural roots. Frequently, this causes far greater difficulties in adapting to a new life in a new country. To exacerbate this, older males have greater difficulty finding gainful employment, placing them at a disadvantage with the pressures of having to learn a new language, acquire new skills, and attain jobs relative to their status, experience, and expectations. The result of a slower pace of acculturation is social isolation from mainstream culture and increased feelings of worthlessness (Beiser, 1987; Bemak & Chung, 2000; Buchwald et al., 1993; Hinton et al., 1997).

Women

In 1980 the United Nations High Commission for Refugees designated refugee women as a high-risk group for developing serious psychological problems due to their premigration war experience of rape and sexual abuse and violence (Refugee Women in Development, 1990). Women who have experienced the following have been identified as being at risk: (a) loss of family members, (b) high rates of rape and sexual abuse that occur during displacement and armed conflict, (c) loss of husbands through war and death resulting in becoming widowed and assuming responsibility as the family provider and caretaker, and (d) loss of their children to starvation, disease, or war (Caspi, Poole, Mollica, & Frankel, 1998; Mollica et al., 1987; Refugee Women in Development, 1990). Given histories of rape trauma, many women and girls face extreme difficulties adjusting to a "more normalized" life in the resettlement country. Adjustment is further complicated by poor educational backgrounds, minimal or no proficiency of the primary language spoken in the country of resettlement, little family and emotional support, and limited access to community resources (Chung, 2000).

For example, gender differences in levels of psychological distress have been found for Southeast Asian refugees with women reporting a significantly higher level of psychological distress than their male counterparts. This was attributed to differences in premigration trauma, such as rape and sexual abuse (Chung & Bemak, 2002). Within the Southeast Asian refugee population Cambodian women are more at risk than other groups. For example, in one study 95% of Cambodian women reported that they had been sexually abused or raped (Mollica et al., 1985). In a community sample of 300 Cambodian refugee women, 22% reported death of a spouse and 53% reported loss or death of other family members (Chung, 2000; Chung & Bemak, 2002).

Children and Youth

Marsella et al. (1994) concluded that the problems of refugees are intensified because most are women and children and often categorized as being at high risk for developing serious psychological disorders. Refugee children, however, appear to be especially vulnerable to the exposure of violence (Boothby, 1988). A study in Sweden indicated that more than 60% of refugee children had been exposed to violence in their countries of origin, either as immediate witnesses or perpetrators (Leyens & Mahjoub, 1989). Similar results were found in Mozambique, where it was reported that a high percentage, ranging from 63 to 88%, experienced some type of violence (Boothby, Upton, & Sultan, 1991). It is therefore not surprising that this population is at risk for developing serious psychological problems. UNCIEF (1996) estimated that 2 million children are killed and 4–6 million are disabled as a result of war and civil unrest.

Another prominent feature of today's conflicts that impacts youth is the personal involvement of civilians. Children are not only victims of violence but are also participants in violent activities (Boothby, 1988; Garbarino, 1990). For example, in Mozambique children captured by the guerrillas had been trained to become killers (Desjarlais, Eisenberg, Good, & Kleinman, 1995). Others witnessed brutality and suffered beatings, threats, and starvation. Many saw their parents killed in front of them while some were forced to do the killings (Desjarlais et al., 1995).

Children who are unaccompanied minors, that is, children and adolescents who were not accompanied by family members during their resettlement, are another group of youth at risk (Nidorf, 1985; Williams & Westermeyer, 1983). These children often suffer from loss of their parents as a result of political and social upheaval or, if their parents are still living, feelings that they have been rejected or abandoned by their parents who remain in their home country. Those who experienced trauma during escape or in the refugee camps may blame their parents for not protecting them and subjecting them to vulnerable and horrific situations. In the resettlement country events such as holidays, receiving letters from home, or reports by the media may trigger increased anxiety, loneliness, homesickness, depression, or feelings of guilt (Chung & Okazaki, 1991). Furthermore, premigration trauma is also a precursor to high school dropout rates and low grade-point averages (Ima & Rumbaut, 1989). In addition, parental stress and depression have been found to negatively impact children's psychological adjustment and academic achievement (Chung & Bemak, 2000; Rumbaut, 1989).

Chapter 3

Culture and Mental Health

CULTURAL BELIEF SYSTEMS

Health has been defined by the World Health Organization (1987) as a "state of complete physical, mental and social well-being" (p. 1). Historically, psychotherapy has focused on fostering mental health, utilizing individual psychotherapy as a means to enhance optimal independent functioning, coping abilities, and adaptation. The dominant Western medical model of mental health focuses on *individuals* and the *individual's* psychopathology. Consistent with this philosophical base are treatment goals that are underscored by individual psychotherapy to promote optimum personal functioning and personal growth and development and mental illness as a disease construct. Thus, the emphasis is on individuality, self, and independence. These methods were originally developed by Europeans and expounded upon by European Americans resulting in effectiveness for European American groups. However, there is a difficulty applying European American models of psychotherapy that are based on concepts emphasizing the self to most refugee groups, given that they are predominantly from collectivistic cultures.

Triandis (1990) differentiated between individualistic and collectivistic cultures. In individualistic cultures social behavior is motivated by personal gain, individual achievement, and personal goals while in collectivistic cultures family, friends, associates, and colleagues are more highly valued and linked with one's goals and behaviors. In collectivist cultures identity is defined by family, community, and social networks, with an emphasis on interdependence rather than independence. Therefore, individuals do not perceive themselves or talk about themselves in the singular but rather within the context of their social networks. For example, South American refugee clients in psychotherapy may refer to "we" instead of "I" when discussing problems. Western psychotherapists may misinterpret this as delusional because Western psychotherapy is based on a set of values and beliefs that contradict the cultural context for refugees. Despite the increased attention given to culture and mental health, basic Western psychological theories continue to focus on individualistic rather than collectivistic cultures. To provide effective mental health interventions in a culturally relevant framework for refugees would thus challenge the basic premise of Western individual psychotherapy.

Kleinman and colleagues (Kleinman, Eisenberg, & Good, 1978; Kleinman & Good, 1985) emphasized that to be effective, psychotherapists must understand and validate the client's conceptualization of mental health within the construct of his or her culture. Concurrently, Psychotherapists must explore differences in cultural beliefs and values as they correspond to beliefs and practices about healing. This is critical for mental health professionals because culture influences the refugees' conceptualization of mental illness as well as other aspects of the mental health process, including the manifestation of mental health problems (Chung & Kagawa-Singer, 1993), help-seeking behaviors (Chung & Lin, 1994), and the expectations for intervention and treatment strategies (Chung, Bemak, & Okazaki, 1997). It is only when mental health professionals understand the cultural belief systems of refugees that they can provide effective and culturally responsive services (Sue, Ivey, & Pedersen, 1996). This is especially important since the refugees' conceptualization of mental illness may differ dramatically from Western views of mental health.

Refugees' worldviews oftentimes differ from those that prevail in the resettlement countries, especially in the developed countries that typically subscribe to Western models of mental health. This results in psychotherapists and refugee clients having different perceptions of causes, diagnosis, and treatment of mental health problems, certainly not a compatible base from which to begin an intervention. For example, a Cambodian refugee may believe that his or her ancestor's spirits return to provide guidance and direction. The deceased relative may be seen and heard and, depending on the message and communication, may even become upset and agitated with the client. Traditionally, Western psychotherapy would define these symptoms as delusional with hallucinations and categorize the individual as having a serious mental illness, resulting in counseling techniques and medication based on the symptomatology (the "hallucination") to treat the underlying psychosis. Indigenous healing methods or a redefinition by Western psychotherapists would approach the same symptoms from a different cultural belief system, incorporating the concept of ancestral spirits as an important and meaningful personal and spiritual communication, potentially contributing to the stabilization of the individual and even the entire family.

According to Pedersen (2000), Western therapies are based on their own cultural assumptions, identified as the tendency to rely on insight and objective consciousness, a progress orientation, value efficiency, a requirement for empirical proof, and a tendency to separate the individual from the context. He contends that inherent in these suppositions are assumptions that the purpose of life is to maximize pleasure and minimize pain, the universe is harsh, uncaring, and unresponsive, the purpose of life is to conquer the universe, human beings are the supreme life form and probably the only intelligent life form, lower organisms exist for the benefit of humans, and only humans are conscious (p. 46). In contrast, indigenous or alternative assumptions by many non-Western societies may have a dramatically different perspective that includes the following assumptions: A newborn infant is the result of previous lives, the self is both individual and cosmic at the same time, social relationships are more important than individualism, maturity requires continuous dependency, personality is molded by duty and guilt sanctions, behavior is molded by parent–child relations, experience is more useful than logic to interpret behavior, rigid authority relationships do not inhibit development, life is dialectical, and truth is paradoxical (p. 47). These implicit and explicit assumptions have bearing on Western attempts at cross-cultural therapeutic treatments for refugee populations.

Furthermore, the Western perspective continues to dichotomize the mind and body, while many non-Western countries that are home to the refugees conceive of the mind and body as integral parts of the whole (Chung & Kagawa-Singer, 1995; Pedersen, 2000). The result of merging mind and body has a profound impact on the conceptualization and manifestation of health and illness and therefore on healing expectations and outcomes. For example, many refugees come from cultures where physical ailments may be a manifestation of psychological problems, so that refugees who complain about headaches or stomach pains may actually be alluding to psychological difficulties. Studies have found that refugees report high frequencies of somatic symptoms with no apparent organic pathology, including headaches, weakness, dizziness, abdominal pain, fatigue, and loss of eyesight (Caspi et al., 1998; Chung & Kagawa-Singer, 1995; Lin, Carter, & Kleinman, 1985; Van Boemel & Rozee, 1992). Refugee clients from non-Western backgrounds frequently exhibit distress through idioms of bodily complaints (Farooq, Gahir, Okeyere, Sheikh, & Oyebode, 1993; Kleinman & Kleinman, 1985; Ohaeri & Odejide, 1994; Roberts, 1994). For instance, it has been suggested that Southeast Asian refugees express depression and other psychological problems in a manner that is consistent with their culture belief system (e.g., Chung & Kagawa-Singer, 1995; Lin, Tazuma, & Masuda, 1979). These studies indicate that groups similar to other Asian populations express psychological distress as neurasthenia, which is comprised predominantly of somatic symptoms (e.g., headaches, weakness, pressure on the chest or head), with depression, anxiety, and psychological dysfunction. Mental illness is highly stigmatized in most Asian cultures and therefore the expression of neurasthenic symptoms is a culturally sanctioned method to express psychological distress (Cheung, 1982; Chung & Kagawa-Singer, 1995; Kleinman, 1982). However, it is also important to acknowledge that although refugees may exhibit distress through somatic channels, they are also capable of discussing their problems in psychological terms (Cheung, 1982; Kinzie et al., 1982; Mollica et al., 1987). Therefore, it is crucial for the mental health professionals working with refugees to be informed, sensitive, and accepting of cultural disparities and to employ culturally based therapeutic interventions and skills that redefine their cultural perspectives and views of mental health to coincide with the refugee's cultural worldview (Kagawa-Singer & Chung, 1994; Pedersen, 1988, 1991; Sue & Sue, 1990). Similarly, it is recommended that mental health professionals present an openness to traditional healing methodologies and at times even forge partnerships with traditional healers to treat specific problems presented by refugees (Bemak & Chung, 2002). This issue will be discussed in detail in Chapter 5.

Simultaneously, the psychotherapist should maintain an awareness of cross-cultural errors in misdiagnosis, underdiagnosis, and overdiagnosis of symptomatology and mental health problems. Again, these errors occur due to lack of knowledge, information, and awareness of the cultural, historical, and sociopolitical background of the refugee client, and simultaneously the psychotherapist may be operating on preexisting stereotypes (Draguns, 2000). For example, research has found that misclassification of mental disorders of ethnic clients in the United States (e.g., African Americans, Latina(o) Americans, and Asian Americans) have been attributed to the psychotherapist's lack of understanding of cultural and/or linguistic differences (e.g., Huertin-Roberts & Snowden, 1993).

Mental health professionals should also be aware that despite the influence of culture on symptom expression and manifestation, similar complaints and symptoms are found across different cultures. However, these symptoms may appear in different patterns and be attributed to a different causation (e.g., Fabrega, 1989; Kirmayer, 1989; Kleinman, 1982; Phillips & Draguns, 1969; Tseng & Hsu, 1969). Therefore, the meaning and symbolic value of similar symptoms may be culture specific and not interchangeable across cultures. For example, as mentioned previously, for Southeast Asian refugees neurasthenia is a culturally sanctioned method of expressing mental illness (Chung & Kagawa-Singer, 1995). The expressed pattern of symptoms, which combine both the somatic and psychological manifestations of distress, is consistent with Southeast Asian nosology and therefore does not fit precisely into a Western framework of mental illness. Other refugee groups, such as those from Arab and Latin American countries, also somaticize psychological distress.

Effective diagnosis without considering the refugee client's conceptualization of mental illness and symptom manifestation will be difficult if not impossible. In fact, discrepant worldviews by the mental health professional and client may lead to inappropriate treatment, premature termination, and even high dropout rates from mainstream mental health services (Chung & Kagawa-Singer, 1995). This is particularly important since identification and characterization of mental illness for the refugee population has generally been conducted using Western measures or diagnostic criteria [as currently embodied in the *Diagnostic and Statistical Manual,* fourth edition *(DSM-IV)*, or the *International Classification of Diseases,* tenth edition *(ICD-10)*]. This has been consistent even though accurate assessment with conceptual equivalence is essential before a cluster of symptoms is labeled with a diagnosis (Good & Good, 1981). An associated issue relates to the generalized use of psychotropic medication. Prescribing medication that is typically used for mainstream Western populations for symptom relief without consideration of ethnic and biological differences may also be problematic (Lin, Inui, Kleinman, & Womack, 1982).

Other cultural beliefs may also influence the psychotherapeutic process. Although the common myth is that refugees from the same country will share common values and culture, their experiences may be markedly different. The socioeconomic class, religious background, experience, education, and value system of refugees from the same country may cause great differences in families and individuals from the same culture. This is evident with conflicting beliefs about issues such as child rearing, gender equity, social status, deference to authority, and the like.

Intracultural variations become even more confusing when mental health professionals find themselves in sharp disagreement with the refugee's belief and value system. Perspectives on responsibility toward one's extended family, gender roles, self-development, perspectives about time, long-range and short-term planning, goal setting, passivity versus action-oriented responses to various life situations, assertiveness, morality, or patterns of verbal and nonverbal communication may all become pronounced as refugee clients struggle with various issues. It is at moments of strong disagreement with client's worldviews and behaviors that professionals must be particularly sensitive and responsive to cultural differences.

To be effective with refugee clients, mental health professionals need to maintain both ascribed and achieved credibility (Sue & Zane, 1987). Ascribed credibility is associated with a mental health professional's position or role, such as, age, gender, or expertise. Achieved credibility, on the other hand, is associated with what the psychotherapist actually does professionally to gain the trust and confidence of the client. Therefore, if mental health professionals have a low ascribed credibility with their clients, they may achieve credibility by displaying cultural sensitivity. For example, if a Somalian refugee client comes to therapy believing that age is important in terms of knowledge and wisdom and is confronted with a young psychotherapist, problems of ascribed credibility may emerge. However, if the psychotherapist in the first session is able to demonstrate cultural sensitivity and erudition, the psychotherapist may be able to gain credibility and prevent the client from premature termination after the first session.

BARRIERS TO MAINSTREAM MENTAL HEALTH SERVICES

Studies have consistently found greater rates of psychiatric disorders among refugees than the general population (e.g., Gong-Guy, 1987; Struwe, 1994). However, there has been a reluctance to seek help from mainstream mental health services (Higginbotham, Trevino, & Ray, 1990; Lin, Masuda, & Tazuma,

1982). Several reasons may be attributed to this, although a primary reason for low utilization of mainstream mental health services is that these services are not culturally responsive (Kagawa-Singer & Chung, 1994; Sue, Fujino, Hu, Takeuchi, & Zane, 1991). Upon entering mainstream mental health services, refugees often encounter unfamiliar and unresponsive environments from waiting rooms to check-in procedures. There may be language barriers between the client and the receptionist and/or psychotherapist, substantiated by findings that the length and outcome of treatment for ethnic minorities were associated with ethnic and language match between therapist and client (Bemak & Chung, 2002; Sue et al.,1991). There may also be important cultural differences in both verbal (e.g., tone and volume of speaking) and nonverbal (e.g., eye contact, personal space) behaviors. For example, the psychotherapist may affectionately pat the head of a Southeast Asian refugee child, a gesture that is culturally considered extremely offensive. This simple touch may precipitate a dynamic in the therapeutic relationship such as emotional or physical withdrawal by the child or adults, which may be interpreted incorrectly by the psychotherapist as psychological withdrawal or resistance. Adding to these differences, there may be a lack of understanding about the actual process of psychotherapy, which most often remains unexplained by the psychotherapist (Bemak & Chung, 2002).

When considering and providing mainstream mental health services for refugees, the cultural frame of reference and subsequent practice must be kept in mind since refugees' help-seeking behavior is influenced by culturally based attitudes (Van Deusen, 1982; Vignes & Hall, 1979). For example, traditional beliefs, superstition, witchcraft, and/or the belief in the supernatural are common barriers to mainstream mental health (Tung, 1983) causing the refugee population to oftentimes rely on indigenous healers and folk medicine (Egawa & Tashima, 1982; Hiegel, 1994; Higginbothom et al., 1990; Muecke, 1983). In fact, more than 75% of the people in the world use complementary or alternative treatments (Micozzi, 1996).

Chung and Lin (1994) found that many Southeast Asian refugees reported concurrent utilization of both traditional and Western mainstream health care methods. They suggested the preferred healing method for this population was the use of traditional methods, and their utilization of mainstream services in the United States was a result of the unavailability of traditional methods. Such behavior suggested a strong need for health and mental health services, yet using mainstream mental health services in resettlement countries as a last resort. This results in longer term problems because by the time refugees finally access mental health services the problem has become acute (Sue, 1993).

Many refugees will seek out indigenous healers, shamans, community leaders, elders, religious and spiritual leaders, and/or family and social support networks prior to contacting mental health professionals. Only after failing to locate or receive help from these sources do they seek out mainstream mental health professionals so that the choice is by default rather than preference (Bemak & Chung, 2002). This presumes a knowledge about mental health services, although many refugees are unaware of the types and availability of these services (Van Deusen, 1982). Another reason for low utilization of mainstream mental health services is inaccessibility (Higginbotham et al., 1990; Lin et al., 1982). Clinics and private offices are frequently located in areas that may be difficult to reach. Sometimes, in urban areas, mental health services are located in poorer communities that refugees perceive as dangerous and thus avoid. Public transportation systems may be complicated and time consuming to use so that the refugee must weight the benefits of spending time and money to receive psychotherapy. Simple tasks such as working out a bus timetable, a bus route, or payment may be confusing and stressful (Bemak & Chung, 2002). This was witnessed recently by the first two authors at a bus stop in San Diego, California, where recent immigrants without English language skills were desperately asking for directions to a mental health clinic at a hospital. They explained that they had been taking buses for 3 hours around the city trying to find the clinic and were completely lost and already 2 hours late.

If refugees overcome these obstacles and actually arrive at a mental health facility, they may be greeted by insensitive receptionists, staff, or professionals. It is confusing for the Salvadorian refugee family who arrives late for a counseling appointment to be told by an unsympathetic secretary or psychotherapist that they should have been on time and will be unable to have an appointment that day. Misunderstandings and dislike for mental health service systems may be created by cultural differences in time, language, tone, and volume used in verbal and nonverbal communication. These discrepancies often trigger a personal response that is culturally based and may relate to past negative experiences.

BILINGUAL AND BICULTURAL INTERPRETERS

Most mainstream mental health services do not have mental health professionals and/or trained bilingual translators who are fluent in the refugee client's native language. Not knowing the native language of the resettlement country may be, but is not necessarily, an obstacle to counseling. When language barriers are addressed with sensitivity, clarity, and awareness, they may be overcome to offer effective mental health assistance. It is important to also mention that although, in some instances, children may act as translators for their families, this is not an effective method of communication with mental health professionals (Chung, Bemak, & Okazaki, 1997).

Without carefully thought out resolutions to language barriers, errors in translation are common. When using bilingual translators, the role and relationship with the mental health professional, as well as expectations and realities of psychotherapy, should be explained carefully. Interpreters who do not understand the intricacies and personal nature of psychotherapy may be embarrassed to accurately translate details and information. Clarifying the role and expectations may lead to a better understanding of the interpreter's responsibilities and subsequent comfort in providing literal translations. An example of misinterpretation was when the second author was asked to clarify a glaring error made by an overly helpful interpreter that caused extreme anxiety for a client and his family. The interpreter understood the concept of severe depression and other forms of mental illness to be as serious as cancer, and therefore communicated to the client and his family that the problem he had was "cancer-like." The family became extremely upset, and the second author was asked to meet and clarify the situation and alleviate the fear and distress.

Sometimes in psychotherapy there is a discussion and exploration of highly personal issues. This may be awkward for an interpreter, who is not comfortable with personal or family private details. This may cause an awkwardness in translation and at times inaccurate information being translated. Sometimes translators may change the client's response in order to be helpful, saying what they believe the client means rather than literally translating content that may be confusing or simply not responsive to the psychotherapist's question. In addition, interpreters may often answer for the client without posing the question to the client because they believe they know the answer (Chung & Okazaki, 1991). This results in inaccurate content and missing information since confusion or incoherence and exact translations have significance in psychotherapy. Difficulties may also arise in confidentiality, poor paraphrasing of questions, and inadequate translation of medical and psychological terms in the client's language.

It is our belief that working with good interpreters is essential providing effective and responsive refugee mental health. To ensure that interventions are accurate and personally and culturally sensitive, it is essential that interpreters/translators are well trained and able to establish a clearly defined partnership with the mental health professional. Thus selecting an interpreter should not be based solely on language ability but requires someone who is both bicultural and understands the fundamentals of mental health interventions and hence their role as a partner in this professional relationship. Being more than translators, bilingual/bicultural mental health workers may be viewed as specialized mental health liasons who are familiar with expectations in Western mental health models and the unique medical and psychological perspectives of their own culture. They know how to convey subtle medical and cultural meanings to the client(s) and psychotherapist and therefore bridge the gap between the language *and* culture of the client and psychotherapist. An established and well-understood therapeutic alliance between the bilingual/bicultural mental health worker and psychotherapist is critical for effectively overcoming the language and cultural barriers and being culturally responsive.

Chapter 4

Acculturation, Postmigration Adjustment Issues, and Mental Health

ACCULTURATION AND MENTAL HEALTH

Difficulties experienced by the refugees as they adjust to a new culture are underscored by the relationship between premigration experiences, mental health problems, and resettlement. The first classic study that investigated the impact of refugee migration on mental illness was conducted by Odegaard in 1932. Originally these studies analyzed admissions rates of clinical populations in psychiatric hospitals and found that immigrants were disproportionately represented (Eitinger, 1960; Hitch & Rack, 1980; Mezey, 1960). Current studies about acculturation generally consider the following dimensions: models of acculturation (which comprise assimilation, integration or biculturalism, rejection, and deculturation), social indicators, stress, and adaptation.

Researchers (e.g., Berry, 1986; Szapocznik & Kurtines, 1980; Wong-Reiger & Quintana, 1987) have concluded that biculturalism or integration produces healthier acculturation outcomes. According to Berry and Kim (1988) the acculturation process can be broken down into five phases that occur on individual and group levels. These phases include precontact, contact, conflict, crisis, and finally adaptation. Being in a particular phase of acculturation depends upon how an individual deals with two fundamental questions: (1) How much of one's cultural identity is valued and retained? and (2) To what extent are positive relations with the dominant culture sought? For detailed descriptions of the models and acculturation phases see Berry (1986) and Berry and Kim, (1988).

Acculturative stress is another concept associated with refugee and immigrant psychosocial adjustment. Acculturative stress is a combination of ameliorating effects of environmental, familial, demographics, and other factors (Miranda & Matheny, 2000) and refers to a unique type of distress that involves adjusting to a foreign country. It includes elements of the acculturation model discussed above, such as changing one's identity, values, behaviors, cognitions, attitudes, and affect (Berry, 1990; Berry & Anis, 1974; Liebkind, 1996; Miranda & Matheny, 2000). For refugees acculturative stress is influenced by multiple factors as stated above, as well as premigration experiences, the social and political context of resettlement society, and postmigration acculturation experiences (Liebkind, 1996).

Premigration trauma adds an additional dimension to acculturation that complicates resettlement and may contribute to mental health problems and psychosocial adjustment. Mollica et al. (1987) categorized four major categories of premigration trauma: (a) deprivation (e.g., of food and shelter), (b) physical injury and torture, (c) incarceration and reeducation camps, and (d) witnessing of torture and killing. These traumatic experiences often place the refugees at risk for serious psychological problems such as anxiety, fear, paranoia and suspicion, grief, guilt, despair, hopelessness, withdrawal, depression, somatization, substance abuse and alcoholism, posttraumatic stress disorder (PTSD), anger, and hostility. In addition, the reeducation and/or refugee camp experiences may contribute to a sense of loss, uncertainty, distrust, skepticism, helplessness, vulnerability, powerlessness, overdependency, violence, crime, and social disintegration.

Unresolved premigration trauma links closely with psychosocial maladjustment and interferes with resettlement. Postmigration issues may also add to acculturation difficulties, such as culture shock and survivor's guilt, that may precipitate feelings of helplessness, hopelessness, and disorientation. The experience of loss may be generalized to all refugees who, by virtue of their refugee experience, are separated and face the loss of nuclear and extended families and community social networks. The arrival into countries of resettlement introduces new cultures and reference groups that are frequently in contradiction to the refugee's culture and experience, since most of the resettlement countries are individualistic rather than collectivistic in nature.

For refugees who primarily come from relationship-oriented societies, this means not only facing a new society that is more likely to be individualistic but simultaneously coming to terms with the loss of their family, community, and social network reference group (Bemak & Greenberg, 1994). Given the contrast between the refugee's native culture and the resettlement country, refugees may encounter difficulties acculturating and may therefore enculturate within their own cultural group as a partial buffer from isolation (Berry, 1990; Casas & Pytluk, 1995). However, refugees cannot ignore and must respond to the influence of the dominant resettlement country's culture (Aponte & Johnson, 2000). Individuals adapt to new cultures differently, depending on personal characteristics and the collective ability of the refugee group to adjust to mainstream culture. On a personal level factors that influence adaptation include coping strategies, ability to handle new and stressful situations, motivation and willingness to adapt, the ability to identify with a new reference group, the acceptance of one's situation and the resettlement country's culture, and the resolution of the past psychological trauma. This is underscored by the collective ability of the refugee group's ability to adjust to the resettlement country's culture that establishes precedence, role models, and practices that ease the way for adaptation. An associated important factor in adjustment is the strength and support of social and family networks.

While adjusting to resettlement countries, refugees may also undergo a search for racial, cultural, and ethnic identity, particularly in light of ethnic, and cultural differences as compared to the mainstream population. During this exploration individuals may become more aware of their racial, ethnic, and cultural selves, leading to a psychological process that ascribes significance and meaning to being a member of a socially defined racial or cultural group. This, in turn, affects the individual's overall self-concept (Helms, 1995; Helms & Talleyrand, 1997; Phinney, 1993), which is crucial to a refugee's mental health as he or she adapts to a new life. Several models have been developed to assess an individual's racial, ethnic, and cultural identity (Cross, 1985; Atkinson, Morten, & Sue, 1998; Helms, 1995) that may be generalized to the refugee population.

The relationship between acculturation and racial and ethnic identity has been recognized as critical variables in understanding mental health in ethnic populations (Aponte & Johnson, 2000) and relate directly to understanding refugees' psychosocial adjustment and mental health. Both acculturation and racial/ethnic identity are complex, multidimensional, multifaceted, and interacting processes that occur at both the individual and group levels (Aponte & Barnes, 1995). Findings demonstrate that both acculturation and racial/ethnic identity are associated with varying degrees of psychological health and adjustment, effecting help-seeking behavior and expectations for treatment outcomes (Aponte & Barnes, 1995; Atkinson et al., 1998; Sue et al., 1995). However, for the refugee population acculturation and racial/ethnic identity is further complicated by the refugee status and premigration trauma.

PSYCHOSOCIAL ADJUSTMENT AND ADAPTATION

Central to refugee acculturation is the issue of psychosocial adjustment. Ben-Porath (1991) described antecedent of flight, the period of flight, and the process of resettlement as key elements in refugee psychosocial adjustment. Within each of the adjustment phases there are potential sources of stress and mental health risks. Mental health professionals who provide counseling for refugees must carefully evaluate and understand the dynamics in each phase of the therapeutic relationship within the framework of past and present experiences. Thus, to be effective with this population the focus must combine premigration, transition, and postmigration and the interaction between each of these critical periods in the refugee's life.

Although refugees come from different home countries with dramatic variations in worldviews, values, and belief systems as discussed in the previous chapter, they also share similar pre- and postmigration experiences (Berrol, 1995). Premigration experiences for many refugees include severe incidents of trauma that may continue to interfere with psychosocial growth and stability and present barriers to adjustment. An example of this is a study on Southeast Asian refugees where no differences were found regarding the effects of premigration trauma on the level of psychological distress between those who had been resettled for 5 years or more and those who had recently arrived (Chung & Kagawa-Singer, 1993).

Similarly there are also common postmigration psychosocial adjustment issues for refugees. During postmigration refugees are confronted with finding housing and employment, being underemployed, language problems, downgrading of socioeconomic status, and profound changes in familial, marital, and gender roles. Tayabas and Pok (1983) identified the first 2 years of resettlement as a crucial period when refugees attempt to meet basic needs such as housing and employment. This period is particularly important since during the early years refugees acquire new skills that facilitate a mastery over the new environment and establish resources from which they can draw upon in the future. Language, housing, and employment are the major initial postmigration problems confronting refugees, and such problems are often presented to psychotherapists (Chung et al., 1997). Mental health professionals cannot ignore these issues since they constitute a foundation for basic survival. How to incorporate these issues into a model for mental health interventions will be presented in the next chapter.

Bemak (1989) outlined a three-phase developmental model of acculturation affecting psychosocial adjustment. Initially in phase I there is an attempt to use existing skills to master the new environment and feel psychologically safe. Phase II involves an integration of former and newly acquired skills that parallels the acculturation process. In phase III there is a growing sense of future and basic mastery of culture and language that accompanies psychological safety. During this phase the refugee begins to consider and plan future realistic and attainable goals and implement strategies to achieve them. It is during this time that refugees acquire skills and establish a foundation for "learning to learn" that paves the way for future psychosocial adjustment and acculturation. The biculturalism emphasized in this and other models has been found to generally produce the most successful and healthy adaptation and acculturation (Berry, 1986; Wong-Reiger & Quintana, 1987).

Adaptation for refugees in the resettlement country not only includes learning new coping skills, and behavioral and communication patterns, but also equally important is the unlearning of some of the "old behaviors." This is particularly important since many refugees learned survival skills that may appear aversive, antisocial, or even pathological in the resettlement country (Stein, 1986). For example, refugees who experienced or witnessed torture, rape, and other incidents

of abuse or death remained alive by acting "dumb," a response typical to survivors of atrocities (Chung & Okazaki, 1991). In fact the Khmer term, *tiing
mooung* ("dummy" personality, puppet, or scarecrow), was identified by Mollica
and Jalbert (1989) as a commonly used descriptor by Cambodians for behavior
under the Khmer Rouge regime. Acting deaf, foolish, confused, stupid, obeying
orders without question or complaint, and being afraid to speak up or show one's
true feelings were a means to avoid torture or execution. The fear of living under
the constant threat of torture or death traumatized many refugees, resulting in behavioral survival strategies. This survival behavior, if continued in the resettlement country, is generally inappropriate and results in further alienation from the
mainstream culture.

Furthermore, the psychological recoil effect phenomenon has also been identified as a coping strategy to deal with traumatic experience (Bemak & Chung,
1998). This phenomenon suggests that for individuals to survive in physically
and psychologically dangerous environments strong defenses are developed
causing emotional numbness to the painful situation. Therefore individuals may
not show any signs of psychological and behavioral reactions to traumatic experiences, regardless if the trauma events are directed at oneself or witnessed and
observed. It is only when individuals are in the resettlement country and feel safe
that the psychological effects of premigration trauma are displayed, making it
critical for psychotherapist to be aware of this phenomenon (Bemak & Chung,
1998).

The abrupt departure that characterizes most refugees' exit from their home
countries leaves them lacking control or the ability to make decisions about their
lives. Essential issues such as where to live, options for work, providing for
one's family, choice of community, and the like become externally determined
rather than self or family selected. Subsequently, there is oftentimes a marked
ambivalence about the actual resettlement that may result in resentment toward
the host country and/or the home country. For example, many Cuban refugees in
the United States hold strong negative feelings toward the government of their
home country. These deeply rooted feelings have also turned against the United
States, their country of resettlement, when the national policies or decisions were
viewed as favorable toward Cuba. Another similar example is in the United
States when some Southeast Asian refugees such as the Hmong felt abandoned
by the United States government during the Vietnam War. Feelings such as these
may contribute to a difficult adaptation process.

SURVIVOR'S GUILT

Survivor's guilt has been identified as a problem common to many refugees
that negatively impacts a healthy psychosocial adjustment (Brown, 1982; Lin et
al., 1982; Tobin & Friedman, 1983). Successfully fleeing from dangerous conditions, many refugees left behind family members and friends who did not
or could not escape. After reaching safety, refugees reported being haunted by

feelings of guilt, especially knowing the danger still facing those who were left behind. The awareness that people who remained at home are alive, possibly suffering, and living in unpleasant conditions may heighten survivor's guilt and contribute to emotional stress. The same response may hold true if there is an absence of information, whereby survivors may be plagued by feelings of intense anxiety and guilt. Survivor's guilt can continue in a spiral of pain, sadness, and guilt that causes barriers to enjoying the safety, success, and sense of well-being in the resettlement country.

SOCIAL SUPPORT

Resettlement in a foreign country may also mean the loss of community support. The customary support system that includes extended family, friends, community members and leaders, and spiritual leaders may be unavailable in the resettlement country. To further compound the situation, in the United States resettlement policy for refugees has been to disperse them throughout the country (Uba, 1994), adding to feelings of isolation and alienation. Furthermore, to economically provide for the family refugees may have several jobs and therefore demanding work schedules that leave little time for social activities. Social isolation may be further exacerbated by cultural taboos on dating and/or peer rejection. For example, Cambodian women who are widowed, separated, or divorced report that they are rejected by their peers because they are perceived as a threat to one's husband (Mollica et al., 1985). Subsequently, family losses and economic responsibilities, coupled with community rejection, cultural isolation, and alienation, may place refugees in an extremely difficult emotional situation with little or no social support (Chung, 2000).

LANGUAGE BARRIERS

Language plays an important part in refugee adjustment in terms of accessing resources and securing employment. Similar to other countries, the United States is a good example of a country that has problems with language acquisition. Over one-third of the 6.3 million refugee and immigrant children in the United States reported difficulties in speaking English (Martin & Midgley, 1994). This is not surprising since many of the refugees came from countries where English was not the official language (Rong & Preissle, 1998).

In the United States English as a second language (ESL) programs provide language training, yet fall short in providing the necessary holistic perspectives to address issues that emerge with cultural language acquisition. Learning a new language symbolizes leaving one's homeland and may be a catalyst for feelings of cultural identity loss. An example of this was the El Salvadorian refugee who struggled with learning English. In a painful moment she explained in Spanish, "To learn English is to forget my country. I don't want to lose myself and speak English!" Another profound example was the Cambodian adolescent, whose mother had been executed during the period of mass genocide under the Khmer Rouge regime. She had a dream one night after migrating to North America in which her mother angrily appeared to her, extolling her to "Stop speaking English. You must speak Khmer! Remember you are Cambodian!"

Although the acquisition of a new language is one of the most important factors in acculturation, surprisingly, it has been found that attendance in language skills classes was a significant predictor of psychological distress for Southeast Asian refugees (Chung & Kagawa-Singer, 1993). An explanation of this may be due to experiencing the frustration of trying to learn a new language that may bring back memories of "better times and easier communication" with neighbors, friends, and family. As one South American refugee in the United States explained in Spanish, "It hurts every time I speak English. My head hurts because I have to constantly think and try to remember what words to use and how to say the words correctly. I have a pain in my heart when I speak English because it reminds me where I am and how I came to be here, it makes me miss my home, English is such a difficult language in so many ways." The struggle to learn the language may exacerbate emotional problems and frustrations in understanding the new environment. Language classes may create feelings of helplessness, exasperation, and cause regressive behavior similar to that of earlier developmental years when, as a child, one was learning to master one's environment. This may evoke questions about self-worth, feelings of inadequacy, and low self-esteem.

It has been suggested that as a result of premigration trauma many refugees have developed emotional and mental fatigue and enormous impairment in their memory and concentration, possibly associated with head injuries. The result of this has been inadequacy and lack of confidence and ability to comprehend a new language or succeed in formalized language training classes (Mollica et al., 1985). This is further complicated since many refugees are illiterate in their own language, making learning a new language even more of a challenge. It has been found that individuals who are literate in their native language achieve literacy in the new language much faster (Raccine, 1984).

Without the context of formal education refugees may find themselves not only having to learn new content areas such as language but simultaneously "learning how to learn" (Chung et al., 1998). Refugee women in particular have expressed this feeling of not understanding anything and compared to their male counterparts are more reluctant to attend language classes (Chung et al., 1998). In addition, refugees who come from cultures with narrowly prescribed gender roles may feel uncomfortable studying with classmates from the opposite sex. This is further complicated when women are reluctant to participate for fear that this may "show up" the men in the class and cause them to lose status.

EDUCATION AND EMPLOYMENT

Many refugees face not only social readjustment problems but also difficulties in becoming financially self-sufficient. This is in large part due to the related issues of education and employment. It was striking to find that in one study Southeast Asian refugees were still dependent on welfare even after an average of 5.5 years of resettlement (Chung & Bemak, 1996). Unemployment and the reliance on welfare may be attributed to differences in work requirements, skills, training, and qualifications that are frequently not transferable to resettlement countries. It is likely that jobs held in countries of origin may not be applicable to the skills needed in a more technologically advanced resettlement country. Consequently, the work and status that refugees previously achieved as a result of their skills and education was often not valued or acknowledged in the resettlement country, creating a situation in which they must "start over."

The marked change in socioeconomic status may cause some refugees to take jobs for which they are overqualified. The result is underemployment, precipitating feelings of low self-worth, and raising questions about the ability to contribute to the family, community, and society. An example of this is the case of a Bosnian surgeon who spoke her native language as well as French and Italian but found herself resettled in an English-speaking country. At home she had been highly respected in the community and successful as a surgeon, spending the last few years working with civilians and soldiers wounded in the war. Because her degree did not meet licensure qualifications in the resettlement country, she was required to take 2 years of residency and then sit for the medical board examinations. At the age of 45, with limited English language skills, this was a difficult challenge for her. To earn money and support her family, she accepted a position in an ethnic bakery that served the Bosnian community where she sometimes saw former patients and friends.

Situations where there is an immediate need to have an income may result in decreased status, embarrassment, low self-esteem, and despair. Achieving professional status in one's home country does not easily transfer to the resettlement country given differences in licensure and credentialing, skill requirements, and competitive markets. Thus there may be added pressure to accept any available job in order to support one's family in the resettlement country and send money back home to other family members. To meet financial obligations refugees are sometimes forced to take more than one job. For many refugee men this is difficult so that they may choose to remain unemployed and welfare dependent and wait for a suitable position that will match their skills rather than experience the loss of status (Chung & Bemak, 2002). Although many refugees make remarkable strides in their adjustment, only a small percentage regained their former socioeconomic status (Lin et al., 1979, 1982).

Financial struggles may also contribute to psychological distress. Studies have found that being on welfare, unemployment, and low levels of English proficiency are predictors to psychological distress for refugees (Chung & Bemak, 1996; Chung & Bemak, 2002; Chung & Kagawa-Singer, 1993; Kinzie & Fleck, 1987). For example, in one study of a community sample of 300 Cambodian women, 22% reported the loss of their spouse and therefore they made the decision to leave Cambodia (Chung & Bemak, 2002). The findings showed that low

English proficiency was a significant distress predictor for this group. Further-more, those who made the decision to leave Cambodia, were more likely to experience psychological distress, which may relate to feelings of guilt about subjecting their families in the United States to financial hardship, especially for those who are fully dependent on welfare.

It is also important for mental health professionals to be aware of the effects of welfare on refugees' psychological well-being. In countries such as the United States, the relationship between welfare and psychological distress in the main-stream population has been well established (e.g., Jahoda, 1982; Kessler, House, & Turner, 1987a, b; Starr & Roberts, 1982). However, little research has been con-ducted on the effects of welfare on refugee populations. In fact it was found with Southeast Asian refugees who were on welfare at any period in their lives, even though they may no longer be on welfare, there was a continued risk for develop-ing psychological distress (Chung & Bemak, 1996). It was suggested that the Asian cultural values of shame and guilt may be a reason for this finding and fur-ther emphasize the importance of examining the effects of welfare for refugee populations (Chung & Bemak, 1996). An unexpected finding in this study pointed to intergroup differences that impact education and unemployment. It was found that unlike the other Southeast Asian refugee groups, Hmong refugees who were no longer receiving welfare were more likely to be at risk for psycho-logical distress (Chung & Bemak, 1996). A suggested explanation to the finding is the unique historical and sociopolitical relationship between the United States, government and Hmong people during the Vietnam War (Chung & Bemak, 1996).

CHANGES IN FAMILY DYNAMICS

Contributing to problems with education and employment are further shifts in family and gender roles. When refugee men are unemployed or underemployed, women may be forced to work. Often, this is contradictory to well-established traditional gender roles and produces a conflict between the values of the culture of origin and those of the host country (Chung & Okazaki, 1991). Paradoxically, changes in gender roles may result in a deterioration of socioeconomic status for refugee men and an improvement for the women, causing shifts in roles and atti-tudes that frequently result in marital conflicts. An example of this was evident with the situation of an Ethiopian wife who attended language classes at night to improve her chances at finding gainful employment and contribute financially to the family. Learning the language of the resettlement country was important but required her to leave home three nights a week, detracting from her traditional duties as a wife and mother. As she gained language proficiency and was ex-posed to the customs and practices of the new culture, she became more indepen-dent and questioned her traditional role as a wife. This dynamic is evident with many refugee women who study or work to contribute financially to the house-hold. There may be identification with, and/or the desire to adopt, the values of the resettlement culture and challenging of traditional gender roles and status as they become more acculturated, resulting in marital disequilibrium and family conflict. Many refugees experience similar situations, resulting in role reversal, confusion, chaos, and marital conflict, challenging generations of well-established family structure.

Since many refugees relocate with their families, the changes in family dynamics are important aspects of psychosocial adjustment. One consequence of migration may be forced changes in childrearing. Disciplinary practices, such as corporal punishment, that may have been commonplace at home prior to migration may be prohibited by laws in the resettlement country (Bemak & Chung, 2002). The laws facing refugees regarding discipline and punishment are reflective of rules for behavior in the resettlement country and may be contrary to the "old country ways." Other laws govern minimum ages for marriage, disallowing the practice of girls being married at an early age. New rules guiding parenting may create confusion and adjustment difficulties within the refugee family, even causing encounters with law enforcement. A good example of this can be seen with the practice of coin rubbing, which is a form of medical treatment used by Vietnamese refugees to release spirits and treat certain illnesses. The treatment requires hard rubbing on the skin with a coin that leaves the skin surface raw and open. The bruises on the skin, which culturally are a sign of care and concern by an adult in the family, have often been mistaken by educators in the resettlement country as evidence of child abuse (Nguyen, Nguyen, & Nguyen, 1987). Such issues present serious dilemmas for refugee parents who may already feel diminished in their stature as parents and restricted from raising their children in ways that have been culturally acceptable for generations.

The impact on family dynamics is significant when children and adolescents learn the language of the resettlement country and acculturate faster than parents and other adults in the family. This is due in large part to youth being immersed in public education and having far greater exposure to mainstream culture. The result of this rapid acculturation is a redefinition of family roles, causing family dysfunction, conflicts, confusion, and painful social restructuring (Bemak & Chung, 2002). The first author observed this with a 14-year-old Vietnamese refugee adolescent who had acquired far better language skills than his parents. In a consultation meeting in a public school, the child assumed the role of translating for his parents, explaining to them everyone's role and the purpose of the meeting and taking an overall lead in bringing his parents to the world of public education. His parents, in turn, were dependent on him and looked to him for guidance and assistance with cultural and language translation.

Adaptation to the host country is in part precipitated by a change in reference groups (Bemak & Greenberg, 1994) that is accompanied by less appreciation and adherence to traditional values. This produces a loss of authority by the adults, intergenerational conflicts about "old" versus "new" value systems, and questions about ethnic and cultural identity. Traditional customs that were handed down for generations are challenged and questioned. An example of this can be seen with Hmong refugees, where there is a tradition of hand embroidery. The embroidery symbolizes a method of storytelling that is passed on through the generations, with the older generation teaching the younger. Hmong youth who resettled in the United States found themselves faced with many opportunities for activities and a much faster pace of life than in Laos. Many of the older women have been concerned by the lack of interest by younger girls in this important tradition, causing intergenerational tension.

This coincides with many refugee children and adolescents who, as they acculturate faster than the adults, perceive their parents and elders differently. Initially, the adults may have been seen as competent, confident, and culturally knowledgeable caretakers and providers who had safely brought them to the new country. This may change during resettlement as the adults face language barriers, employment obstacles, and general confusion about customs and appropriate behaviors, causing them to feel overwhelmed, insecure, and increasingly dependent on their children. During this process the child may lose confidence in the adults as caregivers and providers, inevitably affecting and changing the traditional family structure. In fact, some children may feel ashamed of their parents in the resettlement country because of the lack of language skills, "old-fashioned" dress, and non-Western behaviors, manners, and customs. The effects of premigration trauma exhibited by parents may also affect their interaction and relationship with their children. For example, a Laotian student, who worked on a research project on reeducation camp detainees for the second author, told the second author that she had no respect for and was embarrassed by her father. Subsequently, she told people that her father was dead. She remembered her father in Laos where he was the community leader and respected by all the community members. However, in the United States, he spent most of his time squatting in the corner rocking back and forward and crying uncontrollably. She did not understand her father's transformation from a strong leader to a "vegetable." It was not until she was involved in the research project that she realized that her father was in fact a torture victim, helping her to better understand and accept her father's behavior.

Conflicts between parents and children also emerge regarding cultural practices and customs such as dating, marriage, curfews, extracurricular activities, and the like. Rather than parental edicts being accepted, there may be questions or challenges to their authority, as children attempt to negotiate and discuss issues and values that are sometimes reinforced by schools and peers. This is a significant change in expected behavior for many refugees who may come from cultures where their role is clearly defined without expectations to question authority. Thus, many refugee children face the difficult position of bridging two worlds, acculturating and adopting the customs and behaviors similar to their resettlement country's peer group, while maintaining the role as a child in traditional families. Respectively, parents may want their children to learn the national language and therefore succeed in the resettlement country but are also afraid that their children are losing their traditional culture. In attempts to curtail the youth's adoption of incongruent patterns of behavior and new-world values, some refugee parents try to maintain strict traditional upbringings. Even so, many parents experience the loss of their presumed authority and control.

EDUCATIONAL CHALLENGES OF REFUGEE YOUTH

Refugee children and adolescents encounter challenges in school ranging from personal and cultural adjustment to institutional policies (Huang, 1989; Schapiro, 1987). Moving into a new culture, refugee students may encounter problems in school related to being a foreigner. Speaking the native language with an accent, differences in dress, cultural variances in communication and social interaction, or different habits and foods may elicit prejudicial and discriminatory responses from peers and school personnel. With the documentation of increased violence in schools and communities, refugees may be targets of physical and emotional abuse, harassment, and robbery. School personnel and other mental health professionals may misdiagnose behavior of refugee children who have been exposed to sustained trauma (Freud & Dann, 1951; Pinsky, 1949; UN Educational, Scientific, and Cultural Organization, 1952) that may result in problems in school placements or disciplinary actions. van der Kolk (1987) reported that "traumatized children have trouble modulating aggression and tend to act destructively against others and themselves" (p.16). Similar patterns have also been reported with other refugee populations, for example, Dadfar (1994) with Afghan refugees, Ajdukovic and Ajdukovic (1993) with Croatians, and Boothby (1994) with refugee children in general.

Compounding the personal and cultural challenges faced by refugee students in are the school environment discrepancies in school policies and resources the school environment (Bemak & Chung, 2002). Refugee students have added pressures and difficulties adjusting to the criteria used to measure traditional markers of academic success (Bemak & Chung, 2003). Some of this is based on inflexible standards that are geared for mainstream native-born populations. Another important contributing factor is the inequalities inherent in impoverished urban school systems that house many refugee students. This includes poorly trained teachers, teacher prejudice, unmotivated teachers, lack of instructional resources, overcrowded classes, standardized curriculum that has little relevance for refugees, poor academic tracking that simply clusters refugee students in classes, poor instructional placement, a disparity between home and school life, deficits in instructional material, and cultural biases inherent in the assessment tools (Dana, 2000; Gibson, 1997; McDonnell & Hill, 1993).

In addition, the norms regulating classroom and school behavior are different from those of the home country, the ongoing social and extracurricular life is not easily accessible for newly enrolled refugees, and expectations for academic and personal growth may not fit with life perspectives and worldviews. Many refugee students find themselves in an educational paradigm that values individual competitive success based on grades, test scores, self-performance, tracking, class rank, and winning rather than examining qualitative measures of success such as enjoyment, excitement, interest (Hertzberg, 1998), acculturation, health, social networks, and cultural mastery. For example, the tenth-grade Somalian child in the United States, is expected to meet with a school counselor to define class selections that will have a significant impact on a lifetime of career and work. Choosing a future vocation through academic courses at the age of 15 is quite different from the focus the child had in rural Somalia, where school attendance was irregular and consideration of multiple alternative future vocations was unusual since it was expected that the child would someday do agricultural work.

Another important issue regarding schools is teaching the language of the resettlement country. Predominantly, educational systems in resettlement countries place a major emphasis on language training. Classes, studies, and full attention are typically spent in facilitating language acquisition. What is not considered are the other ramifications of learning a new language that impacts acculturation. For example, in some cases, the foreign language may be taught in ways that reject the refugee student's native language and culture (Bemak & Chung, 2003). In fact, learning English as a second language in the United States, has been called a form of social control (Gonzalez & Darling-Hammond, 1997), whereby a forced and intensive language training approach could precipitate feelings of powerlessness and restimulate premigration trauma. The danger here is the accompanying feelings of frustration, anger, withdrawal, and confusion, resulting in school failure and associated problems acculturating. For an in-depth discussion on counseling refugee and immigrant students in the school refer to Bemak and Chung (in press).

RACISM, PREJUDICE, AND DISCRIMINATION

Another major barrier to psychosocial adjustment for refugees is the experience of racism, prejudice, and discrimination by members and the institutions of the resettlement country. This can be displayed overtly and/or covertly and can be either intentional or unintentional. Discrimination, racism, and prejudice may originate with the resettlement country's attitudes and politically charged issues directed toward the refugee's country of origin. For example, in the United States Afghan, Palestinian and Southeast Asian refugees may encounter racism, prejudice, and/or discrimination related to September 11, and conflicts in the Mideast or the Vietnam War. Furthermore, increasing global political tension and the ongoing terrorist threats toward the United States may result in promoting negative views and attitudes toward specific groups of refugees and therefore hostility and discrimination toward this group.

In addition to existing national attitudes is the state of the economy, which may also contribute to discrimination, racism, and prejudice. Citizens in resettlement countries may perceive refugees as a competitive threat to their jobs and financial livelihood. Refugees may also be considered a financial burden to society, who as a group require government financial support through social service and welfare programs. This may result in targeting refugees as scapegoats, particularly in times of economic and financial hardship.

To compound the situation, some resettlement countries may be homogenous and may not have experiences with people from different ethnic and cultural backgrounds. Members of the resettlement country therefore may hold negative stereotypes and/or are xenophobic toward refugee populations. These attitudes may lead to racism, prejudice, and discrimination toward refugees and hence will effect successful adjustment and adaptation of refugees in the resettlement country.

The experience of racism, prejudice, and discrimination creates psychological distress that affects the daily lives of refugees. This may occur through institutional or individual stereotyping, stigmatization, and labeling and be experienced as teasing, ridiculing, ignoring, disparaging, and belittling behaviors. It may take the form of institutional racism where refugees are denied equal opportunities in employment, education, and housing (Adams, 1990). The experience of discrimination is exacerbated if refugees experienced hostility, suspicion, mistrust, and prejudice during premigration and would become more likely to create "cultural paranoia," a term coined by Jones (1990) to describe the effects of racism, prejudice, and discrimination in resettlement countries.

It has been found that racism, prejudice, and discrimination affect an ethnic person's self-regard and interpersonal relationships (Aponte & Johnson, 2000). In fact, poor self-esteem in ethnic groups has been associated with the psychological consequences of racism, as well as the use of substance abuse, child abuse, domestic violence, and suicide (e.g., Asamen & Berry, 1987; Hughes & Demo, 1989). An outcome of racism and discrimination may be distrust of mainstream institutions, resulting in low utilization of mental health services, all the more reason that psychotherapists acknowledge these experiences in the resettlement country and during premigration as critical issues in psychotherapy.

INTER- AND INTRAGROUP DIFFERENCES

Although refugees, in general, encounter similar pre- and postmigration experiences due to their refugee status, it is important to be aware and understand intergroup differences between and within refugee populations. By assuming that all refugees have the same pre- and postmigration experiences is erroneous and hence leads to ineffective services. This mistake is oftentimes made when refugees come from a specific country or region, for example, Africa, the Balkans, Latin America, or Asia. The circumstances of refugees from specific countries or regions are influenced by the geopolitical, sociopolitical, and historical situations. For example, refugees from parts of Africa are a result of war due to economic reasons, such as the diamond extraction in Sierra Leone and battles for oil in Angola, others are due to civil wars such as the case in Uganda or

Burundi, and others are due to natural disasters, for example, the famine in Ethiopia. These premigration differences within the African refugee population may affect psychosocial adjustment for specific groups.

Even though refugees experience the same war situation, intergroup differences can still emerge. For example, the Vietnam War affected not only Vietnam but also Cambodia and Laos. However, differences emerged in this situation depending on location. For instance, Cambodians experienced genocide orchestrated by the Pol Pot regime and hence have been found to be the most traumatized group within the Southeast Asian refugee population (Chung & Bemak, 2002; Chung, 2000; Mollica et al., 1987). Intragroup differences also occurred, such as the differences between those who escaped Vietnam prior to the fall of Saigon versus the boat people (Nguyen, 1982). Gender differences are also found between and within groups. For example, Southeast Asian refugee women, in general, reported experiencing more psychological distress than male counterparts (Chung et al., 1998). Gender differences were also found in the predictors of distress both between the Southeast Asian refugee groups as well as within specific groups. The study indicates that postmigration psychosocial adjustment is influenced by the unique premigration circumstances and therefore underscores the importance of examining inter and intragroup differences and avoiding the mistake of clustering refugees in one generic category (Chung & Bemak, 2002).

RESETTLEMENT POLICIES: IMPLICATIONS FOR MENTAL HEALTH

Any mental health model that is designed to work with ethnic minority groups must be developed within the context of existing policies and practices that regulate and affect that group. An ongoing political global concern with refugees is their ability to become economically self-sufficient and not create a financial burden on the resettlement country. Resettlement countries outline guidelines, program support, and timelines for refugees to achieve financial autonomy. It is important to note the distinction between countries of first asylum and final resettlement countries. Asylum countries refer to refugee camps or other aggregate living situations that are aimed at providing basic survival needs until determination is made about resettlement or repatriation. The goal of asylum countries is therefore not economic self-sufficiency but to transition the refugee to a receptive country of resettlement.

Although refugee resettlement policies prioritize financial independence, there are some striking gaps that affect long-term positive outcomes. A major deficiency in policy is the neglect of long-term support regarding issues such as education, health, mental health, employment, and job training, especially given language skill deficits. In addition, there is most often not adequate attention paid to pre- and postmigration mental health issues that interfere with successful adaptation. Paradoxically, the pressure associated with the demand for financial independence may contribute to exacerbating mental health problems rather then providing a psychological and cultural foundation from which to resolve past traumatic experiences and make a smoother transition into the new culture. Consequently, resettlement policy goals are frequently hampered by mental health concerns that interfere with achieving economic self-sufficiency.

Chapter 5

Multi-Level Model (MLM) Approach to Psychotherapy with Refugees

Refugees come from different ethnic and cultural backgrounds and are most often unfamiliar with traditional Western mental health services. Studies on ethnic minorities (e.g., Sue et al., 1991) have demonstrated that this population tends to underutilize mainstream mental health services because of a lack of cultural responsiveness. Given the differences in ethnic and cultural backgrounds, which are compounded by the uniqueness of the refugee experience, mental health professionals have an enormous challenge ahead of them to work with this rapidly growing population. To assist refugees to attain a sense of well-being and mental health, we have developed an intervention/prevention model called the Multi-Level Model (MLM) of counseling and psychotherapy with refugees. The MLM was initially conceptualized by Bemak, Chung and Bornemann (1996). The model was later greatly expanded and extended by Bemak and Chung (2002) who both further developed, refined and conceptualized the model in this book. The MLM is specifically applicable to refugee populations across cultures. Inherent in the model is the need for professionals to have unique skills, understanding, and sensitivity to the history, sociopolitical, cultural, psychological realities, deeply rooted trauma, and loss associated with forced migration. This is of particular importance since clinical training and supervision has rarely addressed cross-cultural psychotherapy that incorporates refugee work. The MLM reconceptualizes traditional training within the universal refugee framework of premigration, transition, and postmigration and presents therapeutic applications that are culturally responsive and effective for clinical interventions.

Given the complexity of the refugee experience, the MLM describes issues that need to be carefully considered when providing clinical interventions. Figure 5.1 depicts the skills that are essential for refugees to employ the MLM psychotherapy effectively. To effectively provide psychotherapy for refugees, the psychotherapist must be culturally sensitive and understand the individual's and families' world-view, sociopolitical background, premigration history, and experiences they have had as refugees. They must also understand the extent of identification with their culture of origin, particularly given residency in a new and different country, and the types of barriers that impede successful psychosocial adaptation and adjustment. This requires knowledge of Western psychotherapy and an ability to incorporate such theories and techniques in a culturally sensitive framework.

Since there is frequently a history of trauma, there is a need for the psychotherapist to demonstrate cultural empathy (Chung & Bemak, 2002), maintaining an awareness that traditional Western empathy may be inappropriate and even offensive to many refugee clients. For example, direct eye contact is an appropriate Western method of displaying understanding and empathy, however, for some cultures, such as the Asian culture, direct eye contact is intrusive and offensive. To avoid a continued pattern of premature termination by refugee clients, it is important for psychotherapists to maintain sensitivity and demonstrate cultural empathy.

Racism has been identified as a natural consequence of Westernized individualism (Pedersen, 2000). Mental health professionals who presume that they are free of racism seriously underestimate the social impact on their own socialization and the inherited, in some instances unintentionally covert, racism. In most cases, racism emerges as an unintentional action by well-meaning, right-thinking, good-hearted, caring professionals who are probably no more or less free from cultural biases than other members of the general public (Pedersen, 2000, p. 53). To avoid racism and therefore to be effective with refugee clients, it is also important for psychotherapists to be aware, acknowledge, and understand the ethnic identity of their client, as well, as themselves, this includes white identity (Helms, 1995). Racial and ethnic identity may be an important life issue for refugee clients as they are trying to acculturate. Thus working with a mental health professional who is aware of their clients' and their own ethnic/white identity and its effect on the therapeutic process is crucial. There are difficult questions that psychotherapists must ask themselves to be aware of their own racism and therefore to be effective with refugee populations. Questions such as: What are the effects of countertransference on counseling? What impact does my ethnicity have on the refugee client(s)? Do historical/sociopolitical factors and belief systems about the intersection of race/ethnicity and power relationships impact on the therapeutic relationship? If yes, how? What stereotypes, beliefs, and prejudices do I have about the refugee's cultural background and experiences? Exploring these issues is critical in working with the depth and struggle facing the majority of refugees.

A key issue in adjustment for many refugees is the difficult premigration period that oftentimes leads to posttraumatic stress disorders (PTSD). To work

Figure 5.1
Therapeutic Prerequisites for Effective MLM Application

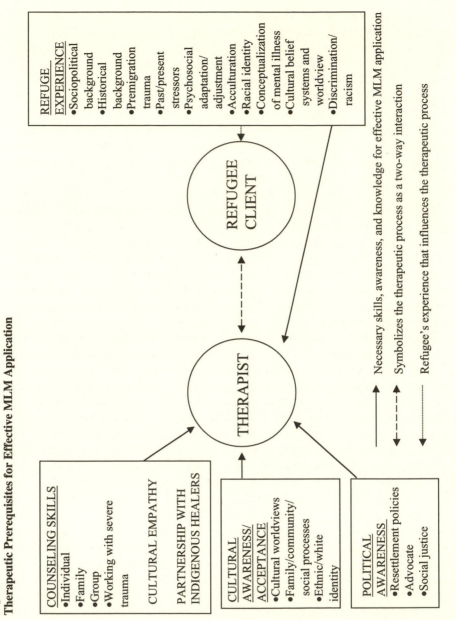

Source: Developed by Bemak and Chung (2002).

effectively with refugees, it is necessary to understand PTSD and the factors associated with severe trauma and to take a multidisciplinary approach that incorporates constructs in psychology, counseling, anthropology, psychiatry, public health, social work, and sociology. Mental health professionals must be willing and able to work with tough and painful premigration issues that precipitate severe trauma that is not always easy, given the depth of past pain and hardship for many refugees. For example, a 26-year-old Cambodian hid and watched her mother and sister being raped and her father and brother tortured and killed by a group of soldiers. The depth of anger and sadness it takes to revisit this story must be openly received by the psychotherapist despite its horror and anguish.

Given the degree of inhumane experiences encountered by some refugees, it is critical that psychotherapist give their clients hope by reducing some of their symptoms. Being exposed and working with this level of trauma requires therapists treating refugee clients to be acutely aware of their reactions to clients' stories of inhumane violence. For example, therapists may be overwhelmed when listening to stories of beatings, executions, or rape, eliciting feelings of horror, anger, and shock. They may become immobilized and withdrawn, unable to effectivly work with their clients. Sometimes, they may experience pity for the client and run the risk of showing hatred of the perpetrators of these atrocities that can interfere with therapy (Kinzie & Fleck, 1987). Given that many refugees come from politically troubled and war-torn countries, the therapist must also ensure that their political beliefs and values do not interfere in the treatment process. An example is the September 11 attacks of the World Trade Center in New York and the Pentagon in Washington, D.C. Strong feelings of loss for the victims and victims' families may contribute to strong political convictions and negative perceptions regarding devout Muslims, causing difficulty in working with Afghan refugees and/or Muslim clients.

Furthermore, given the unique situation of refugees, psychotherapists must also acknowledge that the usual treatment methods for PTSD may not be effective with this population. Similar to Holocaust survivors, the technique of reconstructing and helping victims of PTSD relive their traumatic experiences may not be a useful and beneficial technique for refugees, particularly in light of this group's extreme inhumane experience that may have tapped the limits of human ability to undergo this technique (Draguns, 1996; Kinzie, 1987). Through their work with Southeast Asian refugees Kinzie and Fleck (1987) identified eight universal components of effective intervention specific to refugees diagnosed with PTSD that assist clients in integrating the premigration trauma into postmigration adjustment. A description and commentary on the eight components follows.

First, ensure that the setting where treatment will be taking place is as non-threatening as possible. This requires that the setting should not resemble a jail cell or a place of interrogation or torture. It is recommended that to develop a relationship with their clients, therapists should create a relaxing and nonconfrontational situation, asking questions about health while giving support and immediate feedback. It is also suggested that for refugee women, especially those who have been sexually abused or raped, having a woman present in the room may alleviate anxiety. This component is consistent with the MLM Level I, mental health education, that is discussed below.

Second, therapists need to be aware of the importance of avoidance behavior for clients, since it provides a method of coping and protecting themselves from painfully intrusive thoughts and memories. The denial or suppression of these traumatic events may cause refugee clients to appear unaffected and unmoved by what has happened to them, given the pervasive numbing effects of the trauma. Bemak and Chung (1998) described this as the "psychological recoil effect" (PRE) based on their research with Vietnamese Amerasians (Vietnamese mothers and Americans fathers). It is therefore recommended that therapist slowly and carefully obtain client history without expectations that there will be consistency between the actual experiences of the client and their affective reaction to the event.

Third, therapists should expect an outpouring of emotions. Refugee clients are often numb or focused on somatic or other symptoms in an effort to avoid the past so that when emotions are expressed they may come as a flood of release.

Fourth, due to the nature of PTSD, it is suggested that long-term relationships with clients is necessary. This may involve both periodic intensive treatment when the symptoms are active and briefer contact with the client on an ongoing basis.

Fifth, some symptoms are more disruptive to the client than others, and therefore it is important to determine what initial treatment would give the client the most relief. It is recommended that therapists should focus on sleep disorder and depressed mood.

Sixth, symptoms can increase due to reexperiencing the past, which can be triggered by many sources such as media coverage of events in their home country, family disruption and distress, increased concern about lack of money or food, or pressure of a job and school. It is recommended that therapists assist their clients to relate their symptoms to life events. This technique also helps therapists understand traumatic flashbacks and periods of intensification.

Seventh, it is recommended that therapists obtain assistance from welfare agencies, churches, or refugee agencies and support groups to assist clients in reducing their stress related to problems with housing accommodations and income. Furthermore, it is suggested that therapists utilize the clients' religious or cultural belief systems as an avenue of support while also assisting clients to integrate traditional values with those of the host country. This recommendation is consistent with the MLM Level III, cultural empowerment, discussed below regarding psychotherapists as advocates and change agents for their clients.

Finally, it is recommended of an existential approach to catastrophic stress or brutality. There may be times when there is nothing to say or do except to simply remain with the client in silent companionship. Kinzie and Fleck (1987) state "in the end no words can heal and at times nothing can be added to what has been done or said. Death and the value of life become constant concerns and themes interwoven with life problems of the survivor. Admitting this and helping face it with the client can be one of the most useful and rewarding aspects of therapy" (p. 88).

Thus it is with an understanding of the unique characteristics, traits, and experiences of refugees that we propose the MLM of psychotherapy. The MLM takes into account cross-cultural issues relevant to different refugee groups, such as cultural conceptualization of mental illness and cultural belief systems and worldviews. It also takes on the complexity of the refugee's historical and sociopolitical background, premigration traumas, past and present stressors, the acculturation process, psychosocial factors in adapting to a new culture, and issues of discrimination and racism encountered in resettlement. The MLM is a psychoeducational model that incorporates affective, behavioral, and cognitive intervention and prevention strategies that are rooted in cultural foundations and relate to social and community processes. Figure 5.2 illustrates the four phases of the MLM: Level I, mental health education; Level II, individual, group, and/or family psychotherapy; Level III, cultural empowerment; and Level IV, indigenous healing.

It is important to emphasize that there is no fixed sequence to implementing the MLM levels, so they may be used concurrently or independently. The interrelationship of the four levels is essential for attaining the desired goals of psychotherapy, although each level may be considered independent of the other levels. The mental health professional may utilize a level at any stage of the therapeutic process or use elements of a level anytime throughout the treatment process. For example, although it is important to discuss Level I at the beginning of the session, this could be revisited at any period during the psychotherapeutic process to reclarify the psychotherapist's role or the aim of psychotherapy. Emphasis and utilization of any one level or combination of levels are based upon the assessment of the psychotherapist. Furthermore, the MLM is not a model that requires additional resources or funding.

LEVEL I: MENTAL HEALTH EDUCATION

This level focuses on educating client(s) about mainstream mental health practices and interventions. Refugees are typically not familiar with mental health services nor have expectations for what happens in therapy. This is especially true since many of the refugees come from cultures where professionals are directive and prescriptive and personal problems are not usually shared with people outside the family network. Critical in Level I is establishing a therapeutic relationship, which has been recognized as an essential ingredient of effective psychotherapy (Whol, 2000). However, a key to developing trust and rapport is to discuss and present these issues in a culturally sensitive manner without making assumptions about the knowledge base of refugee clients. In fact, refugees may need more time to explore and discuss these issues (Root, 1998), which can take place within the framework of Level I discussions.

Figure 5.2
Multi-Level Model of Psychotheraphy for Refugees

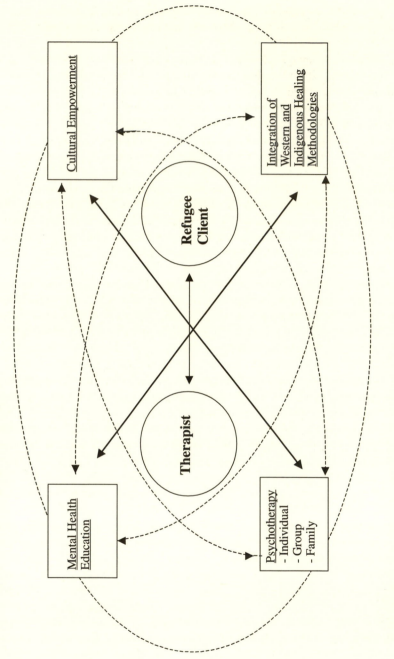

——— Indicate mutually exclusive utilization of an MLM level

- - - - Indicate interrelation between MLM levels and the concurrent utilization of MLM level

Source: Developed by Bemak and Chung (2002).

Included in these discussions are "mental health basics." Clarification is made regarding such issues as time boundaries for sessions, types of questions asked during intake assessments, the appropriateness of personal discussion and disclosure, the lack of a relationship between government officials and psychotherapy, confidentiality, the role of the professional, the role of an interpreter, different psychotherapeutic techniques, interpersonal space, relationship boundaries, and use or nonuse of medications. Refugee clients may feel less awkward or uncomfortable participating in the therapeutic relationship after discussing these important and relevant fundamentals of mental health. Thus Level I provides information, education, and clarification for the individual, group, or family about the process of psychotherapy and the mental health encounter.

It is important to note that Level I is a two-way process. While educating, providing, and clarifying the parameters of psychotherapy, the psychotherapist is gathering information about the client('s) mental health belief system and cultural views about help-seeking behaviors for use and application in other MLM levels. For example, a Salvadorian refugee shared that while escaping the fighting and traveling through Mexico he became highly agitated seeing spirits of family members who were killed in the fighting. Similar to the spiritual healer his family had worked with in El Salvador, he was introduced to a *curanderismo*, who helped calm the spirits anger. Hearing his story becomes a window into understanding client expectations, familiar practices, and previous mental health history. Bridging the divide between the client and psychotherapist's conceptualization of mental illness is central to effective interventions (Kleinman, 1980) and includes an exploration of the etiology, course, help-seeking behavior, and treatment outcomes as well as culturally unique symptom manifestation and preferred treatment expectations and outcomes.

Another important consideration during Level I is the history of premigration distrust that follows many refugees and may cause resistance and fear in psychotherapy. Mental health professionals must understand the origin of these behaviors and aim to cultivate a safe environment, not making the mistake of viewing the mistrust, suspicion, reluctance, confusion, and skepticism displayed by refugee clients as pathological resistance. Rather, these characteristics were oftentimes a survival strategy that meant the difference between life and death. Thus, a culturally sensitive introduction regarding the psychotherapeutic process can reduce client fears and mistrust.

LEVEL II: PSYCHOTHERAPY

Level II is based upon applying more traditional Western individual, group, and family therapy in culturally responsive ways and being able to work with clients who have experienced severe trauma. The mental health professional must make an assessment about the client's needs and then determine which type of psychotherapy and what techniques would be most suitable for that particular client in that particular situation. Although traditional Western techniques are foreign to most refugee clients, Zane and Sue (1991) demonstrated applicability of individual and family therapy to several culturally distinct groups. Techniques must be founded on basic cultural attributes and incorporate an understanding of cultural norms and practices with Western-based interventions, rather than emphasize Western techniques rooted in psychodynamic theory, which is alien to many refugees. An example of this is Kinzie's (1985) recommendation for psychotherapists to be more directive and active with Southeast Asian refugees.

There have been a number of other recommendations for therapeutic techniques that are effective in cross-cultural refugee work. Cognitive-behavioral interventions have been used successfully with refugees (Bemak & Greenberg, 1994; Egli, Shiota, Ben-Porath, & Butcher, 1991) and identified as applicable for Asian refugees because of its compatibility with Buddhism (De Silva, 1985; Mikulas, 1981) and ability to reorient to the present and move beyond painful premigration memories and anxiety about the future (Beiser, 1987). There has also been consistency between cognitive-behavioral therapy and the Hispanic culture (Arce & Torres-Matrullo, 1982; Comas Diaz, 1985; Stumphauser & Davis, 1983).

The MLM Level II also incorporates other techniques. Storytelling and projective drawing have assisted previously traumatized children regain control over their lives (Pynoos & Eth,1984). Family therapy has also been found to be an effective and culturally sensitive intervention (Bemak, 1989; Szapocznik & Cohen, 1986). Bemak and Timm (1994) presented a Cambodian refugee case study in which dreamwork played a central role in therapy, while moral development with a focus on strongly valued cultural traits such as honesty with Haitian refugees (Charles, 1986) was found to be an effective intervention. Other techniques that may be employed in counseling include gestalt, relaxation, narrative therapy, role playing, and psychodrama.

To employ culturally relevant techniques, there must be an awareness and knowledge of counseling theory, therapeutic processes, and models of prevention and intervention. Given the history of persecution, trauma, and forced migration that many refugees faced, it is vital to understand and consider the refugee's background as it impacts present psychological functioning and be able to work with PTSD. Many political governments or groups intruded into the lives, families, and communities of refugees, creating a distrust and fear of authority. Daily survival necessitated a hypersensitivity to the motives of those seeking personal information. Thus, being asked highly personal and blunt questions by a mental health professional may be experienced as dangerous, threatening, and inappropriate. Since psychotherapy requires personal self-disclosure and a level of intimacy with the psychotherapist, trust must be cautiously fostered, keeping in mind the client's worldview based on premigration history. An example of this is the Bosnian adolescent who hid and watched in silence as his mother was repeatedly raped. He knew that if he yelled out or tried to protect her, he would certainly face severe beatings and possibly his own death. When he first met a psychotherapist, he had blunted affect, was reluctant to express any feelings or opinions, and mistrusted the "true" motives of the psychotherapist.

Given that most refugees come from collectivist cultures, we would strongly recommend group and family work to foster interdependence in social and family networks (Morris & Silove, 1992; Rectman, 1997). Although there is little research on group or family therapy with refugees, based on the authors' experience and informal reports from national and international colleagues, these therapeutic modalities are viewed as key elements in the MLM. The curative factors of group work identified by Yalom (1985) that have applicability for refugees are universality, altruism, and corrective emotional experiences. These healing factors have been used in refugee group therapy to resolve painful psychological issues. Examples of beneficial group therapy with refugees include refugee children in group counseling discussing their shared experience of a traumatic event (Galante & Foa,1986), sharing in group therapy with traumatized refugee clients (Friedman & Jaranson,1994), and a year-long therapy group for Southeast Asians that incorporated discussions about somatizations, cultural conflicts, and loss while maintaining loosely constructed time boundaries (Kinzie et al., 1988). Therefore, the MLM recommends using group therapy since this technique is in line with the refugee's cultural background.

The strong family bonds for most refugees and the necessity of family adaptation in countries of migration leads us to also recommend family therapy as a natural means of addressing problems from a family systems perspective. The cultural importance of the refugee family, especially within the context of being placed as a unit in a new and strange country, results in the MLM embodying family counseling as a major therapeutic intervention. Since families in collectivist cultures are typically defined as an extended unit, family therapy with refugee populations may work with extended families. It is essential that professionals who provide family therapy for refugee populations must have a clear understanding and knowledge about the background and traditional relationships and roles of families prior to migration. In Western countries family therapy most often includes parents and children. In comparison, in the MLM, we recommend evaluating the inclusion of grandparents, aunts, uncles, cousins, and friends who are identified as part of the family, and even more distant relatives. Having determined who family members are, it is crucial that the psychotherapist be aware of family hierarchy and appropriately address and acknowledge those who warrant greater respect by virtue of their role in the family. Examples of family therapy as an effective intervention during the postmigration period with refugees, describing the benefit of working with family relationships, family dynamics, communication patterns, and roles have included work by Bemak (1989), Charles (1986), Lee (1989), and Szapocznik and Cohen (1986).

Diagnoses

It is also important to note that Western-based frameworks of diagnoses [e.g., the *Diagnostic and Statistical Manual*, fourth edition (*DSM-IV*) and the *International Classification of Diseases* (*ICD1-0*)] may not be culturally sensitive to refugee populations. As mentioned previously, given the cultural influence in conceptualizing mental health problems and symptom manifestation, it is often-times the case that patterns of symptoms do not correspond exactly with discrete classifications of Western disorders. However, psychotherapists may try to make sense of culturally expressed symptomatology and force them into discrete categorizations, resulting in erroneous diagnoses and subsequently ineffective treatment (Chung & Kagawa-Singer, 1995). Research has shown that the mis-classification of psychiatric disorders of ethnic clients in the United States (Asian Americans, African Americans, and Latina(o) Americans has been due to the psychotherapist's lack of understanding of cultural and/or linguistic differences (e.g., Baskin, Bluestone, & Nelson, 1981; Huertin-Roberts & Snowden, 1993). Therefore, the mental health professional must become knowledgeable about how refugees conceptualize mental illness and express their distress before effective diagnosis and treatment can take place. This includes the awareness of ethnocentric biases inherent in diagnostic categories (Chung & Kagawa-Singer, 1995).

LEVEL III: CULTURAL EMPOWERMENT

MLM's Level III, cultural empowerment, provides another important dimension in the healing of the refugee client. Cultural empowerment is a critical element in postmigration, assisting refugees to gain a better sense of cultural and environmental mastery. Refugees who present themselves to mental health professionals may have pressing survival needs related to resettlement such as finding housing, securing employment, learning English, and understanding aspects of the social services system that may have far more immediacy than delving into intrapsychic and interpersonal problems or psychosocial adjustment issues. The frustration and stress of not understanding how systems work, how to access services, or where to go for assistance with certain problems related to education, finances, health, or employment may be a predominant issue that must be resolved before other psychological problems can be explored. Psychotherapists may be instrumental in providing information about these resources.

Since most refugees are also involved with other service systems, there is a need for multiagency information sharing. To fully understand and assist with what is going on with child protective services, social services, juvenile services, housing, schools, and medical services, it is important for the mental health professional to ensure that information is available to them. For example, many refugees acquire health problems due to histories of starvation, poor nutrition, unsanitary living conditions, disease, and camp experiences. These health problems are sometimes confusing and frightening to refugees, who may lack the medical knowledge to understand the physical symptoms and long-range course of their medical condition. This was true for a Vietnamese refugee who was diagnosed with hepatitis and was told he could not engage in "sexual activity or contact" with anyone. He was highly agitated and did not understand what the physician meant nor how long this would last. To clarify this situation, the MLM recommends that mental health professionals have access to this information so that it can be discussed in psychotherapy.

The MLM also suggests that mental health professionals become proactive and assume a social advocacy role related to governmental resettlement policies and practices and basic human rights that are troublesome and unfair and present problems for refugee clients. Inherent in this more active stance is the assumption that social justice is an integral component of psychotherapy. To neglect issues that present themselves regularly to refugees that are inequitable, unfair, discriminatory, or a violation of their human rights is unconscionable. This requires attention to issues such as family reunification, welfare benefits, social services, financial support for heating or electricity costs, and housing benefits that may present difficult barriers that impede a healthy adjustment. Thus it is recommended that psychotherapists incorporate social advocacy based on a value for social justice and equity into their definition of intervention to ensure that discrimination and unfair treatment is addressed. It is important to note that this should not involve additional time beyond therapeutic sessions with clients but should be built into psychotherapy. For example, making phone calls together or writing letters to agencies may be a valuable use of time in therapy.

A final aspect of cultural empowerment is acquiring skills to deal with racism, discrimination, and oppression that may be encountered in the resettlement country. As previously discussed, the host society may not welcome nor accept refugees, especially during economic hardship or perceived competition for resources. This hostility and rejection is exacerbated when the host society does not understand or accept the refugee's customs or behaviors, precipitating negative reactions toward them. The negativity may result in individual and/or institutional racism that makes acculturation more difficult and is substantiated by the literature that clearly documents the ill effects of racism on psychological well-being (e.g., Aponte & Johnson, 2000; Asamen & Berry, 1987; Hughes & Demo, 1989).

Thus, we strongly believe that mental health professionals must be attuned and highly sensitive to the difficulties inherent in adapting to a new culture and expand beyond traditional roles to provide case management-type assistance, guidance, and resource information that will empower the refugee. In the MLM, the psychotherapist is not expected actually to become the case manager for the client. Rather, they assume responsibilities as a "cultural systems information guide and advocate," assisting the refugee with relevant information about how systems work, how to problem solve within those systems, and what new coping strategies are needed to master the new culture. This may require the psychotherapist to function in this capacity over an extended period, with the long-term goal of enabling the client to develop knowledge and skills to deal with the new system. The resultant mastery of these skills by the client creates successful experience and cultural empowerment.

LEVEL IV: INTEGRATION OF WESTERN
AND INDIGENOUS HEALING METHODOLOGIES

Level IV of the MLM, indigenous healing, integrates Western traditional and nontraditional healing methodologies. It has been acknowledged by the World Health Organization (1992) that an integration of Western traditional mental health practice and indigenous healing results in more effective outcomes. The use of alternative healing methodologies is widespread throughout the world. For example, it has been reported that approximately one third of the United States population, half of those in Europe, and more than three quarters of people worldwide regularly utilize some form of alternative or indigenous (non-Western) method of healing (Micozzi, 1996).

According to Pedersen (2000), Western and non-Western approaches to healing are becoming more complementary as the fields of counseling and psychology give increasing attention to this area. Despite this knowledge, indigenous practices are typically disregarded by Western mental health professionals, who lack the knowledge and experience to understand this cross-cultural work. There is a need for professional training and receptivity to non-Western, culturally bound forms of healing that would support and enhance the psychotherapeutic process with refugee clients. One cautionary note here is that not all indigenous healers are legitimate; Western practitioners must be mindful and carefully ascertain their genuineness before collaborating with them in the therapeutic process.

It is also critical that psychotherapist establish a relationship with community leaders, priests, monks, healers, and other significant community members. These community members play an important role in assisting the psychotherapist in learning about a refugee client's cultural background, as well as other cultural perspectives on health and mental health issues. Significant community members also can assist the psychotherapist in educating the community regarding psychotherapy and mental health practices.

Four approaches of indigenous healers have been identified: (a) physical treatments, (b) magic healing methods, (c) counseling, and (d) medications (Hiegel, 1994). To form "treatment partnerships" with indigenous healers, it is important that the mental health professionals understand and accept these traditional cultural practices that ensure the refugee the rich combination of healing sources from the culture of origin and the culture of resettlement. Religious and spiritual leaders may also become essential in indigenous healing, particularly when working with families and communities that are highly spiritual. One example of this was with a refugee Muslim family from Iraq who were in a period of bitter tension regarding the wife's growing autonomy. The psychotherapist learned that they were an extremely religious family. Working together with the head of the nearby mosque in a treatment partnership, the therapist was able to ensure spiritual guidance for the family that was consistent with the family therapy. Another example is the case of one of thousands of Southeast Asian refugee women who was raped during the war, escaped, and lived in a refugee camp. Although she was Buddhist, there is no Buddhist healing ritual for rape. The Western psychotherapist spoke with the local monks to express the pain and frequency of rape for a number of refugee women and asked about the possibility of developing a healing ritual for the cleansing of rape. This treatment partnership facilitated new practices by the monks that would balance the psychotherapy work.

These examples point toward the need for receptivity to culture-bound practices by making referrals to indigenous healers and the willingness to explain and discuss problems in treatment partnerships. For those mental health professionals who work with refugees, it is necessary that they are knowledgeable and have access to healers and community elders and cooperate with them during treatment (Chan, 1987; Hiegel, 1994). Of equal importance for mental health professionals is to acknowledge that their clients may prefer indigenous methods or want to combine Western with indigenous treatment techniques, and that a number of them may use both methods concurrently without the knowledge of the psychotherapist (Chung & Lin, 1994).

A key to working successfully with traditional healers is the nature and quality of the relationship that is established with them. The relationship must be based on genuine mutual respect, trust, understanding, and confidence so that traditional healers feel free to act without concern for the success or failure of their treatments, or the constant need to explain to the psychotherapist the reasons behind their methods. It is important to remember that traditional healers are respected and trusted by their community even though some behaviors may seem odd to the mental health professional, such as the tendency for indigenous healers to boast about their ability and protect their image (Hiegel, 1994). Thus, to form value-free and judgment-free treatment partnerships with a genuine acknowledgment that both healing methodologies are beneficial and aim toward the same goal of mental health is important.

Although the MLM highly recommends psychotherapists to work collaboratively and in partnership with indigenous healers, it is also necessary to mention a few words of caution. It is important that psychotherapists not assume that all refugee clients prefer traditional healing as the treatment of choice. This model suggest that psychotherapists should explore this type of treatment with their clients only when the client initiates this discussion, when the client's social network recommends this type of intervention, or when it is clear from the sociocultural background and history of the client that this type of intervention would be beneficial. Thus, it is necessary for psychotherapists to fully explore and investigate the validity, reliability, and effectiveness of traditional healing as an effective intervention as well as the credibility of the traditional healer.

References for Part I

Adams, P.L. (1990). Prejudice and exclusion as social traumata. In J.D. Noshpitz & R.D. Coddington (Eds.), *Stressors and the adjustment disorders* (pp. 362–391). New York: Wiley.

Aponte, J., & Barnes, J.M. (1995). Impact of acculturation and moderator variables on the intervention and treatment of ethnic groups. In J.F. Aponte, R. Young Rivers, & J. Wohl (Eds.), *Psychological intervention and cultural diversity* (pp. 19–39). Needham Heights, MA: Allyn & Bacon.

Aponte, J., & Johnson, L.R. (2000). The impact of culture on intervention and treatment of ethnic populations. In J. Aponte & J. Wohl (Eds.), *Psychological intervention and cultural diversity* (pp. 18–39). Needham Heights, MA: Allyn & Bacon.

Ajdukovic, M., & Ajdukovic, D. (1993). Psychological well-being of refugee children. *Child Abuse and Neglect, 17*, 843–854.

Arce, A., & Torres-Matrullo, C. (1982). Application of cognitive behavioral techniques in the treatment of Hispanic patients. *Psychiatric Quarterly, 54*, 230–236.

Asamen, J.K. & Berry, G.L. (1987). Self-concept, alienation, and perceived prejudice: Implications for counseling Asian Americans. *Journal of Multicultural Counseling and Development, 15*, 146–160.

Atkinson, D.R., Morten, G., & Sue, D.W. (Eds.). (1998). *Counseling American minorities* (5th ed.). Boston: McGraw-Hill.

Baker, R. (1992). Psychosocial consequences for tortured refugees seeking asylum and refugee status in Europe. In M. Basoglu (Ed.), *Torture and its consequences* (pp. 83–106). Cambridge: Cambridge University Press.

Balian, K. (1997). *Overview of issues and the United Nations roles.* Paper presented at the meeting on Survivors of Torture: Improving Our Understanding Conference. Washington, DC.

Baskin, D., Bluestone, H., & Nelson, M. (1981). Mental illness in minority women. *Journal of Clinical Psychology, 37*(3), 491–498.

Beiser, M. (1987). Changing time perspective and mental health among Southeast Asian refugees. *Culture, Medicine, and Psychiatry, 11*, 437–464.

Bemak, F. (1989). Cross-cultural family therapy with Southeast Asian refugees. *Journal of Strategic and Systemic Therapies, 8*, 22–27.

Bemak, F., & Chung, R.C-Y. (1998). Vietnamese Amerasians: Predictors of distress and self-destructive behavior. *Journal of Counseling and Development, 76*(4), 452–458.

Bemak, F., & Chung, R.C-Y. (1999). Vietnamese Amerasians: The relationship between biological American father and psychological distress, and self-destructive behavior. *Journal of Community Psychology, 27*(4), 443–456.

Bemak, F., & Chung, R.C-Y. (2002). Counseling and psychotherapy with refugees. In P.B. Pedersen, J.G. Draguns, W.J. Lonner, & J.E. Trimble (Eds.), *Counseling across cultures*, (5th ed., pp. 209–232). Thousand Oaks, CA: Sage.

Bemak, F., & Chung, R.C-Y. (2003). Working with children and families from recent immigrant groups (2nd ed., pp. 84–101.) In P. Pedersen & J. Carey (Eds.), *Multicultural counseling in schools*. Needham Heights, MA: Allyn & Bacon.

Bemak, F., Chung, R.C-Y., & Bornemann T.H. (1996). Counseling and psychotherapy with refugees. In P.B. Pedersen, J.G., Draguns, W.J. Lonner, & J.E. Trimble (Eds.), *Counseling across cultures* (4th ed., pp. 207–231). Thousands Oaks, CA: Sage.

Bemak, F., & Greenberg, B. (1994). Southeast Asian refugee adolescents: Implications for counseling. *Journal of Multicultural Counseling and Development, 22*(4), 115–124.

Bemak, F., & Timm, J. (1994). Case study of an adolescent Cambodian refugee: A clinical, developmental and cultural perspective. *International Journal of the Advancement of Counseling, 17*, 47–58.

Ben-Porath Y. (1991). The psychosocial adjustment of refugees. In J. Westermeyer, C. Williams, & A. Nguyen (Eds.), *Mental health services for refugees* (pp. 1–23) (DHHS Publication No. ADM 91-1824). Washington, DC: U.S. Government Printing Office.

Berrol, S.C. (1995). *Growing up American: Immigrant children in American then and now*. New York: Twayne.

Berry, J.W. (1986). The acculturation process and refugee behavior. In C.L. Williams & J. Westermeyer (Eds.), *Refugee mental health in resettlement countries* (pp. 25–37). Washington, DC: Hemisphere.

Berry, J.W. (1990). Psychology of acculturation. In R.W. Brislin (Ed.), *Applied cross-cultural psychology* (pp. 232–253). Newbury Park, CA: Sage.

Berry, J.W., & Anis, R.C. (1974). Acculturative stress: The role of econology, culture, and differentiation. *Journal of Cross-Cultural Psychology, 5*, 382–406.

Berry, J.W., & Kim, U. (1988). Acculturation and mental health. In P.R. Dasen, J.W. Berry, & N. Sartorius (Eds.), *Health and cross-cultural psychology: Toward applications* (pp. 207–236). Newbury Park, CA: Sage.

Boothby, N. (1988). Without moral restraint: Children in the midst of war. *Social health review: Special report*. Washington, DC: U.S. Committee for Refugees.

Boothby, N. (1994). Trauma and violence among refugee children. In A.J. Marsella, T. Bornemann, S. Ekblad, & J. Orley (Eds.), *Amidst peril and pain: The mental health and well-being of the world's refugees* (pp. 239–259). Washington, DC: American Psychological Association.

Boothby, N., Upton, P., & Sultan, A. (1991). *Children of Mozambique: The cost of survival*. Washington, DC: U.S. Committee for Refugees.

Bottinelli, M. (1990). *Psychological impact of exile: Salvadoran and Guatemalan families in Mexico*. Washington, DC: Center for Immigration Policy and Refugee Assistance.

Brown, G. (1982). Issues in the resettlement of Indochinese refugees. *Social Casework,*
 63, 155–159.
Buchwald, D., Manson, S.M., Ginges, N.G., Keane, E.M., & Kinzie, D. (1993). Prevalence of depressive symptoms among established Vietnamese refugees in the
 United States. *Journal of General Internal Medicine, 8,* 76–81.
Carlson, E.B., & Rosser-Hogan, R. (1991). Trauma experiences, posttraumatic stress, dis-
 sociation and depression in Cambodian refugees. *American Journal of Psychiatry,*
 148, 1548–1551.
Caspi, Y., Poole, C., Mollica, R.F., & Frankel, M. (1998). Relationship of child loss to
 psychiatric and functional impairment in resettled Cambodian refugees. *Journal of*
 Nervous and Mental Diseases, 186(8), 489–491.
Casas, J.M., & Pytluk, S.D. (1995). Hispanic identity development: Implication for research
 and practice. In J.G. Ponterotto, J.M. Casas, L.A. Suzuki, & C.M. Alexander (Eds.),
 Handbook of multicultural counseling (pp. 155–180). Thousands Oaks, CA: Sage.
Catanzaro, A., & Moser, R.J. (1982). Health status of refugees from Vietnam, Laos, and
 Cambodia. *Journal of American Medical Association, 247,* 1303–1308.
Cervantes, R., Salgado, V., & Padilla, A. (1988). Posttraumatic stress in immigrants from
 Central America and Mexico. *Hospital and Community Psychiatry, 40,* 615–619.
Chan, F. (1987, April). *Survivors of the killing fields* Paper presented at the Western Psy-
 chological Association Convention, Long Beach, CA.
Charles, C. (1986). Mental health services for Haitians. In H.P. Lefley & P.B. Pedersen
 (Eds.), *Cross-cultural training for mental health professionals* (pp. 183–198).
 Springfield, IL: Charles C. Thomas.
Cheung, F.H. (1982). Psychological symptoms among Chinese in urban Hong Kong.
 Social Science and Medicine, 16, 1339–1334.
Chung, R.C-Y. (2000). Psychosocial adjustment of Cambodian refugee women: Implica-
 tions for mental health counseling. *Journal of Mental Health Counseling, 23(2),*
 115–126.
Chung, R.C-Y., & Bemak, F. (1996). The effects of welfare status on psychological dis-
 tress among Southeast Asian refugees. *Journal of Nervous and Mental Disease,*
 184(6), 346–353.
Chung, R.C-Y., & Bemak, F. (2000). Vietnamese refugees' levels of distress, social support, and acculturation: Implications for mental health counseling. *Journal of*
 Mental Health Counseling, 22(2), 150–161.
Chung, R.C-Y., & Bemak, F. (2002). Revisiting the California Southeast Asian mental
 health needs assessment data: An examination of refugee ethnic and gender differences. *Journal of Counseling and Development, 80,* 111–119.
Chung, R.C-Y., & Bemak, F. (2002). The relationship between culture and empathy in
 cross cultural counseling. *Journal of Counseling and Development, 80,* 154–159.
Chung, R.C-Y., & Kagawa-Singer, M. (1993). Predictors of psychological distress among
 Southeast Asian refugees. *Social Science and Medicine, 36(5),* 631–639.
Chung, R.C-Y., & Kagawa-Singer, M. (1995). Interpretation of symptom presentation
 and distress: A Southeast Asian refugee example. *Journal of Nervous and Mental*
 Disease, 183(10), 639–648.
Chung, R.C-Y., & Lin, K.M. (1994). Helpseeking behavior among Southeast Asian
 refugees. *Journal of Community Psychology, 22,* 109–120.
Chung, R.C-Y., & Okazaki, S. (1991). Counseling Americans of Southeast Asian descent:
 The impact of the refugee experience. In C.C. Lee & B.L. Richardson (Eds.),

Multicultural issues in counseling: New approaches to diversity (pp. 107–126). Alexandria, VA: American Association for Counseling and Development.

Chung, R.C-Y, Bemak, F., & Kagawa-Singer, M. (1998). Gender differences in psychological distress among Southeast Asian refugees. *Journal of Nervous and Mental Disease, 186*(2), 112–119.

Chung, R.C-Y, Bemak, F., & Okazaki, S. (1997). Counseling Americans of Southeast Asian descent: The impact of the refugee experience. In C.C. Lee (Ed.), *Multicultural issues in counseling: New approaches to diversity* (pp. 207–232). Alexandria, VA: American Counseling Association.

Clinton-Davis, L., & Fassil, Y. (1992). Health and social problems of refugees. *Social Science and Medicine, 35*, 507–513.

Coleman, D.A. (1995). International migration: Demographics and socioeconomic consequences in the United Kingdom and Europe. *International Migration Review, 29*(1), 155–180.

Comas-Diaz, L. (1985). Cognitive and behavioral group therapy with Puerto Rican women. A comparison of group themes. *Hispanic Journal of Behavioral Sciences, 7*, 273–283.

Cox, D.R., & Amelsvoort, A.V. (1994). *The wellbeing of asylum seekers in Australia: A study of policies and practice with identification and discussion of the key issues.* Melbourne: Centre for Regional Social Development, La Trobe University.

Cross, W.E., Jr. (1985). Black identity: Rediscovering the distinction between personal identity and reference group orientation. In M.B. Spencer, G.K. Brookins, & W.R. Allen (Eds.), *Beginnings: The social and affective development of Black children* (pp. 155–171). Hillsdale, NJ: Lawrence Erlbaum.

Dadfar, A. (1994). The Afghans: Bearing the scars of a forgotten war. In A.J. Marsella, T. Bornemann, S. Ekblad, & J. Orley (Eds.), *Amidst peril and pain: The mental health and well-being of the world's refugees* (pp. 125–139). Washington, DC: American Psychological Association.

Dana, R.H. (2000). Psychological assessment in the diagnosis and treatment of ethnic group members. In J.A. Aponte & J. Wohl (Eds.), *Psychological intervention and cultural diversity* (pp. 59–74). Needham Heights, MA: Allyn & Bacon.

De Silva, P. (1985). Buddhism and modern behavioral strategies for the control of unwanted intrusive cognitions. *The Psychological Record, 35*, 437–443.

Desjarlais, R., Eisenberg, L., Good, B., & Kleinman, A. (1995). *World mental health: Problems and priorities in low-income countries.* New York: Oxford University Press.

Displaced people: When is a refugee not a refugee. *The Economist*, March 3, 2001.

Draguns, J.G. (1996). Ethnocultural considerations in the treatment of PTSD: Therapy and service delivery. In A.J. Marsella, M.J. Friedman, E.T. Gerrity, & R.M. Scurfield (Eds.), *Ethnocultural aspects of posttraumatic stress disorder: Issues, research and clinical applications* (pp. 459–482). Washington, DC: American Psychological Association.

Draguns, J. (2000). Psychopathology and ethnicity. In J.F. Aponte & J. Wohl (Eds.), *Psychological intervention and cultural diversity* (pp. 40–58). Needham Heights, MA: Allyn & Bacon.

Dube, K.C. (1968). Mental disorder in Agra. *Social Psychiatry, 3*, 139–143.

Egawa, J.E., & Tashima, N. (1982). *Indigenous healers in Southeast Asian refugee communities.* San Francisco: Pacific Asian Mental Health Research Projects.

Egli, A., Shiota, N., Ben-Porath, Y., & Butcher, J. (1991). Psychological interventions. In J. Westermeyer, C. Williams, & A. Nguyen (Eds.), *Mental health services for refugees* (pp. 157–188). Washington, DC: U.S. Government Printing Office.

Eitinger, L. (1960). The symptomatology of mental disease among refugees in Norway. *Journal of Mental Science, 106,* 315–326.

El-Sarraj, E.R., Tawahina, A.A., & Heine, F.A. (1994). The Palestinians: An uprooted people. In A.J. Marsella, T. Bornemann, S. Ekblad, & J. Orley (Eds.), *Amidst peril and pain: The mental health and well-being of the world's refugees* (pp. 141–152). Washington, DC: American Psychological Association.

Fabrega, H. (1989). Cultural relativism and psychiatric illness. *Journal of Nervous and Mental Disorders, 177*(3), 415–425.

Farias, P. (1991). Emotional distress and its sociopolitical correlates in Salvadoran refugees. *Culture, Medicine and Psychiatry, 15,* 167–192.

Farooq, S., Gahir, M.S., Okeyere, E., Sheikh, A.J., & Oyebode, F. (1993). Somatization: A transcultural study. *Journal of Psychosomatic Research, 39,* 883–888.

Fawzi, M.C.S., Pham, T., Lin, L., Nguyen, T.V., Ngo, D., Murphy, E., & Mollica, R.F. (1997). The validity of posttraumatic stress disorder among Vietnamese refugees. *International Society for Traumatic Stress Studies, 10*(1), 101–108.

Freud, A., & Dann, S. (1951). An experiment in group upbringing. *Psychoanalytic Study of the Child, 6,* 127.

Friedman, M., & Jaranson, J. (1994). The applicability of the posttraumatic stress disorder concepts to refugees. In A.J. Marsella, T. Bornemann, S. Ekblad, & J. Orley (Eds.), *Amidst peril and pain: The mental health and well-being of the world's refugees* (pp. 207–228). Washington, DC: American Psychological Association.

Galante, R., & Foa, D. (1986). An epidemiological study of psychic trauma and treatment effectiveness for children after a natural disaster. *Journal of the American Academy of Child Psychiatry, 25,* 33–57.

Garbarino, J. (1990, April 3). *Children and youth in war zones: coping with the consequences.* Testimony prepared for the U.S. Senate Committee on Human Resources, Subcommittee on Children, Family, Drugs, and Alcoholism, Washington, DC.

Garcia-Peltoniemi, R. (1991). Epidemiological perspectives. In J. Westermeyer, C.L. Williams, & A.N. Nguyen (Eds.), *Mental health services for refugees* (DHHS Publication No. ADM 91–1824, pp, 24–41). Washington, DC: U.S. Government Printing Office.

Gibson, M.A. (1997). Complicating the immigrant/involuntary minority typology. *Anthropology and Education Quarterly Review, 28*(3), 431–454.

Gong-Guy, E. (1987). *The California Southeast Asian Mental Health Needs Assessment.* Asian San Francisco: Community Mental Health Services. Unpublished Manuscript.

Gonzalez, J.M., & Darling-Hammond, L. (1997). *New concepts for new challenges: Professional development for teachers of immigrant youth.* Washington, DC: Center for Applied Linguistics.

Good, B.J., & Good, M.J.D. (1981). The meaning of symptoms: A cultural hermeneutic model of clinical practice. In L. Eisenberg & A. Kleinman (Eds.), *The relevance of social science for medicine* (pp. 165–196). Dordrecht, Holland: Reidel.

Hauff, E., & Vaglum, P. (1995). Organized violence and the stress of exile: Predictors of mental health in a community cohort of Vietnamese refugees three years after resettlement. *British Journal of Psychiatry, 166,* 360–367.

Healey, J. (1993). *Countdown to the 1993 World Conference on Human Rights* (Fundraising letter). Amnesty International USA.

Helms, J.E. (1995). An updated of Helm's white and people of color racial identity models. In J.G. Ponterotto, J.M. Casas, L.A. Suzuki, & C.M. Alexander (Eds.), *Handbook of multicultural counseling* (pp.199–217). Thousand Oaks, CA: Sage.

Helms, J.E., & Talleyrand, R.M. (1997). Race is not ethnicity. *American Psychologist, 52*, 1246–1247.

Hertzberg, M. (1998). Having arrived: Dimensions of educational success in a transitional newcomer school. *Anthropology & Educational Quarterly, 29*(4), 391–418.

Hiegel, J.P. (1994). Use of indigenous concepts and healers in the care of refugees: Some experiences from the Thai border camps. In A.J. Marsella, T. Bornemann, S. Ekblad, & J. Orley (Eds.), *Amidst peril and pain: The mental health and well-being of the world's refugees* (pp. 293–310). Washington DC: American Psychological Association.

Higginbotham, J.C., Trevino, F.M., & Ray, L.A. (1990). Utilization of curanderos by Mexican Americans: Prevalence and predictor findings from HHANES 1982–1984. *American Journal of Public Health, 80 Supplement*, 32–35.

Hinton, W.L., Tiet, Q., Tran, C.G., & Chesney, M. (1997). Predictors of depression among refugees from Vietnam: A longitudinal study of new arrivals. *Journal of Nervous and Mental Disease, 185*(1), 39–45.

Hitch, P.J., & Rack, P.H. (1980). Mental illness among Polish and Russian refugees in Bradford. *British Journal of Psychiatry, 137*, 206–211.

Huang, L.N. (1989). Southeast Asian refugee children and adolescents. In J.T. Gibbs & L.N. Huang (Eds.), *Children of color: Psychological interventions with minority children* (pp. 278–321). San Francisco: Jossey-Bass.

Huertin-Roberts, S., & Snowden, L. (1993). *Comparison of ethnographic descriptors of depression and epidemiological catchment area data for African Americans.* Paper presented at the 18th Annual American Anthropology Association Meeting, Washington, DC.

Hughes, M., & Demo, D.H. (1989). Self-perceptions of Black Americans: Self-esteeem and personal efficacy. *American Journal of Sociology, 95*, 135–159.

Ima, K., & Rumbaut, R. (1989). Southeast Asian refugees in American schools: A comparison of fluent English-proficient students. *Topics in Language Disorders*, 54–74.

Jahoda, M.M. (1982). *Employment and unemployment: A social psychological analysis.* New York: Cambridge University.

Jenkins, J. (1991). The state, the body, and political violence: The embodiment of fear and anxiety among Salvadoran women refugees. *Culture, Medicine and Psychiatry, 15*, 139–165.

Jones, N. (1990). Black/White issues in psychotherapy. *Journal of Social Behavior and Personality, 5*, 305–322.

Jupp, J. (1994). Australian immigration and settlement: History and current trends. In I.H. Minas, & C.L. Hayes (Eds.), *Migration and mental health: Responsibilities and opportunities* (pp. 3–11). Melbourne: Victorian Transculturay Psychiatry Unit.

Kagawa-Singer, M., & Chung, R.C-Y. (1994). A paradigm for culturally based care in ethnic minority populations. *Journal of Community Psychology, 22*, 192–208.

Karadaghi, P. (1994). The Kurds: Refugees in their own land. In A.J. Marsella, T. Bornemann, S. Ekblad, & J. Orley (Eds.), *Amidst peril and pain: The mental health and well-being of the world's refugees* (pp. 115–124). Washington, DC: American Psychological Association.

Kessler, R.C., House, J.S., Turner, J.B. (1987a). Unemployment and health in a community sample. *Journal of Health and Social Behavior, 28*, 51–59.

Kessler, R.C., Turner, J.B., & House, J.S. (1987b). Intervening processes in the relationship between unemployment and health. *Psychological Medicine, 17*, 949–961.

Kinzie, J.D. (1985). Overview of clinical issues in the treatment of Southeast Asian refugees. In T.C. Owan (Ed.), *Southeast Asain mental health: Treatment, prevention, services, training, and research* (pp. 113–135). Washington, DC: National Institute of Mental Health.

Kinzie, J.D. (1987). The concentration camp syndrome among Cambodian refugees. In D.A. Ablin & M. Hood (Eds.), *The Cambodian agony* (pp. 332–353). Armonk, NY: M.E. Sharpe.

Kinzie, J.D. (1993). Posttraumatic effects and their treatment among Southeast Asian refugees. In J. Wilson & B. Raphael (Eds.), *International handbook of traumatic stress syndromes* (pp. 311–320). New York: Plenum.

Kinzie, J.D., & Fleck, J. (1987). Psychotherapy with severely traumatized refugees. *American Journal of Psychotherapy, 41*, 82–94.

Kinzie, J.D., Manson, S., Do.V., Nguyen, T., Anh, B., & Pho, T. (1982). Development and validation of a Vietnamese language depression rating scale. *American Journal of Psychiatry, 139*(10), 1276–1281.

Kinzie, J.D., Frederickson, R.H., Ben, R., Fleck, J., & Karls, W. (1984). Posttraumatic stress disorder among survivors of Cambodian concentration camps. *American Journal of Psychiatry, 141*(5), 645–650.

Kinzie, J.D., Leung, P., Bui, A., Ben, R., Keopraseuth, K.O., Riley, C., Fleck, J., & Ades, M. (1988). Group therapy with Southeast Asian refugees. *Community Mental Health Journal, 23*(2), 157–166.

Kinzie, J.D., Boehnlein, J., Leung, P., Moore, L., Riley, C., & Smith, D. (1990). The prevalence of PTSD and its clinical significance among Southeast Asian refugees. *American Journal of Psychiatry, 147*, 913–917.

Kirmayer, L.J. (1989). Cultural variation in the response to psychiatric disorders and emotional distress. *Social Science & Medicine, 28*(3), 327–339.

Kleinman, A. (1980). *Patients and healers in the context of culture*. Berkeley: University of California Press.

Kleinman, A. (1982). Neurasthenia and depression: A study of somatization and culture in China. *Culture, Medicine & Psychiatry, 6*, 117–190.

Kleinman, A., & Good, B. (1985). *Culture and depression: Studies in the anthropology and cross-cultural psychiatry of affect and disorder*. Berkeley: University of California Press.

Kleinman, A., & Kleinman, J. (1985). Somatization the interconnections in Chinese society among culture, depressive experiences, and the meaning of pain. In A. Kleinman & B. Good (Eds.), *Culture and depression*. Berkeley, CA: University of California Press.

Kleinman, A., Eisenberg, L., & Good, B. (1978). Culture, illness and care. *Annals of Internal Medicine, 88*, 251–258.

Kozaric-Korvacic, D., Folnegovic-Smalc, V., Skringjaric, J., Szajnberg, N., & Marusic, A. (1995). Rape, torture and traumatization of Bosnian and Croatian women: Psychological sequelae. *American Journal of Orthopsychiatry, 65*, 428–433.

Lee, E. (1989). Assessment and treatment of Chinese-American immigrant families. *Journal of Psychotherapy, 6*(102), 99–122.

Leyens, J., & Mahjoub, A. (1989). *The mental health of refugee children exposed to violent environments.* Unpublished manuscript, Refugee Studies Programme, Oxford, England.

Liebkind, K. (1996). Acculturation and stress: Vietnamese refugees in Finland. *Journal of Cross Cultural Psychology, 27,* 161–180.

Lin, K.M., & Masuda, M. (1983). Impact of the refugee experience: Mental health issues of the Southeast Asians. In *Bridging cultures: Southeast Asian refugees in America* (pp. 32–52). Los Angeles: Special Services for Groups—Asian American Community Mental Health Training Center.

Lin, E.H., Carter, W.B., & Kleinman, A.M. (1985). An exploration of somatization among Asian refugees and immigrants in primary care. *American Journal of Public Health, 75,* 1080–1084.

Lin, K.M., Inui, T.S., Kleinman, A.M., & Womack, W. (1982). Sociocultural determinants of the help-seeking behavior of patients with mental illness. *Journal of Nervous and Mental Disease, 170*(2), 78–85.

Lin, K.M., Masuda M., & Tazuma, L. (1982). Adaptational problems of Vietnamese refugees: Part III. Case studies in clinic and field: Adaptive and maladaptive. *Psychiatric Journal of University of Ottawa, 7*(3), 173–183.

Lin, K.M., Tazuma, L., & Masuda, M. (1979). Adaptational problems in Vietnamese refugees. *Archives of General Psychiatry, 36,* 955–961.

Marsella, A.J., Bornemann, T.H., Ekblad, S., & Orley, J. (Eds.) (1994). *Amidst peril and pain: The mental health and well-being of the world's refugees.* Washington, DC: American Psychological Association.

Marsella, A.J., Friedman, M., & Spain, H. (1993). Ethnocultural aspects of PTSD. In J. Oldham, M. Riba, & A. Tasman (Eds.), *Review of psychiatry* (Vol. 12, pp. 157–181). Washington, DC: American Psychiatric Press.

Martin, P., & Midgley, E. (1994). Immigration to the United States: Journey to an uncertain destination. *Population Bulletin, 49*(2), 2–46.

Matusuoka, J. (1993). Demographic characteristics as determinants in qualitative differences in the adjustment of Vietnamese refugees. *Journal of Social Service Research, 17*(4), 1–21.

McDonnell, L.M., & Hill, P.T. (1993). *Newcomers in American schools—Meeting the educational needs of immigrant youth.* Santa Monica, CA: RAND.

Mezey, A. (1960). Personal background, emigration and mental health in Hungarian refugees. *Journal of Mental Science, 106,* 618–627.

Micozzi, M.S. (1996). *Fundamentals of complementary and alternative medicine.* New York: Churchill Livingstone.

Mikulas, W. (1981). Buddhism and behavior modification. *The Psychological Record, 31,* 331–342.

Miranda, A.O., & Matheny, K.B. (2000). Socio-psychological predictors of acculturative stress among Latino adults. *Journal of Mental Health Counseling, 22,* 306–317.

Mollica, R.F. (1986, August). *Cambodian refugee women at risk.* Paper presented at the American Psychological Association annual meeting, Washington, DC.

Mollica, R.F., & Jalbert, R.R. (1989). *Community of confinement: The mental health crisis on Site Two: Displaced persons' camps on the Thai-Kampuchean border.* Boston: Committee on World Federation for Mental Health.

Mollica, R.F., & Lavelle, J. (1988). Southeast Asian refugees. In L. Comas-Diaz & E.H. Griffith (Eds.), *Clinical guidelines in cross-cultural mental health* (pp. 262–303). New York: Wiley.

Mollica, R.F., Lavelle, J., & Khuon, F. (1985, May). *Khmer widows at highest risk*. Paper presented at the Cambodian Mental Health Conference: A day to explore issues and alternative approaches to care. New York.

Mollica, R.F., McInnes, K., Pham, T., Fawzi, M.C.S., Murphy, E., & Lin, L. (1998). The dose-effect relationships between torture and psychiatric symptoms in Vietnamese ex-political detainees and a comparison group. *Journal of Nervous and Mental Disease, 186*, 543–553.

Mollica, R.F., Wyshak, G., & Lavelle, J. (1987). The psychosocial impact of war trauma and torture on Southeast Asian refugees. *American Journal of Psychiatry, 144*(12), 1567–1572.

Morris, P., & Silove, D. (1992). Cultural influences in psychotherapy with refugee survivors of torture and trauma. *Hosptial & Community Psychiatry, 43*(8), 820–824.

Muecke, M.A. (1983). In search of healers. Southeast Asian refugees in the American health care system. *Cross-cultural Medicine, 139*(6), 835–840.

Muecke, M.A. (1992). New paradigms for refugee health problems. *Social Science and Medicine, 35*, 515–523.

Murphy, H.B. (1977). Migration, culture and mental health. *Psychological Medicine, 7*, 677–684.

Nguyen, S. (1982). Psychiatric and psychosomatic problems among Southeast Asain refugees. *Psychiatric Journal of the University of Ottawa, 7*(3), 163–172.

Nguyen, N., Nguyen, P.H., & Nguyen, L.H. (1987). *Coin treatment in Vietnamese families: Traditional medical practice vs. child abuse*. Unpublished manuscript.

Nicholson, B.F. (1997). The influence of premigration and postmigration stressors on mental health: A study of Southeast Asian refugees. *Social Work Research, 21*, 19–31.

Nidorf, J.F. (1985). Mental health and refugee youths: A model for diagnostic training. In T.C. Owan (Ed.), *Southeast Asian mental health: Treatment, prevention, services, training and research* (pp. 391–429). Washington, DC: NIMH.

O'Brien, L.S. (1994). What will be the psychiatric consequences of the war in Bosnia? *British Journal of Psychiatry, 164*, 443–447.

Odegaard, O. (1932). Emigration and insanity: A study of mental disease among the Norwegian born population of Minnesota. *Acta Psychiatrica et Neurologica Supplement, 4*, 1–206.

Ohaeri, J.U., & Odejide, O.A. (1994). Somatization symptoms among patients using primary health care facilities in a rural community in Nigeria. *American Journal of Psychiatry, 151*, 728–731.

Pedersen, P.B. (1988). *A handbook for developing multicultural awareness*. Alexandria, VA: American Association for Counseling and Development.

Pedersen, P.B. (1991). Multiculturalism as a generic approach to counseling. *Journal of Counseling and Development, 70*, 6–12.

Pedersen, P.B. (2000). *A handbook for developing multicultural awareness* (3rd ed.). Alexandria, VA: American Association for Counseling and Development.

Pernice, R., & Brook, J. (1994). Relationship of migrant status (refugee or immigrant) to mental health. *International Journal of Social Psychiatry, 40*, 177–188.

Phillips, L., & Draguns, J. (1969). Some issues in intercultural research on psychopathology. In W. Caudill & T.Y. Lin (Eds.), *Mental health research in Asian and the Pacific* (pp. 21–32). Honolulu: East-West Center Press.

Phinney, J.S. (1993). A three-stage model of ethnic identity development in adolescence. In M.E. Bernal & G.P. Knights (Eds.), *Ethnic identity: Formation and transmission among Hispanics and other minorities* (pp. 61–79). Albany: State University of New York Press.

Pinsky, L. (1949). *The effects of war on displaced children.* Unpublished materials. World Federation for Mental Health, National Committee for Mental Hygiene. Second World Mental Health Assembly, New York. [Available from Centre for Documentation of Refugees, Untied Nations High Commissioner for Refugees ((UNHCR), Geneva, Switzerland.]

Pompfret, J. (2001). Evading border guards, Afghan refugees also dodge relief workers. *Washington Post, October 23*, A16.

Pynoos, R., & Eth, S. (1984). Children traumatized by witnessing acts of personal violence: Homicide, rape or suicide behavior. In S. Eth & R. Pynoos (Eds.), *Posttraumatic stress disorder in children* (pp. 17–44). Washington, DC: American Psychiatric Press.

Raccine, M. (1984). Why literacy in the native language: The cause of adult Haitian illiterates. *Paper of Social Sciences, 4*, 61–77.

Ramsay, R., Gorst-Unsworth, C., & Turner, S. (1993). Psychiatric morbidity in survivors of organised state violence including torture: A retrospective series. *British Journal of Psychiatry*, 162, 55–59.

Rechtman, R. (1997). Transcultural psychotherapy with Cambodian refugees in Paris. *Transcultural Psychiatry, 34*(3), 359–375.

Refugee Women in Development, (1990). *What is a refugee?* (Available from RefWID, Washington, DC.)

Roberts, S.M. (1994). Somatization in primary care: The common presentation of psychosocial problems through physical complaints. *Nurse Practitioner, 19*(47), 50–56.

Rong, X.L., & Preissle, J. (1998). *Educating immigrant students: What we need to know to meet the challenges.* Thousands Oaks, CA: Corwin.

Root, M.M. (1998). Facilitating psychotherapy with Asian American clients. In D.R. Atkinson, G. Morten, & D.W. Sue (Eds.), *Counseling American minorities* (5th ed., pp. 214–234). New York: McGraw-Hill.

Rumbaut, R.G. (1989). Portraits, patterns and predictors of the refugee adaptation process: A comparative study of Southeast Asian refugees. In D.W. Haines (Ed.), *Refugees and immigrants: Cambodians, Laotians, Vietnamese in American* (pp. 138–190). Totwa, NJ: Rowman & Littlefield.

Sack, W.H., Him, C., & Dickason, D. (1999). Twelve-year follow-up study of Khmer youths who suffered massive war trauma as children. *Journal of American Academy of Child Adolescent Psychiatry, 38*, 1173–1179.

Schaprio, A. (1987). Adjustment and identity formation of Lao refugee adolescents. *Smith College Studies in Social Work, 58*(3), 157–181.

Starr, P.D., & Roberts, A.E. (1982). Community structures and Vietnamese refugee adaptation: The significance of context. *International Migration Review, 16*, 595–618.

Stein, B.N. (1986). The experience of being a refugee: Insights from the research literature. In C.L. Williams & J. Westermeyer (Eds.), *Refugee mental health in resettlement countries* (pp. 5–23). Washington, DC: Hemisphere.

Struwe, G. (1994). Training health and medical professionals to care for refugees: Issues and methods. In A.J. Marsella, T. Bornemann, S. Ekblad, & J. Orley (Eds.), *Amidst peril and pain: The mental health and well-being of the world's refugees* (pp. 311–324). Washington, DC: American Psychological Association.

Stumphauser, J., & Davis, J. (1983). Training Mexican-Americans mental health personnel in behavior therapy. *Journal of Behavior Therapy and Experimental Psychiatry, 14*, 215–217.

Sue, S. (1993). The changing Asian American population: Mental health policy. In J.D. Hokoyama & D. Nakanishi (Eds.), *The state of Asian Pacific American: A public policy report. Policy issues to the year 2020* (pp. 79–93). Los Angeles: LEAP Asian Pacific Public Policy Institute and UCLA Asian American Studies Center.

Sue, D.W., & Sue, D. (1990). *Counseling the culturally different: Theory & practice* (2nd ed.). New York: Wiley.

Sue, S., & Zane, N., (1987). The role of culture and cultural techniques in psychotherapy: A critique and reformulation. *American Psychologist, 42*(1), 37–45.

Sue, S., Chun, C., & Gee, K. (1995). Ethnic minority intervention and treatment research. In J.F. Aponte, R. Young Rivers, & J. Wohl (Eds.), *Psychological interventions and cultural diversity* (pp. 266–282). Boston: Allyn & Bacon.

Sue, S., Fujino, D., Hu, L., Takeuchi, D., & Zane, N. (1991). Community mental health services for ethnic minority groups: A test of cultural responsive hypothesis. *Journal of Consulting and Clinical Psychology, 59*(4), 533–540.

Sue, D.W., Ivey, A.E., & Pedersen, P.D. (Eds.) (1996). *A theory of multicultural counseling*. Pacific Grove, CA: Brookes/Cole.

Szapocznik, J., & Cohen, R.E. (1986). Mental health care for rapidly changing environments: Emergency relief to unaccompanied youths of the 1980 Cuba refugee wave. In C.L. Williams & J. Westermeyer (Eds.), *Refugee mental health in resettlement countries* (pp. 141–156). New York: Hemisphere.

Szapocznik, J., & Kurtines, W. (1980). Acculturation, biculturalism, and adjustment among Cuban-Americans. In A.M. Padilla (Ed.), *Recent advances in acculturation research: Theory, models, and some new findings* (pp. 914–931). Boulder, CO: Westview.

Tayabas, T., & Pok, T. (1983). The arrival of the Southeast Asian refugees in America: An Overview. In *Bridging cultures: Southeast Asian refugees in America* (pp. 3–14). Los Angeles: Special Services for Groups—Asian American Community Mental Health Training Center.

Tobin, J.J., & Friedman, J. (1983). Spirits, shamans and nightmare death: Survivor stress in a Hmong refugee. *Journal of Orthopsychiatry, 53*, 439–448.

Triandis, H. (1990). Cross cultural studies of individualism and collectivism. In Berman, J. (Ed.), *Cross-cultural perspectives* (pp. 41–134). Lincoln and London: University of Nebraska Press.

Tseng, W., & Hsu, J. (1969). Chinese culture, personality formation and mental illness. *International Journal of Psychiatry, 16*, 5–14.

Tung, T.M. (1983). Psychiatric care of Southeast Asians: How different is different? In T.C. Owan (Ed.), *Southeast Asian mental health: Treatment, prevention, services, training and research* (pp. 5–40). Washington, DC: NIMH.

Uba, L. (1994). *Asian Americans: Personality patterns, identity, and mental health*. New York: Guilford.

United Nations. (1995). *Notes for speakers: Social development*. New York: Department of Public Information, United Nations.

United Nations Children's Emergency Fund (UNICEF). (1996). *The state of the world's children*. New York: United Nations Children's Emergency Fund.

United Nations Convention Relating to the Status of Refugees. (1951, July 28). U.S.T.6259, T.I.A.S. No. 6577, 189 U.N.T.S. 137.

United Nations Educational, Scientific, and Cultural Organization (UNCESO). (1952). *The psychological and social adjustment of refugee and displaced children in Europe.* Geneva, Switzerland: Author.

United Nations High Commissioner of Refugees. (1998). *UNHCR statistics.* (Available at http://www.unhcr.ch/refword/refworld/refbib/refstate/1998.)

United Nations High Commissioner of Refugees. (2001). The wall behind which refugees can shelter: 50th anniversary, The 1951 Geneva convention. *Refugees, 2*(123), 2–31.

Van Boemel, G., & Rozee, P.D. (1992). Treatment for psychosomatic blindness among Cambodian refugee women. In E. Cole, O.M. Espin, & E.D. Rothblum (Eds.), *Refugee women and their mental health: Shattered societies, shattered lives* (pp. 239–266). New York: Harrington Park Press.

van der Kolk, B.A. (1987). *Psychological trauma.* Washington DC: American Psychiatric Press.

Van Deusen J. (1982). Part 3. Health/mental health studies of Indochinese refugees: A critical overview. *Medical Anthropology, 6,* 213–252.

Van Velsen, C., Gorst-Unsworth, C., & Turner, S. (1996). Survivors of torture and organized violence; Demography and diagnosis. *Journal of Traumatic Stress, 9,* 181–193.

Vignes, A.J., & Hall, R.C.W. (1979). Adjustment of a group of Vietnamese people to the United States. *American Journal of Psychiatry, 136,* 442–444.

Watanabe, S. (1994). The Lewisian turning point and international migration: The case of Japan. *Asian and Pacific Migration Journal, 3*(1), 134–143.

Weine, S.M., Becker, D.F., McGlashan, T.H., Laub, D., Lazrove, S., Vojvoda, D., & Hyman, L. (1995). Psychiatric consequences of "ethnic cleansing": Clinical assessments and traumatic testimonies of newly resettled Bosnian refugees. *American Journal of Psychiatry, 152,* 536–542.

Weisaeth, L., & Eitinger, L. (1993). Posttraumatic stress phenomena. Common themes across wars, disasters, and traumatic events. In J. Wilson & B. Raphael (Eds.), *International handbook of traumatic stress syndromes* (pp. 69–78). New York: Plenum.

Westermeyer, J. (1986). Migration and psychopathology. In C.L. Williams & J. Westermeyer (Eds.), *Refugee mental health in resettlement countries* (pp. 39–59). Washington, DC: Hemisphere.

Widgren, J. (1988). The uprooted within a global context. In D. Miserez (Ed.), *Refugees: The trauma of exile* (pp. 1–9). Dordrechts: Martinus Nijhoff.

Williams, C.L., & Westermeyer, J. (1983). Psychiatric problems among adolescent Southeast Asian refugees. *Journal of Nervous and Mental Disease, 171*(2), 79–85.

Wohl, J. (2000). Psychotherapy and cultural diversity. In J. Aponte & J. Wohl (Eds.), *Psychological intervention and cultural diversity* (pp. 75–91). Needham Heights, MA: Allyn & Bacon.

Wong-Reiger, D., & Quintana, D. (1987). Comparative acculturation of Southeast Asian and Hispanic immigrants and sojourners. *Journal of Cross-Cultural Psychology, 18*(3), 345–362.

World Health Organization. (1992). *Refugee mental health: Draft manual for field testing.* Geneva: Author.

World Health Organization, Division of Mental Health. (1987). *Care for the mentally ill: Components of mental health policies governing the provision of psychiatric services*. Geneva: Author.

Yalom, I. (1985). *The theory and practice of group psychotherapy* (3rd ed.). New York: Basic Books.

Zane, N., & Sue, S. (1991). Culturally responsive mental health services for Asian Americans: Treatment and training issues. In H. Myers, P. Wohlford, P. Guzman, & R. Echemendia (Eds.), *Ethnic minority perspectives on clinical training and services in psychology* (pp. 49–58). Washington, DC: American Psychological Association.

Part II

Case Studies and Innovative Multicultural Interventions: Multi-Level Model of Psychotherapy for Refugees

Introduction

Part II presents 19 case studies (Chapters 6–24) of refugees from different cultural backgrounds. The cases include a mix of gender and a variety of age groups. The facts and names in the case studies have been altered to maintain confidentiality and ensure privacy. Although the case studies are based in the United States, the refugee situations described are common to other resettlement countries and may be applied to other resettlement countries throughout the world.

Each case study will be comprised of five components: (a) a description of the situation, (b) critical incident, (c) key clinical issues, (d) sequence of events, and (e) the application of the Multi-Level Model of Psychotherapy for Refugees. Interventions discussed using the Multi-Level Model (MLM) of Psychotherapy are designed specifically for refugee populations, taking into account premigration trauma and experiences, migration, and postmigration acculturation issues within the context of a culturally responsive intervention framework that emphasizes group and family work.

The case studies are intentionally not ordered in any particular format but are presented in random order with different ages, gender, ethnicity, and presenting problems. To assist the reader in identifying which case studies may be of primary interest, a summary of each case will be presented below giving the country of origin, ethnicity, age, gender, and a short summary of the presenting problem.

Case Study of Vu, a 16-year-old Cambodian male (Chapter 6): Vu has been in the United States for 6 months and arrived as an unaccompanied minor. He lives with his foster parents and their 12-year-old son. Vu has become progressively withdrawn and isolated from his foster family, causing tensions in the home and questions about Vu's residential placement.

Case Study of Amir, a 35-year-old Bosnian male (Chapter 7): Three years ago Amir arrived alone in the United States. He was involved in the war in Bosnia and was a victim of torture. Recently he has shown signs of posttransmatic stress disorder (PTSD).

Case of Vinh, a 26-year-old Black Amerasian male (Chapter 8): Vinh has been living with his sponsoring family since his arrival 8 months ago. Vinh described an extremely difficult life in Vietnam that is manifesting in problems with his sponsoring family.

Case Study of Niborom, a 35-year-old Cambodian woman (Chapter 9): Four years ago Niborom came to the United States with three children and her 25-year-old cousin. Her adolescent children are having problems in school, and Niborom has become emotionally involved with a 54-year-old white American male. This has led to serious emotional distress and suicidal ideation for Niborom as well as family and community problems.

Case Study of Khadra, a 16-year-old Somali female (Chapter 10): Khadra came to the United States with her mother, seven brothers, and two sisters after her father and uncle were murdered during the civil war. A shooting in her community brought back memories of her life in Somalia, causing new and different problems for Khadra.

Case Study of Tran, a 48-year-old Vietnamese male (Chapter 11): Tran has been in the United States for almost 20 years. During the war Tran lost contact with his family and wandered from village to village until he escaped just before the fall of Saigon. Recently Tran has been experiencing delusions that have affected his daily life.

Case Study of Eleni, a 36-year-old Ethiopian woman (Chapter 12): Eleni migrated to the United States 3 years ago with her husband and two sons. Eleni witnessed family members being tortured during the war and carries the secret of being raped in Ethiopia. As her family struggles with adjustment, this has become a more pronounced problem for her and her family.

Case study of Hector, a 15-year-old El Salvadorian male (Chapter 13): Hector, his parents, and two sisters have been in the United States for 11 months. Resettlement has been difficult for Hector and his family. He has no friends and there is a great deal of tension in the family. Accusations that Hector has been stealing have precipitated more serious mental health concerns.

Case Study of Sokhany, a 55-year-old Cambodian woman (Chapter 14): Sokhany lives with her youngest and only surviving 25-year-old daughter. In Cambodia Sokhany witnessed her husband and three sons being tortured and killed. A sudden crisis of Sokhany's daughter has forced her to face her dependency and difficulties adjusting to the United States.

Case Study of Matilda, a 17-year-old Albanian female (Chapter 15): Matilda migrated with her parents and sister after witnessing fighting, killing, and numbers of people suddenly disappearing. After living with such a different reality in Albania, Matilda is facing conflicts about adjusting to life in the resettlement country.

Case Study of Toan, a 17-year-old Vietnamese male (Chapter 16): Toan lives with his foster parents and is a good student. He is at odds with his foster parents about short- and long-term goals and his continued relationship with his biological family who remain in Vietnam.

Case Study of Natasha, a 23-year-old Russian woman (Chapter 17): After a difficult life in Russia, Natasha migrated to the United States 2 years ago to live with someone she called "Aunt." When her aunt abandoned her, she moved in with an American family who has pressured her to better acclimate. Natasha is struggling with unresolved premigration issues and becoming increasingly alienated.

Case Study of Tam, a 17-year-old Lao female (Chapter 18): Tam arrived in the United States with her parents, uncle, and two younger brothers 4 years ago. The death of her father during an accident caused the family to move in with her uncle. Sexual abuse by Tam's uncle has caused serious problems for Tam and her family.

Case Study of Khaled, a 38-year-old Palestinian male (Chapter 19): Khaled arrived in the United States with his wife and two sons. Before migrating, Khaled was accidentally shot and paralyzed, affecting his work as a medical doctor. Since arriving in the United States Khaled has been depressed and angry, unable to reestablish his life-style or sense of purpose.

Case Study of Juanita, a 15-year-old Cuban female (Chapter 20): In Cuba Juanita had been sexually abused by a close family friend. After arriving in the United States with her family 2 years ago, Juanita remains angry and unresolved about this past experience and recently found herself in a serious situation that forces her to address these issues.

Case Study of Ru, a 16-year-old Vietnamese male (Chapter 21): Ru is an unaccompanied minor who was denied permission to move from his third foster placement to an apartment with friends. Ru is angry and prone to violent rages, needing help adjusting.

Case Study of Mustafa, a 41-year-old Somali male (Chapter 22): Mustafa came to the United States with his wife and younger brother 3 years ago. Since that time relatives from Somalia have joined his family, putting pressure on Mustafa to support the extended family. Mustafa is concerned about how to meet his obligations, causing pronounced family strife.

Case Study of Nusreta, a 15-year-old Bosnian female (Chapter 23): Nusreta arrived in the United States with her parents and younger brother. Because of her painful and abusive experiences in Bosnia, Nusreta is having significant mental health and adjustment problems in the United States.

Case Study of Faisal, a 16-year-old Iraqi male (Chapter 24): Faisal, coming from a wealthy Muslim family, arrived in the United States 4 years ago with his mother, four younger siblings, and his grandparents. The family has been struggling financially and were joined 3 years ago by Faisal's father who had been detained and tortured. The broken spirit of his father has caused great pain and turmoil for Faisal and his family.

Chapter 6

Case Study of Vu, a 16-year-old Cambodian

DESCRIPTION

Vu is a 16-year-old Cambodian male who came to the United States 6 months ago. Since his English is poor, he communicates through his bilingual case-worker who works at the local community agency. He explained to his case-worker that in Cambodia he lived with his "aunt" and her family. He has not been willing to talk much more about his background, but the caseworker believes that Vu's biological parents are deceased and his "aunt" was not biologically related to him.

Arriving in the United States as an unaccompanied minor, Vu was placed in a foster home by an agency that helps refugees adjust to the United States. The home is in a middle-class suburban neighborhood 30 miles from a nearby middle- sized city. In the home, he shares a room with his foster parent's biological 12-year-old son whom Vu describes as, "all right but he always wants to follow me around. He won't let me touch his stereo." Vu feels that his relationship with his foster parents is fine, explaining that "they're ok, I guess. I don't know . . . they're nice people." In contrast Vu's foster parents describe him as increasingly uncommunicative, withdrawn, and resistant to family activities, including eating dinner together.

Vu spent his first 3 months in the United States exclusively with his foster family. During the fourth month he began to spend time with other Cambodians in the community. He shared with his caseworker doubts about ever being able to make American friends. "My English is so bad. I will never know any of the American students. They will never talk to me." His foster parents believe they understand his concerns, since both of them were children of Italian immigrants, were first-generation college graduates, and now worked as teachers in a local suburban school. They thought their extended family would welcome Vu, given their own background as immigrants, but were very surprised by the intolerant reaction of their family toward Vu. This was evident when they went to the wedding of a cousin in a nearby town and received what they described as a "cold shoulder" reception.

Vu's increasing resistance to participate in family activities finally prompted his foster parents to ask the sponsoring agency for help. His father explained: "It just isn't working out . . . . He's a good kid, I guess, but he's just not talking. He was really a good kid when he first got here, but now, I don't know . . . he's changed. He's just different." The agency has recommended family therapy even though Vu has been threatening to live independently. "I don't want to live with anyone anymore . . . it's not my foster parents. I just want to go by myself." His foster parents have been more insistent. "We want him to stay with us. He is like our son. But we need help. It's hard right now being under the same roof with him!" Tensions have increased, with Vu confiding to his caseworker that he overheard his foster mother arguing on the phone, and his name was mentioned a few times.

CRITICAL INCIDENT

The critical incident happened on a Saturday night. Vu had agreed to a weekend curfew of midnight. When he did not arrive home, his foster parents became concerned and waited up for him. Finally, at 4:00 A.M., Vu returned home. His foster parents were worried and angry, demanding an explanation and wanting to know why he had not called them. Vu told them he was out with friends at a party and refused to discuss any more details. It was at this point that his foster parents decided that this was the "last straw" and it was impossible to keep going like this. The next day they called the agency to request help and support.

SEQUENCE OF EVENTS

Vu and his foster parents enjoyed the first 3 months after his arrival without significant problems. In the fourth month Vu began to go out with newly found Cambodian friends and spend less time with his foster parents. Although they continued to encourage Vu to participate in social and school activities, Vu progressively withdrew from the family. He told the caseworker about his preference to live alone, complaining about restrictions at home such as "times at night that he must be home." The caseworker tried to explain to Vu what it was like to live in "an American foster home," but Vu continued to "stubbornly" insist on wanting his independence.

The caseworker described Vu as not very well adjusted and immature and has concerns that without adequate support and guidance Vu could easily get into trouble. Gradually Vu has become even more isolated from his foster family, sometimes refusing to join them at the table for supper and weekend activities. It has become more difficult to communicate with him, especially with his growing stubbornness and focus on independence.

KEY CLINICAL QUESTIONS

1. How does it feel for 16-year-old Vu to share a room with a 12-year-old American? How does he feel that his foster brother will not let him use his stereo?

2. The caseworker thinks that Vu may get "into trouble" on his own. In Vu's opinion, why?

3. When Vu and his foster parents argue, how does it begin and then escalate? A more detailed description of the interaction patterns would be helpful in determining what is actually taking place and how each family member contributes to the growing tension.

4. What happened to Vu's biological family? Are they still alive or is it unknown?

5. How did Vu escape from Cambodia? What happened?

6. What was Vu's relationship to his biological parents and how does this effect his response to his foster parents?

7. What does Vu really want at this time? Where is he going and how does this fit into his hope for the future, if at all?

8. Why is Vu increasingly withdrawing from his foster family? What feelings does he associate with his behavior? Not joining the family for supper or activities connotes more than just wanting independence.

9. What are Vu and his friends doing together? Are any of the activities dangerous or illegal or potentially leading to more serious problems?

10. What is Vu's vision of living independently? What does he imagine it would be like?

11. What does Vu like and dislike about the United States? It would be helpful to explore a 6-month retrospective assessment.

MULTI-LEVEL MODEL (MLM) OF PSYCHOTHERAPY INTERVENTION

Level I: Mental Health Education

Vu has only been in the United States for 6 months. He comes from a country where there was a history of political oppression and tremendous fear about expressing feelings or thoughts about oneself or the surrounding world. Therefore, prior to introducing mental health interventions, it is critical to explain to Vu the purpose and course of psychotherapy. Clarifying the role and responsibility of the caseworker and the psychotherapist and explaining carefully whom they work for and issues of confidentiality would be important as a starting point with Vu. A clear definition of role expectations and objectives for counseling would also be essential in establishing trust and rapport.

Level II: Individual, Group, and Family Therapy

Vu is in his first home placement since leaving Cambodia. It is his entry point into the United States and the aim is that this first living situation be experienced as a positive cultural transition to his "new country." Therefore, coming to terms with the problems in the foster home is an important objective and will establish a foundation for his life in the new culture. Thus it is recommended that Vu and his foster family participate in family therapy.

In family therapy it would be important to contextualize Vu's situation. He has been in the United States for 6 months. During the initial adjustment phase to a new culture there is a "honeymoon" period. In Vu's situation, he is just at the ending stages of a 6-month honeymoon period and has recently made friends with other Cambodians. This has resulted in behavioral changes at home, impacting his relationship with his foster parents. This developmental period is crucial for the family and Vu to discuss and understand, especially as he acclimates outside the home environment.

Rules, restrictions, and subsequent expectations for adolescent behavior are very different from culture to culture and would be important to discuss in family therapy. We do know that in Cambodia Vu was living with an aunt who was not believed to be a biological relation. Without more information from Vu it is difficult to ascertain what his role and expected behavior was within his "aunt's household." Family therapy could assist in clarifying the cultural differences regarding family rules. Vu's foster parents believe they must monitor Vu's life and social network assuming responsibility to establish guidelines for a 16-year-old adolescent. It is unclear from Vu's background whether or not in living with his aunt there were similar adult expectations, although we know that he experiences his foster parents' inquiries and demand for information about his social activities as highly intrusive. Thus the issues of child–adult relationships, family obligations, and subsequent rules would be helpful to address.

Another important issue to explore in family therapy would be the role and impact of the extended family. In both the Italian and Khmer (Cambodian) cultures extended families are important. The family wedding certainly had an impact on Vu's foster parents and Vu who all received a "cold shoulder." It would be helpful to discuss the effect of the family gathering on everyone and explore Vu's reaction to being rejected and ignored by the extended family.

It would also be beneficial to explore with Vu what is going on for him with regards to his life and living situation within the context of family therapy. It may be that there are residual issues related to the loss or absence of his family of origin, that rules and structure remind him of unpleasant situations in Cambodia, or his younger foster brother may bring back memories of his own childhood. At this point it is unclear to everyone in the family and would be helpful to discuss.

In family therapy it would be important to redefine roles, expectations, responsibilities, and relationships within the family. This clarification would assist everyone in reformulating the "new" family constellation and assist the foster parents and their son in accommodating Vu, while simultaneously assisting Vu to understand terms and boundaries of being in a new family. In the short term the reexamination of the family has the potential to disrupt the status quo for the family, but the longer term goals are to yield healthier relationships and changes that would meet the expectations and fantasies about including a newcomer into the family and being a new member of the family For Vu, on a short-term basis, he would have a stronger base from which to acculturate into a strange and different society, while on a long-term basis his adjustment would potentially have a happier and healthier foundation.

If it is determined that some of the difficulty with Vu related to his background in Cambodia, it may be helpful to explore, with the support of his foster parents, relevant key clinical questions about his childhood and upbringing. Examining a potentially painful and traumatic background may require strong support for Vu, which could be offered by his foster parents. Long term, it would be critical that Vu addressed these issues in order to facilitate a better adjustment to his new home country.

Level III: Cultural Empowerment

An important long-term goal for Vu may be to become more autonomous within his foster home, followed by living with his friends at a later time. It is likely that he is unaware of the realities of independent living in the United States. Therefore, rather than directly challenging his goals as unrealistic or listing obstacles, it would be helpful for the psychotherapist to assist Vu in understanding the United States culture from firsthand experience. Subsequently the psychotherapist might familiarize Vu with realities of independent living such as costs and electric, heat, water, telephone, or gas bills. The psychotherapist may provide Vu with information about how to visit or call any of these companies so he can inquire about setting up services including initial fees and billing procedures. Renting an apartment is also an alien concept for Vu and the psychotherapist may help Vu read through apartment advertisements and provide guidance about how to find apartments for rent and issues such as security deposits and a lease. All of this would better enable Vu to know what it means to live independently and give him a realistic framework to reevaluate his situation.

Level IV: Indigenous Healing

It is unclear to the psychotherapist what Vu holds as his spiritual beliefs and/or religious practices. Understanding this information is important because it provides a basis for knowing what Vu believes, which would assist in resolving troubling issues. For example, if the psychotherapist determines that Vu is a Buddhist, then a monk may be of help to him in coming to terms with projected anger toward his foster parents. Work with the monk would not supercede his psychotherapy, but rather be an added dimension in his healing that is culturally appropriate and could supplement the counseling.

Chapter 7

Case Study of Amir, a 35-year-old Bosnian

DESCRIPTION

Amir is a 35-year-old Bosnian refugee from a Muslim background. He arrived in the United States by himself 3 years ago and is living with a Bosnian family in an urban area that has a large Bosnian community. During the war in Bosnia Amir was involved in fighting, until he was captured and tortured. After 3 months he escaped and fled the country. Most of his family was killed during the war, except for his grandparents and brother and sister who still live in Bosnia. His family in Bosnia is dependent on him for living expenses, so every month he sends money home to them.

Although Amir came from a middle-class family in Bosnia, he now works as a driver for a bakery. In Bosnia he had been studying chemistry with the intention to secure a job that could help support his family. When Amir first arrived in the United States, he took English as a second language (ESL) classes in the hope of going to college and continuing his studies in chemistry. Because of the financial obligation to his grandparents and siblings in Bosnia, Amir decided to postpone taking additional English classes and spend his time working to earn more money. Since his English is limited, his only option was unskilled labor.

Amir's grandparents in Bosnia constantly write to him asking for more money, describing the deteriorating living conditions, how they were hungry and just barely surviving, and how lucky he was to have escaped to America where there is wealth and opportunity. Although Amir is struggling financially and personally in the United States, he remains reluctant to let his surviving family know about the resettling difficulties. Instead, he writes letters to them describing what he thinks they would like to hear—how exciting and good life is for him, his success at work, the difficulty of college courses (he is not taking any classes), friends, and good wages. Amir harbors guilt for having escaped the terrible conditions when most of his family was killed. Sometimes he finds himself thinking, "Now that I am able to make money, I can send it back to my family. They have such a hard life there, compared to me."

Through his work, Amir was exposed to another way of life, delivering bakery goods to large parties in the wealthy area of the city. Each time he saw the opulence of the homes and food, Amir began to think more about being wealthy. He became obsessed about becoming rich, thinking about sending large sums of money to his family or even flying them to a "big home in the U.S." that he would buy. He once tried to set up a business after sending away for material about how to become a millionaire, but this did not work and he lost 700 hard-earned dollars. Lately Amir has been having bad headaches and stomach aches, feeling lonely, and missing his family.

Amir's focus on supporting his family and long hours at work leaves little time for other activities. In Bosnia he would frequently join friends and family in their homes for food and coffee, laughing, joking, and eating all afternoon and evening. Nowadays he is isolated, works hard, and stays more by himself. On weekends he watches television and visits bars away from the Bosnian community, drinking and occasionally picking up a woman for a one-night relationship. Typically he finds himself alone the next day and most weekends.

CRITICAL INCIDENT

One Saturday evening Amir found himself accidentally invited by a group of Bosnians to someone's home for coffee. Although he felt unsure about going, he agreed to join. Once there, Amir found himself in the midst of a group of people who were familiar with each other, laughing and joking about themselves and their lives. Although Amir did not know anyone there very well, he immediately felt comfortable and was reminded of his life in Bosnia before the fighting began. As the night progressed and the hour became late Amir found himself laughing and joking with his new friends, something he had not done for many years.

Later that evening at home, he began to think about his life in Bosnia, and people who had died such as his parents, two brothers, aunts, uncles, the elderly couple next door in his village, and friends. He became more and more upset as he reflected on his past life and began to cry for the first time in many years. Memories raced through his mind, and he lay in bed the entire night, gently sobbing and remembering things he had not thought about in years. When he got out of bed in the morning he felt scared, disoriented, and confused. Several days later, the intensity of these feelings remained and his head and stomach had a "lot of pain."

SEQUENCE OF EVENTS

When Amir escaped, he was hungry, physically ill, and hurt from psychological and physical torture. He narrowly got away, almost being killed more than once. When he arrived back at his village, he found that most of his family and the residents were gone, many having been killed. Without much thought, Amir fled his village and after a series of harrowing experiences, eventually migrated to the United States.

Trying to survive, Amir never reflected back on his days in Bosnia. He tried to put thoughts of torture, hunger, and his family out of his mind, but sometimes he had bad dreams and painful headaches. For years he had stayed away from the Bosnian community and the local mosque, trying to forget his past and the painful memories. Finally, when he joined a group of Bosnians one Saturday night, he found himself remembering and thinking about his life and all the things that had happened to him.

KEY CLINICAL QUESTIONS

1. Is Amir at all religious? If yes, has he been to the mosque or been continuing his daily prayers?

2. Gently begin to explore with Amir his experience of torture. Has he ever spoken with anyone about what happened?

3. How has he personally reconciled with the death of family, friends, or neighbors? What more needs to be done to come to terms with these painful losses?

4. What happened to Amir while he was fleeing Bosnia?

5. What is Amir's relationship with his surviving grandparents, brothers, and sisters?

6. What holds Amir back from sharing with his family the difficulties of living alone in the United States?

7. Does Amir remain interested in pursuing studies in chemistry? If yes, what longer term goals would be helpful to establish?

8. Can it possibly fit into Amir's life at the moment to study English? What would be the pros and cons of including a course of language study?

9. Amir is interested in earning money. Explore realistically how he might work toward better achieving that goal. Also, examine the amount he needs for current living expenses and how much he is able to send back to his family in Bosnia.

10. Discuss with Amir the lack of contact with a Bosnian social network. Does he want to spend more time with Bosnians? If no, why? If yes, how can that happen?

11. What about a more meaningful significant relationship? Explore this with Amir.

12. What is the root of Amir's tears? Explore.

MULTI-LEVEL MODEL (MLM) OF PSYCHOTHERAPY INTERVENTION

Level I: Mental Health Education

Traditionally, Muslims do not share mental health problems with strangers. Generally, family members of the same gender assist others with problems. Therefore, visiting a mental health professional and telling him/her deep inner thoughts and feelings would be strange for Amir. Providing information about the context for personal sharing outside the family with a professional, the structure and form of that encounter, and confidentiality would be important issues to define with Amir. Clarification about the role and relationship of the psychotherapist would be essential given Amir's experience as a victim of torture.

Level II: Individual, Group, and Family Therapy

In Bosnia helping others with mental health problems is done typically through social networks. This happens in the community in one's home with a group of friends and family, usually over coffee and food. When considering mental health problems there is a word that aptly describes how it is conceptualized in Bosnia. The word is *prolupao*, which can be translated as "when a car needs some work to make it move again." Thus, the psychological problems that someone faces warrant repair since they are only temporary problems that require some attention that will fix them. This perspective is very different than viewing a car as seriously broken and needing perpetual repairs for as long as it may keep running (pathological), although one never knows when it will permanently stop functioning. Thus, to think of mental health problems as simply being somewhat "off track" and needing some minor repair to set things straight would be more aligned with a Bosnian conceptualization of mental health.

Given this context, it is recommended that Amir participate in group therapy that happens in the community in someone's home or a community setting that can maintain privacy and confidentiality. This would require a culturally sensitive group therapist who is able to work cooperatively with community leaders to establish a safe and homelike environment for healing. Thus the group therapy would be structured in a culturally appropriate manner that is less formal, gathering together in someone's home with food and coffee, recreating social encounters and settings where problems were oftentimes addressed in the home country. Amir could join a group, sit in a living room, and discuss (including joking, laughter, and stories that poke fun at oneself as is customary in Bosnia) problems he is facing. Discussions may include bad dreams, loss of concentration, aspirations for a better life, supporting surviving relatives in Bosnia, isolation, and acculturation. Loss of family and community would also be important topics that could be shared collectively. It would also be important to explore physical symptoms such as Amir's headaches and stomachaches, discussing how these may be manifestations of deeper rooted psychological problems.

Level III: Cultural Empowerment

It would be beneficial for Amir to find out about English language classes. It would be helpful to know about times and locations when classes are offered, associated costs, and tuition support. In addition, it may be helpful for Amir to know about immigration policies, family reunification policies, and financial assistance that may support his relatives immigrating to the United States. This information would define what type of assistance the local and federal government would provide and what steps one must take rather than speculate about what it would require to bring his grandparents and brother and sister to the new country.

Level IV: Indigenous Healing

There may be some individuals known in the community as "wise" or helpful to the Bosnian community when individuals are having problems. Given the pre-migration torture, a harrowing escape, and tremendous losses, Amir may greatly benefit from someone in the Bosnian community who has helped others with these issues. In addition, there may be a Sheik in the Muslim community who can provide guidance and speak about the Qu'ran (Koran) as it relates to Amir's healing.

Chapter 8

Case Study of Vinh, a 26-year-old Black Amerasian

DESCRIPTION

Vinh is a 26-year-old Black Amerasian. He has been living in a home with his sponsor family since his arrival in the United States 8 months ago. Vinh's sponsoring family is African American and specifically requested from the local agency to host a Black Amerasian. There are four people in the family including the wife, a librarian, the husband, a mechanic, and two biological daughters aged 16 and 13.

When asked about why they wanted to host a Black Amerasian, the husband spoke about his experience in Vietnam and the desire to "contribute to resolving that mess." On two occasions in the second and fifth months the couple called the agency to ask about establishing stricter rules for Vinh, indicating their commitment to "stick it out with him and bring him into their family." Even so, they are upset by Vinh's "lack of respect and disregard for their family and house rules."

Vinh described his life in Vietnam as "difficult." He entered an orphanage at age 7 after being abandoned by his mother "on the streets of the city." He experienced prejudice and rejection in Vietnam and attended only 3 years of school. In Vietnam he worked at odd jobs that lasted only short periods of time. As he described his life in Vietnam, it was confusing and unclear how he lived or earned a living. Vinh cannot read or write, speaks limited English, and claimed most of his childhood and adult life was spent "hanging out on the streets." Vinh has been looking for a job, but because of his poor English was having difficulty finding employment. He started to attend English language classes at night school two times per week but was "bored and not really interested."

Vinh has a small social network. He has a group of three Amerasian friends with whom he spends most of his time. He has no contact with anyone back in Vietnam and avoids discussion about his mother. Vinh once commented that he would like a girlfriend but has not met anyone since his arrival in the United States.

CRITICAL INCIDENT

One Saturday night Vinh became upset at the sponsoring couple for asking him about his plans. With very broken English and nonverbal gestures he angrily told them that he had been independent for years and did not have to tell "anyone" where he went or what he did. When they insisted that he did have some responsibility to them as a family and did not want their children corrupted by alcohol or drugs in their home, Vinh became very upset and angry. He slammed his fist against a file cabinet and stormed out of the house.

SEQUENCE OF EVENTS

It has been increasingly difficult over the last 3 months for Vinh and his sponsoring family to get along. He has been increasingly off on his own and more openly disrespectful when they have challenged him or asked him to be accountable for his actions. Two times in the last 6 weeks Vinh had come home with alcohol on his breath, leaving his sponsoring family unsure what to do. "We don't know what to do with him. He's doing some things we don't like and he's not listening. He is becoming a bad influence on our two daughters. We really want him to stay—he's like one of us now, but not if he's going act like that."

KEY CLINICAL QUESTIONS

1. What was it like to be a Black Amerasian in Vietnam?
2. What is it like to live with a family? What is it like to live with an African American family given that his unknown biological father was an African American?
3. Does Vinh identity himself as Vietnamese, African American, or biracial?
4. How has Vinh dealt with racism and discrimination in Vietnam and the United States?
5. What issues is the sponsoring husband, who is a Vietnam veteran, working through by hosting Vinh and wanting him to become part of the family? How does the sponsoring wife fit into this?
6. What are the expectations of the host family for Vinh?
7. What are Vinh's expectations for living with his host family?
8. What was the orphanage like for Vinh in Vietnam?

9. How has Vinh made a living for the past decade, once leaving the orphanage?

10. What does Vinh feel toward his biological mother?

11. Does Vinh want to learn English?

12. What is going on with Vinh's drinking?

13. What would the sponsoring family like to happen at this point?

14. Vinh indicated that he wanted a girlfriend. Has he made any strides in this area?

MULTI-LEVEL MODEL (MLM) OF PSYCHOTHERAPY INTERVENTION

Level I: Mental Health Education

Despite the problems that Vinh faced during premigration, he has never received counseling. It would be important to explain to him issues such as confidentiality, privacy, the potential benefits, and possible outcomes, as well as the role and expectation for both Vinh and the psychotherapist.

Level II: Individual, Group, and Family Psychotherapy

Vinh's sponsoring parents are particularly committed to him but have concerns about his more recent behavior. Given their care, the importance of family in the Vietnamese culture, and the rejection of Vinh by his biological mother resulting in him being placed in an orphanage, it is recommended that Vinh and his sponsoring family enter family therapy. In part, this recommendatin is due to the sponsoring family strongly embracing Vinh, telling friends and family members that they have "adopted" him. Their commitment and care may make this an ideal situation for family work, potentially teaching Vinh how to live in a family environment and assist the family with how to incorporate a new member. Especially important in the family therapy is identifying and understanding issues that are interfering with a more harmonious relationship. For example, Vinh may be having difficulty with intimacy given that his mother abandoned him or there may be background issues for his sponsoring father that would be helpful to examine in therapy.

In family therapy it is recommended to explore premigration issues. Research has found that Black Amerasians have experienced significant racism and discrimination in Vietnam and subsequently greater degrees of psychological distress during postmigration. Vinh has only been in the United States for 8 months and may be ending the "honeymoon" period. His life as an orphan beginning at the age of 7 and his mother's abandonment of him leave him without a background of living with a family and unsure of how to manage expectations, responsibilities, consequences, and family intimacy. These issues would be crucial for the entire family to explore and assist with a cross-cultural understanding of how racism contributes to current issues.

Night school studying English is also a new experience for Vinh. He only attended school for 3 years in Vietnam, so that simply learning about how to study and be a student are new experiences. These fundamentals must be discussed and taught to Vinh rather than simply "diving" into school and studying. Strategies to understand the "culture of school" may be helpful to explore in therapy, supported by his sponsoring parents and their daughters.

Another cross-cultural issue that would be beneficial to explore relates to the fact that the Vietnamese community has not generally accepted Amerasians, particularly Black Amerasians. Vietnam is a homogeneous society, and the Amerasians were not only biracial but representations of the Americans, the nation that was at war with Vietnam. It is therefore unrealistic to expect that coming from Vietnam, speaking Vietnamese, and knowing the culture leads to acceptance by the Vietnamese community in the United States. Issues such as belonging, where one fits, and how this relates to a sponsoring family and community in the resettlement country are core issues.

In turn, the sponsoring husband may have unresolved issues about his experience in Vietnam and expectations for Vinh that may be unrealistic. The husband's comments about "resolving that mess" would be helpful for the family to understand, clarifying his motivation. It would also be helpful to examine his wife's reaction to her husband's strong interest in sponsoring a Black Amerasian since unexpressed issues about requesting a Black Amerasian from Vietnam may contribute to some of the current confusion and conflict about living together.

Another important issue that may be helpful to explore in family therapy relates to racial identity. As mentioned earlier, there has been significant prejudice against Black Amerasians in Vietnam, which would not have created an environment for Vinh to explore his biracial identity. Family therapy would be a means to assist Vinh in this exploration, especially given his closeness and support of an African American family. What is it like for him to learn about his heritage? What are the positive aspects? What are the struggles? Is he comfortable or uncomfortable with this process? Is his self-image changing? These are essential questions that Vinh must face as he looks at his biracial identity for the first time outside of Vietnam.

Family therapy could also address Vinh's anger and alleged drinking, especially since this affects the entire family system. What is he so angry about? How does this affect his sponsoring family? What can be done about this from a family systems perspective? How can his sponsoring family help? The short-term aim is to establish strategies for Vinh to control his angry outbursts, with a longer term emphasis on resolving the deeper core issues that precipitate the anger.

Finally, family therapy could address the deeply rooted experience of Vinh regarding discrimination in Vietnam and now, possibly, in the United States. It is striking that Vinh does not have Vietnamese friends in the United States, but only spends time with a few Amerasians. This may be due to discrimination of Amerasians in Vietnam that has carried over to postmigration and may be especially helpful to explore. In family therapy members of his sponsoring family may also share similar experiences of racism and discrimination and responses to this type of behavior they have used that may prove to be insightful for Vinh.

Level III: Cultural Empowerment

Vinh is probably not aware that there are laws that were adopted to protect him from discrimination in the United States. This information may be important for Vinh to gain a perspective about the cultural values and beliefs in the United States and know that legally (although not always practically) there is protection from discriminatory behavior. This legal information can aid the psychotherapist to more effectively work with Vinh and his sponsoring family to discuss proactive steps to confront racism and discrimination. For example, if Vinh is rejected from a job because of perceived discrimination the psychotherapist can assist Vinh with strategies to challenge these situations, explore how the host family might assist Vinh, and even advocate for Vinh in certain situations.

Level IV: Indigenous Healing

In Vietnam Vinh was rejected by his mother. His American father was unknown to him, so he was left to fend for himself. Furthermore, Vietnam is a patriarchal society with family and social relations being a cornerstone of the culture. Yet, Vinh was without relatives while living there. Therefore, it may be essential for Vinh to undergo a culturally based healing ritual, related to his mother and ancestors. This could be done with a monk, who could, in Vietnamese, work with Vinh's spirit and ancestral lineage to heal and bring harmony to all. This would be done in conjunction with family therapy.

Chapter 9

Case Study of Niborom, a 35-year-old Cambodian

DESCRIPTION

Niborom is a 35-year-old Cambodian woman who came to the United States with three children and her 25-year-old female cousin 4 years ago. Her children aged 17, 15, and 12 are having problems in school, including absenteeism, not turning in homework assignments, inattentiveness in class, and tardiness. Although Niborom has attended numerous meetings with school and social service officials, there has not been any improvement in her children's performance.

Niborom is living in a medium-sized town that is a cluster site for Cambodian refugees. In addition to involvement with the sponsoring social services agency Niborom receives sponsorship from the local church. Six months ago she became emotionally involved with a 54-year-old white male, Tom, from the church, causing strong negative reactions by her cousin and children. They were embarrassed by their mother/cousin's relationship with Tom and avoided spending time at home by staying at other Cambodians' homes until late at night. The children claimed that many of the Cambodians are taunting them, calling them names and socially ignoring them. Niborom is no longer welcomed in the Cambodian community, with many of her former friends saying that she is having a relationship with an *American*, who is "as old as her father." Her cousin tried to convince Niborom to end the relationship, but she refused, explaining that "Tom is the only person who knows my pain and how afraid I am here." When Tom is not around or working, Niborom spends most of her time alone. "Before I enjoyed very much the time with my Cambodian friends, now everything is different."

Niborom's English language skills are minimal and may relate to her being unemployed. During the past month she has become more confused. "I don't know anymore. I just don't know." The loss of her support system in the Cambodian community is affecting Niborom and she has felt increasingly alone. "All day I just look out the window or watch TV. It is not so good." More recently she is feeling acutely alone, rejected by her children and cousin as well as the Cambodian community. For the past few weeks she has been talking about ending the relationship with her friend and dying. It was at this point that her friend brought her to see a psychotherapist known for his work with the Cambodian community.

CRITICAL INCIDENT

Although the situation has been escalating for 3 weeks, it became a crisis when Niborom invited Tom for dinner one night. The children would not talk to him and midway through dinner left the house angrily telling their mother in Khmer that they were going to move out of the house. Niborom started crying uncontrollably and talked about dying and "ending this misery." Since that time she has been unresponsive to her boyfriend and the children, spending most of her time in her room with the door closed.

SEQUENCE OF EVENTS

Niborom has been lonely since coming to the United States and upset about the struggle she has raising her children. Despite assistance from the church, the sponsoring agency, her cousin, and to some degree by the Cambodian community, she has felt "empty." Six months ago Tom, a parishioner in her church, invited her out for lunch. She enjoyed meeting an American and had laughed for the first time in years. Following the lunch he started to call her and they began dating. With passing months Niborom became more dependent on Tom and recently asked him for advice about her three children. Tom helpfully offered to speak to the children and school officials. Three weeks ago Niborom invited Tom for dinner to speak with the children. When he raised the subject of their behavior at school, they became very quiet, refused to eat, and left the table (this was very unusual behavior for them). The next day they told their mother that Tom was not welcome in their home and that they would like to move to another home. Several days later Niborom was brought to the psychotherapist.

KEY CLINICAL QUESTIONS

1. Is Niborom suicidal? Explore this is depth.
2. What is the perceived origin of the problems that Niborom's children are having in school prior to Tom's presence?
3. Has Niborom been studying English?

4. Why are Niborom's children and the community so against her relationship with Tom?

5. Is there anyway to bridge the cultural divide with the Cambodian community? How could Niborom reconnect with her community?

6. Explore Niborom's relationship with her children and the impact of her husband's absence.

7. What happened to Niborom's former husband? Is he alive or deceased? If deceased, did he die during the Pol Pot regime when millions of people were massacred? If he is still alive, where is he?

8. How was Niborom's relationship with her husband?

9. What was the children's relationship with their biological father?

MULTI-LEVEL MODEL (MLM) OF PSYCHOTHERAPY INTERVENTION

Level I: Mental Health Education

Niborom has been immersed in the Cambodian culture and has had little contact with the American culture, other than Tom, her new boyfriend. Her English skills are poor and she is unemployed. She has minimal knowledge about psychotherapy. Therefore, it is important to inform her about the counseling process so that she has a clear understanding and expectations.

Level II: Individual, Group, and Family Therapy

The Cambodian society prioritizes family and social relationships. One of the major current problems for Niborom is rejection by her cousin and daughters. This has been very painful and caused Niborom to talk about dying. Therefore, given the cultural context and extreme problems within her family system, family therapy is recommended as the intervention strategy.

Within family therapy there could be an exploration of the impact of the absence of the children's biological father as well as relationships between Niborom and her children and Niborom and her cousin. The role of her cousin within the current family constellation would be helpful to discern. It would also be important, within a cultural framework, to explore the response to Tom by the children and cousin.

Maintaining a cultural framework for norms in family relationships, it would be helpful to determine patterns of communication within the family. Disrespect toward a parent is unusual in Cambodia, making this dynamic important to examine and discuss. How are people expressing dislike for something (such as Tom) to each other? What level of disagreement is permissible to express and how is this shared? How would family members want to share difficult issues such as this with each other? Could Tom ever have a part in the family dynamics? Questions such as these would be important to address in family therapy.

Level III: Cultural Empowerment

A major decision facing Niborom is whether or not to remain in the relationship with Tom and try and resolve this with her family. To assist her with this decision, it may be important for her to know and understand about biracial couples in the United States. What kind of discrimination do they face and to what degree is it accepted or tolerated? If she and Tom did become more serious, it is helpful for Niborom and Tom to know what are their respective cultural norms for formal and informal rules and laws regarding relationships of biological children with parental significant others? What are customary dating relationships in the United States and Cambodia, and how does this impact the family and community? These issues would be important, especially in melding two separate cultural views and a larger family system together. In addition, understanding about practice and expectations for dating relationships would be particularly important since Niborom knows only about Cambodian culture norms. Thus clear expectations and norms would be helpful for Niborom to know and process with her psychotherapist.

Level IV: Indigenous Healing

There may be an absence of cultural rituals that remain barriers to Niborom's mental health. For example, proper burial and words to deceased loved ones (in the event her husband is deceased) are important in aiding them to move on to the next life and for the ones left behind to find inner harmony. This may be contributing to Niborom's problems with her children and relationship with Tom, especially if she has not worked with a monk to properly address her deceased ancestors. Furthermore, since Niborom is crossing between two cultures as she develops her relationship with Tom, it is important to pay respects to practices in her own culture in order to peacefully move on. Thus, it may be very helpful for Niborom to visit with a Buddhist monk for his assessment and intervention with her current problems, including her suicidal ideation. This would best be done in conjunction with family psychotherapy.

Chapter 10

Case Study of Khadra, a 16-year-old Somali

DESCRIPTION

Khadra is a 16-year-old refugee from East Somalia who has been in the United States for 1 year. She came to the United States with her mother, seven brothers, and two sisters after her father and uncle were murdered by bandits in her home town during the civil war. The same bandits who murdered her father and brother also took all the families' property, leaving them penniless and hungry with only the clothes they were wearing. In their escape from their home country Khadra remembers being without food for days and fearing that her mother, brothers, and sisters would die.

Khadra's family is religious and continues to abide by the precepts of Islam as practicing Muslims. Khadra believes their faith was the reason that her family lived, with Allah watching over them. When they arrived in the United States, no one in the family, including Khadra, spoke English nor knew anything about the American culture. They often speak together about how the United States is so different than the war years in Somalia. Although Khadra has been in the United States for only 1 year, she learned English very rapidly and is almost fluent. Khadra and her siblings enjoy their lives in the United States. Of all her brothers and sisters Khadra likes school the most and studies very hard. She enjoys spending nights practicing English with her mother, who is learning English in an English as a second language (ESL) class at a local community center. Khadra hopes to become a doctor so she can help people when they "have accidents or are wounded in fighting."

The medium-sized city where Khadra's family lives has a large Somali community. Khandra is easygoing and friendly, and does not have any difficulty making friends. "People are very nice here and I like to speak with them," she shared with the agency social worker. "It is so much better than back home, where everyone was fighting and many times I was very scared and did not trust so many people."

Life has been fairly easy for Khadra and her family since settling into an apartment in a housing project and learning about how to survive in America, a place far less dangerous than Somalia. She knows how to walk to the local grocery that caters to the Somali population, how much food should cost, which parts of her neighborhood are unsafe after dark, and understands (easily) how to work American gadgets such as toilets and water facets in sinks. She even has a favorite candy bar with peanuts and chocolate. During the past year Khadra has gained a sense of comfort, feeling like she has a better idea of the world around her until one day 2 months ago when something happened that reminded her of Somalia. Since that day Khadra has been nervous, unable to concentrate, has difficulties in falling sleep, finds it hard to study English, and has been losing weight.

CRITICAL INCIDENT

Approximately 3 months ago something changed in Khadra's neighborhood. She noticed it after a few days, but could not figure out what was happening. There were different men standing around near the grocery store and the nearby liquor store, and many cars were stopping to talk to them. One of Khadra's friends said that she thought they were selling drugs and had been chased out of another neighborhood, but she was not sure. Khadra was confused because for the past year these men were not around her neighborhood and now they were there every day.

One afternoon coming home she passed by three of these men talking in the shadow of a building near the grocery store. Khadra walked by quickly, always feeling a little nervous around them, although she did not know why. As she went by, she saw a car slowly come around the corner. She saw two men in the car point guns and start shooting at the three men. Khadra dropped to the ground and saw the men start running in her direction. She was scared. Two of the men were shot and killed only 15 meters away from her, similar to what happened to her father and uncle. The other one got away. Khadra just lay on the ground, scared and crying. Since that day 2 months ago, she felt like her life has changed. "I thought America was different. It's not. It's the same as home."

SEQUENCE OF EVENTS

Everything in the United States was "coming together" for Khadra. Her English was improving rapidly, the bad dreams about what happened to her father and uncle were less frequent, and more recently even her mother laughed occasionally when they studied English together. There was even a 17-year-old Somali boy who Khadra thought liked her, and whenever he smiled at her she felt special. She had met with her school counselor just 3 weeks ago and learned about a local community college where she could continue to study English while taking classes. Even if it was a few years away, her school counselor suggested thinking about studying there as a first step to becoming a doctor.

When the shooting happened, Khadra's world shattered. A flood of memories came back, and she began to worry about her mother, brothers, and sisters' welfare. She felt responsible for them since she was the only one who witnessed the shooting and "knew how dangerous it really was outside." It was at this point 2 months after the shooting when Khadra was not eating or sleeping very well, not laughing anymore, and not concentrating on her schoolwork, that her mother found out about a local mental health agency to help with problems such as these.

KEY CLINICAL QUESTIONS

1. Has Khadra ever spoken about what happened to her father and brother? If yes, with whom?
2. What was it like escaping from her town in Somalia?
3. What role does Khadra play in her family? Is this role longstanding?
4. Who has supported Khadra's mother? Is there a community support network that has been helpful?
5. What role does Islam play in the lives of Khadra and her family at this time? How do they maintain their religious practice?
6. What does Khadra believe needs to happen for her to feel better?
7. What happens to Khadra when she has difficulty concentrating What is she thinking about?
8. What will constitute a safe environment for Khadra

MULTI-LEVEL MODEL (MLM)
OF PSYCHOTHERAPY INTERVENTION

Level I: Mental Health Education

Given the importance of social networking in the Somali community, it would be essential that Khadra and her family understand that psychotherapy is confidential. It would also be important for Khadra and her family to understand how family therapy works and what are the goals of therapy.

Level II: Individual, Group, and Family Therapy

The shooting incident on the street precipitated memories of the loss of Khadra's father, uncle, and very likely many other people. This incident, in fact, changed the entire course of life events for the whole family. Given the family-based nature of the Somali community, a systems-based approach of family therapy is recommended.

It could be suggested that family therapy begin with a focus on postmigration. How are they adjusting? What is life like for them in the United States? What are still some of the difficult aspects of adapting and living in the new country? Probing these issues tackles the difficulties with acculturating while concurrently establishing trust and rapport with the psychotherapist in order to work together on the more painful premigration issues.

Premigration issues would concentrate on the violence and terror that was personally experienced and observed. This would be critical to the family since they lost the husband/father who was the caretaker and patriarch. Not only was he killed, but his brother also died at the hands of soldiers. This left a vacuum in the family, necessitating dramatic shifts ranging from migration to a new country to Khadra's mother becoming the financial provider and caretaker. Furthermore, everyone in the family had witnessed brutality and murder, and several of them had seen the murder of their father and brother. In many respects Khadra's response to the shooting in the United States triggered buried feelings and memories about these past incidents.

In family therapy it would be important to hear family member's stories about their experience in Somali. This must be done according to their timing and readiness to share deep-rooted painful memories and cannot be forced. The storytelling or sharing is culturally appropriate where this style of communication is an accepted aspect of everyday life. In family therapy the storytelling could be supplemented with sharing and analyzing dreams, which are culturally believed to have significance and meaning. Dreams may be especially important in helping to come to terms with the death of family members and friends.

It may be helpful for Khadra to also participate in group therapy with other members of the Somali community. This may prove to be highly beneficial since many members of the community share the same premigration experiences and loss of loved ones. It may be helpful for the psychotherapist to establish links with the community to develop a community-based support group that would explore premigration trauma and acculturation.

Level III: Cultural Empowerment

Khadra was not sure what the men on the street corner were doing or why they were shot. A friend had explained that it might be related to drugs, but Khadra remained unsure. To regain a sense of security about her environment, it would be crucial that there is an explanation and meaning attributed to the community around her apartment. Determining that, in fact, these men were known to be dealing drugs and how that works in the United States would be important information for Khadra and her family. Furthermore, providing them with an understanding about why they suddenly appeared in her neighborhood 2 months ago (it was determined that they had been "pushed" out of their old area) and helping to comprehend the context for the violence would be important information.

A second area of cultural mastery important for Khadra would be to clearly explain what is required to study medicine. Khadra was not clear that she could even attend a community college that would eventually lead toward a medical degree while further developing her English skills. Khadra was worried that her English would be the impediment for earning the degree. Thus, a clear pathway to reach this goal would be important, along with grade and course requirements.

Finally, the psychotherapist could assist Khadra and others in family therapy and group therapy about what to do in situations that are dangerous. For example, refugees may not be aware of how to call the police or emergency medical services. Skills such as how to make emergency 911 phone calls are very important resources to have for Khadra and other refugees from Somalia.

Level IV: Indigenous Healing

Traditional medicine in Somalia is typically practiced by "traditional doctors" who are usually elderly men in the community. Their skills are learned from older family members, who pass the skills of healing down through generations. The basis for cure is to remove the spirits residing in the patient that are causing the illness. Angry spirits lead to sickness.

With this as a fundamental belief system for illness and healing in the Somali culture, it is important that there is communication with the spirits to facilitate healing for Khadra and her family. In addition to family therapy, it may be very helpful to visit an elderly traditional doctor in the community and go through rituals to appease the spirits. Ceremonies might involve reading the Koran, eating special foods, or burning incense in attempting to appease the spirits of the father and uncle as well as neighbors and friends who were killed.

Chapter 11

Case Study of Tran, a 48-year-old Vietnamese

DESCRIPTION

Tran is a 48-year-old Vietnamese male who has been in the United States since 1980 and is currently unemployed. Before escaping to the United States Tran was working as an engineer fixing roads and bridges during the war in Vietnam. One day when he was working 50 miles away from his village the fighting became very intense. He could not return to his village and lost contact with his family. He spent several months wandering from village to village in the Vietnamese countryside until he finally escaped just before the fall of Saigon in 1975. Tran's training and background was not recognized in the United States, forcing him to look for unskilled or semiskilled positions. Periodically he does temporary work, earning a minimal salary, although he has expressed a desire to have full-time employment "like it was in Vietnam." He was hired twice during the past 20 years in permanent positions, but each position lasted only several months until he lost the job. Tran complains that most employers are prejudiced against "people like me because my English is not so good," although many of his friends believe that he is very proficient in English.

Tran sporadically looks for full-time employment and feels desperate after many rejections. He maintains his inability to secure a job is due to his English, even though he studied English in the refugee camp and has good English language skills according to his caseworker in the local sponsoring agency. Recently, he decided to attend an advanced language training class offered two nights a week. He goes regularly and aspires to enroll in a university extension course next year to study engineering. Tran is somewhat resentful and feels he has no choice. "Why must I study engineering again? This was my work. I don't need more study!"

Tran does not know anything about his family in Vietnam, having never been able to trace them. He currently lives in a rented apartment with three other Vietnamese men. He appears to be extremely intelligent, articulate, and friendly on a one-to-one basis. In groups he is aloof and tends to keep to himself stating clearly, "I don't like groups of people." He hopes to save enough money to get married someday and have a family.

Tran's social network is small. Although he knows a large number of people in his community, he is not close to anyone. He spends weekends mostly by himself except when one of his three roommates invites him to a party or social gathering. Usually he would go but prefers to stay at home watching television or sitting in his room. Tran does not have a significant relationship with a female or male companion and never speaks about dating or his family in Vietnam since being in the United States.

CRITICAL INCIDENT

Tran enrolled in an advanced 6-week English as a second language (ESL) class. After so many failed attempts at securing employment, Tran reluctantly decided that improving his English could help him "get a job and then someday study engineering." The English class focused on interviewing skills, telephone communication, and writing resumes. During the fourth week, the class was role-playing interviewing skills. To more effectively learn these skills, the class assignment was to tape the role-plays and then critique them as an entire class.

In class Tran became increasingly annoyed, making sarcastic comments and interrupting taping and discussions about his classmate's tapes. The teacher tried to calm him down but he would not listen. Up to this point Tran had gotten along well with his classmates, but his interruptions and attitude caused his classmates to tell him to "be quiet and stop it." This only made him more agitated. Tran refused to participate in the role-play, but the teacher finally shamed him into participating. During the role-play Tran lost control, stood up, and began yelling, "I know what you want, I'm not going to tell you anything." At that point he began aggressively pushing chairs and tables around the room.

SEQUENCE OF EVENTS

Six weeks prior to attending the ESL classes Tran had gone to the dentist complaining about a severe toothache. He claimed that the dentist implanted a listening device in his tooth that could be regulated by people in positions of authority. He explained: "When they turn on the device my thoughts and conversations with other people are being monitored." He shared his concern with two of his roommates and twice commented to them, "Ssshh…remember they can hear us."

KEY CLINICAL QUESTIONS

1. What happened in Vietnam when the war broke out and Tran was wandering from village to village?

2. What was Tran's escape from Vietnam like?

3. What does Tran believe happened to his family in Vietnam?

4. What does Tran believe are the reasons why he was fired from the two jobs he held in the United States?

5. Tran describes his employers and potential employers as prejudiced. How does he experience this? What does his perceived prejudice do to him?

6. What is it like for Tran to be a student in an advanced English class?

7. Explore in depth Tran's reaction to being a student of engineering again? How is this affecting him?

8. Explore with Tran his family in Vietnam? This is important, especially since Tran has not commented or shared any information about his family life in Vietnam.

9. Would Tran like to have more friends? If yes, why? If no, why not?

10. Explore Tran's goal of having a wife and child? What does this image look like to him and what would it require to achieve this goal? Does he believe that he must make any changes in his life for this to happen?

11. What happened in ESL class with the videotaping that so upset Tran?

12. Discuss his belief that the dentist implanted a listening device in his tooth. What are "they" listening for, who are "they," what will "they" do with the information?

MULTI-LEVEL MODEL (MLM) OF PSYCHOTHERAPY INTERVENTION

Level I: Mental Health Education

Given the escalation of Tran's emotional difficulties and behavior, it would be helpful for him to receive professional help to work through his problems. Since Tran has had no previous contact with the mental health system, it would be important to clearly explain to him the goals, purpose, and process of psychotherapy. This is especially significant given Tran's concerns about his mistrust toward people in authority and that he is being "controlled." Issues such as confidentiality would be important to introduce and reinforce during psychotherapy.

Level II: Individual, Group, and Family Therapy

Although the Vietnamese culture is based on family and social relationships, Tran is fairly alone. It is recommended that Tran enter group therapy to work on adjustment issues, especially in light of his social isolation. This group could include other refugees where a focus would be on the relationship of premigration problems to current functioning. Relevant issues for Tran would include his loss of status as an engineer, difficulty finding or maintaining employment in the United States, discrimination, not achieving his professed goal of having a family, believing his English is poor, and fears about being monitored by people in positions of authority. The group format would allow Tran to explore these issues with others with the potential to gain insight from peers about his problems. This requires skillful facilitation, given his delusional thinking that underscores deeply rooted anxiety and pain.

In group therapy a discussion of memories, feelings, and situations from premigration days in Vietnam would be essential. For Tran this would include examing what happened to him when he lost his job in Vietnam and his subsequent difficulties as he wandered the countryside. The fact that he never mentions his family network in Vietnam makes this important to explore. It would also be helpful to discuss with Tran the change from having an established job as an engineer in Vietnam to his struggle in the resettlement country to find and keep even an unskilled job where he experiences discrimination. What has happened in terms of his pride, sense of self-image and worth, and social status as a result of these changes?

His struggle to find work in the United States is a metaphor for other difficulties adjusting to the new culture. It would be helpful to examine how he is adapting, what is working, and what is problematic for him. Important in this discussion would be an exploration of English language proficiency, which research has shown to be closely correlated with better adjustment and psychological well-being. Another aspect of acculturation to bring into group therapy is his delusional thinking that the dentist implanted a listening device in his tooth. A thorough examination in the group context about his delusional belief system may be extremely beneficial. In addition, the psychotherapist must take into account Tran's experience of discrimination and work with Tran to acknowledge and address his feelings and reactions.

Tran stated that someday he wanted a wife and family. It might be helpful for the psychotherapist to explore when "someday" is, how he imagines he would achieve this goal, and why is he "holding off" now. Questions to explore with Tran could include the following: What does he need to do differently to accomplish this goal? Is he creating the opportunities to meet women? Are his social skills adequate to begin and maintain a dating relationship? The balance of discussing past, present, and future would be meaningful for Tran, who may be struggling with all three of these issues.

Level III: Cultural Empowerment

Tran has been having a difficult time finding employment. It would be helpful to ensure that he is knowledgeable about unemployment and social service benefits while he is trying to secure work. In addition, information about employment offices and laws regulating discrimination practices would be important for Tran to know in order to understand his legal rights.

Level IV: Indigenous Healing

Depending on what emerges in psychotherapy, Tran may benefit from working with an elder in the community or Vietnamese monk. If Tran has not come to terms with the loss or death of family or friends in Vietnam and any other traumatic events that he may have encountered, it may be helpful for him to work with someone who can facilitate culturally sanctioned healing rituals. This could bring peace and an inner balance for Tran, which are crucial for adaptation to the United States and moving ahead to establish his own family.

Chapter 12

Case Study of Eleni, a 36-year-old Ethiopian

DESCRIPTION

Eleni is a 36-year-old Ethiopian woman who migrated to the United States 3 years ago and lives with her husband and two sons in a large urban city. Her husband works long hours as a taxi driver while Eleni works in a factory. Eleni's next door neighbor told her that there were better paying jobs at another site if "you speak English." Soon after Eleni began English as a second language (ESL) night classes but had nowhere to leave her two small children since her husband worked the night shift. She took the children with her to class but was upset about the cost and danger of the bus ride. In class she was sometimes distracted by her children who became bored and tired during the 2-hour class. Usually the children would play quietly or sleep at the back of the class, but sometimes, when they were really tired or irritable, she had to take them out of class and try to settle them down.

There were also money problems that always seemed to leave one or two bills left unpaid each month. Each week the family had just enough money to live on, and it was Eleni's responsibility to manage the shopping. Since money was a problem, Eleni and her family lived in a low-income neighborhood. Sometimes Eleni was afraid to be home alone in the evening, especially when she heard people fighting and yelling outside. Even though her day started at 7:00 A.M. when the children woke up, her husband expected her to be the dutiful wife when he arrived home at 10:00 or 11:00 at night and prepare food and care for his needs. Eleni complained, "I am tired all the time. I don't know what to do!"

Eleni has a good social network in the city where she lives, with a number of Ethiopian friends and her older sister who lives nearby. She regularly gets together with a group of women and on weekends the families join together for picnics and other activities. Her friends agree that "people talk too loud here" and many of them are also afraid to go outside, especially at night.

CRITICAL INCIDENT

Money has always been a problem for Eleni and her family. Recently, the factory where she worked lost a major contract and decreased the working hours by 25% for employees. With less income, the financial problems for Eleni's family have gotten worse. There is even less money for food. Sometimes Eleni does not eat so her children and husband have enough food. Her husband has been complaining about eating the same type of food over and over again and is blaming Eleni for their financial problems. Recently he was angry at her and told her that instead of going to language classes and spending more money she should take an evening job. That same evening her husband refused to eat the food and left for a friend's home "where you can find a different taste!" Eleni was angry and scared and did not know what to do.

SEQUENCE OF EVENTS

During the war the village where Eleni and her husband lived was invaded. Eleni watched her father receive a severe beating from a group of men. It was during the same invasion that several men raped her in the field near the village. Eleni and her husband did not speak about this incident but Eleni confided to her older sister, who lives nearby, that she believes her oldest child may be from the rape. Eleni's husband occasionally drinks and one time recently yelled at Eleni, "If you had done things differently all that wouldn't have happened back there!" Eleni did not know what he meant but was too afraid to ask him. She feels as if things are closing in on her. Not having enough food reminds her of being hungry all the time during their last few months in the village when the fighting was getting closer. "It's like that time and I'm getting more and more scared."

KEY CLINICAL QUESTIONS

1. What is the experience like for Eleni to continue to be the "dutiful wife" in the United State?
2. In addition to people in the United States "talking too loud," what other things does Eleni find difficult in terms of cultural differences and adjustment?
3. Is there a possibility that any of her friends could take care of the children when she attends ESL classes?
4. Would Eleni be willing to talk about the rape in a safe environment that would maintain confidentiality?

5. How did watching her father severely beaten impact her?

6. Explore Eleni's feelings and reactions to the possibility of her eldest son being conceived during the rape.

7. What does Eleni think is the origin of her fears? Did she always feel like this?

8. Explore Eleni's relationship with her husband?

MULTI-LEVEL MODEL (MLM)
OF PSYCHOTHERAPY INTERVENTION

Level I: Mental Health Education

Eleni has never been to a mental health professional and has no understanding of what happens in psychotherapy. It would be very important, especially given the secrets she carries about the rape, pregnancy, and questions regarding the biological father of her oldest son that the therapeutic relationship is very carefully described to her. Information about confidentiality, being able to speak about one's deepest thoughts and concerns, an explanation about how this process can be helpful, and clearly defined role expectations for her as the client and expectations for the psychotherapist would be essential.

Level II: Individual, Group, and Family Therapy

Given the depth of Eleni's concerns, it may be helpful to begin with individual therapy and move toward couple therapy at a later date. Initially there must be an emphasis on establishing rapport and trust between the psychotherapist and Eleni. She has been carrying around culturally taboo secrets and must find a very safe environment so she feels safe enough to disclose and explore these issues. Concerns that would be helpful to initially address in individual counseling would focus on immediate problems such as strategies to manage the current family financial crisis, an exploration of her relationship with her husband given the demands of living in the United States, and realistic choices about taking language classes at this time. An examination of both short-term and long-term goals and subsequent ramifications would be helpful.

As a therapeutic alliance was forged and there was a focus on exploring more immediate concerns, it may be helpful to introduce deeper premigration issues. For example, if Eleni is speaking about not being able to talk with her husband about ESL classes, it might be timely to explore how long it has been difficult for her in a culturally sensitive and respectful framework. Questions such as "What can you speak with him about?," "Are there things that you feel you can't talk about with him?," or "What is it like to not be able to speak with him about those things and keep things privately inside yourself?" would be helpful in the exploration. It is critical to keep in mind that this exploration must be done within a cultural context that appreciates the values and structure that is inherent in Ethiopian marriages. It may also be helpful and culturally appropriate to speak in metaphor or use story telling with Eleni to approach the issue of being raped, since it might be too difficult to speak directly about this powerful and painful experience.

Once Eleni has addressed premigration trauma and postmigration adjustment issues, it may be helpful to invite her husband into the therapy sessions for couple counseling. Having them work together to tackle current financial problems, concerns about taking ESL courses, childcare, and residual issues from premigration that interfere with their current functioning as a family residing in the United States would all be important therapeutically. An emphasis on structural family therapy would assist in redefining roles within the context of short- and long-term family goals.

Level III: Cultural Empowerment

It may be unclear to Eleni and her family about temporary assistance that is available to help them through this difficult financial period. They may be eligible for food stamps and free school lunches until Eleni is able to find a full-time job. In addition, there may be support for Eleni to take language classes, including transportation and childcare costs. Providing this information to Eleni and her family would give them information about the U.S. culture that may not have been available before their current financial crisis. This could be instrumental in reducing the current family tensions and bringing them through a rough time when Eleni's hours at work have been reduced and the family income is lower.

Level IV: Indigenous Healing

In the Ethiopian community there is an elderly man recognized for his healing powers. He has successfully worked with many members in the community, helping them heal through a certain kind of sorcery that is known to be very powerful. It might be extremely beneficial for Eleni to undergo traditional healing from a cultural framework while concurrently seeing a Western mental health professional for counseling. The combination of these two healing methodologies may be extremely potent in addressing the depth of the premigration trauma, that is, the rape and witnessed torture and abuse, as well as the contemporary issues facing the family.

Chapter 13

Case Study of Hector, a 15-year-old El Salvadorian

DESCRIPTION

Hector is a 15-year-old male from El Salvador who was accused of stealing from classmates in school. He has been in the United States for 11 months and has no friends. He is seeing the school counselor on a weekly basis to receive emotional support since he seems lonely and sometimes depressed.

His background is somewhat confusing with vague and conflicting information. Some of his relatives were killed while fighting in El Salvador, but the details remain elusive. Hector appears to be pleasant and somewhat submissive to teachers. He does not have any friends and his peers describe him as "a little strange and withdrawn." Hector has been approached several times by peers to join them in activities but has rejected these friendly overtures preferring to remain aloof and continues to eat lunch by himself. In contrast, when he plays sports in gym class he is particularly aggressive, and once during a soccer game he forcefully ran into another boy and seriously injured him. Most of Hector's time outside of school is spent at home in the apartment watching television.

Hector came to the United States with his parents and two sisters. He is the middle child. His younger sister is 14 while his older sister is 17 and the only family member who speaks fluent English. His older sister is frequently absent from school and is failing all her classes. The school counselor believes she will drop out of school in the near future. Hector, on the other hand, attends daily. His teachers have commented that he is always "neat and clean but wears the same clothes every day."

Although the family lives in a town where there is a small Latino population, they feel isolated and miss the sense of community they had in El Salvador. They do not like the colder climate and report having a difficult time "paying all the bills." Although a church group and sponsoring agency are assisting them, Hector and his family remains distrustful and most often avoid their sponsors and caseworker (a Latina from Puerto Rico).

CRITICAL INCIDENT

One day in gym Hector was ill. He was granted permission to go to the nurse's office and went to change into his clothes in the locker room. Later that period three classmates claimed that money was missing from their lockers. When questioned, Hector vehemently denied taking it and became angry. He refused to speak with the school counselor, threatening in Spanish to "never return to this stupid school" and left the building.

SEQUENCE OF EVENTS

There have been increasing arguments at home between Hector's parents and his older sister. Hector reported to the school counselor, "It is too difficult to be at my home. They are always arguing . . . then my parents tell my older sister to be like me and go to the school. I don't be in the middle! I care for my sister, but it is between them. . . . She say she might leave. I worry about this." The school counselor believes that Hector is more and more upset about his sister and parents and seems to be withdrawing even further. The school counselor is also aware that the electricity was cut off this past month for a few days and Hector didn't do his homework "because we have no light." It is her general impression that the home problems have been escalating in the past month and relate to accusations of Hector stealing in the locker room and 2 weeks before in homeroom.

KEY CLINICAL QUESTIONS

1. Does Hector want friends?
2. Why is Hector isolating himself from his peer group?
3. Did Hector have friends in El Salvador? If yes, what makes things different now?
4. What, if any, was the impact of the war in El Slavador on Hector? Were any of his experiences traumatic?
5. What members of his family were killed in the war in El Salvador? How did this affect Hector?
6. To attempt and gain an understanding of Hector's value system, it would be helpful to explore socially acceptable and unacceptable behaviors. This may assist in probing Hector's thoughts about stealing rather than to address it directly.
7. What is Hector's relationship with his older sister? What does he think is going on with her at this time? How does he feel about her behavior?

8. How is home life going for Hector?

9. How would Hector describe his relationship with his parents?

MULTI-LEVEL MODEL (MLM) OF PSYCHOTHERAPY INTERVENTION

Level I: Mental Health Education

Hector already has an awareness of the counseling process since he is seeing the school counselor weekly. This is helpful since Hector and his school counselor can now explain together to his family what happens in psychotherapy and family therapy, since this will be recommended for the larger family.

Level II: Individual, Group, and Family Therapy

Individual support for Hector has been built in with his school counselor. It is also evident that the older daughter is having problems and there are financial concerns. At this point it is unclear how the younger daughter is doing in school or in the family, making her noticeably absent. Thus, the recommendations for Hector and his family would be to enter family therapy and for Hector to participate in group counseling. The recommendation for family therapy could be presented by the school counselor, describing the process and potential benefits.

Family therapy would initially focus on systemic issues related to the older daughter's problems with school and Hector's possible stealing. It would also be important to discuss the psychological effects of poverty on the family, which is evident with their struggle to pay bills in a timely fashion. In addition, family therapy could address premigration trauma. Although it is unclear what effect the war had on family members, this would be important to explore, especially since El Salvadorians highly value extended family and social networks. An exploration of premigration trauma would therefore be essential to understand the impact on acculturation and psychological adjustment, particularly as it affects family dynamics.

Group counseling for Hector also has the potential to be highly beneficial. Hector is withdrawn, has minimal contact with peers, and thus is inexperienced within a social context. It is recommended that Hector participate in a multiethnic group of similar aged immigrant and refugee males who have been having some adjustment problems in school. This may help him gain insight into his behavior and interpersonal relations.

Level III: Cultural Empowerment

One known fact about Hector's family is that they have been unable to meet utility payments, which has affected Hector's schoolwork. They have been in the United States for less than 1 year and may not have information about financial assistance for such things as heat, electricity, phone, and water. It would be important to educate them about their rights and the necessary steps for not losing basic services. This requires knowledge about which agencies to call, where to go and fill out forms, public transportation routes and information, and expectations for support. Learning this information provides the beginning of cultural mastery.

Level IV: Indigenous Healing

It is important to determine the family's perspective on help-seeking behavior and healing. Clearly, this family is struggling with adjustment to the United States given allegations about Hector stealing, problems with his older sister, and parental arguments. Within the Latino community the local priest from El Salvador is recognized for his work helping with personal and family problems. It may be that in conjunction with the family therapy and group counseling, that a culturally based healing intervention with the El Salvadorian priest would be highly beneficial for the family. His work would be based on the religious belief system of Hector and family members and would be culturally based on the religious healing practices in El Salvador. He may include practices such as reading from the Bible to address present difficulties in adjusting to the resettlement country to assisting with the healing necessary for coming to terms with family members and loved ones who were killed during the war.

Chapter 14

Case Study of Sokhany, a 55-year-old Cambodian

DESCRIPTION

Sokhany is a 55-year-old Cambodian woman who lives with her youngest and only surviving child, a 25-year-old daughter. They arrived in the United States 13 years ago after spending 6 years in a refugee camp in Thailand. Sokhany had witnessed her husband and three sons being tortured and eventually killed by Khmer Rhouge soldiers just before her escape from Cambodia.

Sokhany had lived in the countryside in Cambodia and explained that "I had never traveled to the city." Even after living many years in the United States, she still speaks poor English. Sokhany recently told her caseworker that "I will always be lost in this country." She does not work and depends on her daughter's income to survive. Her daughter works long hours washing dishes in a restaurant, dropped out of English as a second language (ESL) classes some years ago and spends her weekends at home with her mother. Sokhany spends days alone at home, looking out the window and drinking tea throughout the day. "I am scared to go out there without my daughter . . . she knows how to walk around and all the different places we need to go." Sokhany is also afraid of other things. "I don't like the dark . . . I always keep my light on just in case . . . it helps." Although her daughter bought her a bed she preferred to sleep on the floor. "I'm afraid I could slip away and fall off . . . how can you stay balanced sleeping?" There were other difficulties for Sokhany in adjusting to the United States. "The weather is too cold and the people here . . . they're strange. I don't understand them at all . . . and the food, it is not too good." Sokhany has not made many friends in the United States except for a few women from the Cambodian community.

CRITICAL INCIDENT

While walking home from work one night Sokhany's daughter was hit by a drunken driver. The daughter had initially been in intensive care but was recently moved to a recovery unit. The hospital was eight blocks from Sokhany's home. Sokhany was highly anxious going to and from the hospital and wanted to stay at the hospital with her daughter. She was confused when staff at the hospital would not let her sleep with her daughter at nights, not understanding why "a mother couldn't be with her sick daughter." More recently when Sokhany met with her caseworker, she would burst into tears and sob for long periods of time.

SEQUENCE OF EVENTS

Initially, the United States was terrifying to Sokhany. She spoke little English and could not understand the different way of doing things that were "so different than Cambodia." She was scared to go out into the community, especially since a few times people who were just standing around on the street had made loud comments to her that she did not understand. More recently her daughter and the caseworker had been helping her to go outside more. She had been gaining some confidence and after many years had gone to the local corner grocery store on a few occasions. Her confidence had been building.

Concurrently, her daughter had begun to participate in community activities. She had gone to a dance, a festival, and a birthday party. This was different than before; for most of the years they had lived in the United States she had just worked and come home to keep her mother company. A few weeks ago she convinced her mother to join her at one of the Cambodian festivals, which was a major change in behavior.

KEY CLINICAL QUESTIONS

1. What happened to Sokhany (and her daughter) as a result of witnessing the death of her husband and sons in Cambodia? Has she ever spoken about this with anyone? If not, it might be very important to gently assist her in talking about this horrible experience.

2. How has Sokhany coped with the killing of her family? What strategies has she employed to continue her life?

3. What does Sokhany envision for her daughter? What is her future?

4. What does Sokhany envision for herself? What kind of life is she leading? How would she like her life to be realistically, given that she is now in the United States?

5. What is Sokhany afraid will happen if she goes out alone? What is the basis for her fears?

6. Explore Sokhany's fear of the dark. Does this have anything to do with the killing of her husband and sons?

7. How does Sokhany feel about her social network? Is it satisfactory or would she like to be more socially active?

8. Discuss with Sokhany her crying related to her daughter's accident. It may be that the tears and long periods of crying relate to more than just her daughter's hospitalization and have deeper roots.

9. Is sleeping on the floor somehow a symbol for not letting go of Cambodia and adjusting to the United States? How can she sleep peacefully in the United States?

MULTI-LEVEL MODEL (MLM)
OF PSYCHOTHERAPY INTERVENTION

Level I: Mental Health Education

As with other clients, it would be essential that Sokhany understand the process, anticipated benefit, and role of the psychotherapist in the counseling relationship. This would be especially relevant for Sokhany since she has had little or no contact with the American culture and may be highly confused by a mental health professional asking personal questions about her life.

Level II: Individual, Group and Family Therapy

Given the extent of premigration trauma and acculturation difficulties Sokhany has in the United States. it is recommended that Sokhany participate in group therapy with other refugee women who have experienced premigration trauma. This is strongly recommended given Sokhany's isolation and dependency on her daughter and the appropriateness with the Cambodian culture where there is an emphasis on community and social relationships. This would assist Sokhany to work on her long-standing unresolved personal issues within a social framework, which is applicable for the Cambodian culture.

Given her isolation and alienation from the Cambodian community, it would be suggested that the group be comprised of refugee women who experienced trauma during premigration and are having difficulties adjusting in the resettlement country. The group format would allow Sokhany and others to share their experiences in a safe environment. Hearing and helping each other and describing their inner pain and sadness in a group setting has the benefit to normalize their reactions and reduce the isolation of living with the trauma.

Within a group of this nature it is recommended that the initial focus is on safe and less threatening aspects of the client's lives, such as problems in adjustment. As group members gain an understanding of the process of group work and therapeutic trust is established, other more anxiety producing topics that relate to postmigration could be introduced into the sessions. For example, it would be important that Sokhany talk about her dependency on her daughter, fear of the dark, fear of going out of her apartment, language difficulties, sleeping on the floor, shopping, loneliness, and the like. A group format would be invaluable for Sokhany to discuss her current crisis with her daughter, who is her "cultural life-line" and the fact that for many years her life has essentially been on hold.

Since many refugee women similar to Sokhany have had a very difficult past, it is essential that trust and cohesion is established prior to speaking about the pain and horror during premigration. Thus it would be recommended that the group transition from postmigration difficulties to premigration memories that are less threatening. For example, what was the daily routine like in their home countries before any difficulties, who do they remember, and what special memories do they have. After entering the world of premigration that was comfortable and safe, more difficult experiences can be introduced. In Sokhany's case, this would include the witnessing of her three sons and husband who were tortured and murdered, fighting and death in her village, 6 years in a refugee camp, and other experiences that she may recall.

After the difficult exploration of these issues in the group, it would be helpful for group members to examine the future. For Sokhany a critical issue is to determine her desire to change. How would she like to change her life? What would she like to happen for her daughter and herself? How can she facilitate this and what steps would she need to take? It is only after Sokhany and other members of the group have come to terms with the past and present, can they establish goals to move forward.

Following group therapy and the recovery of Sokhany's daughter, it is recommended that Sokhany and her daughter engage in family therapy. This would be helpful in redefining their relationship, which at this time is too enmeshed. Roles, responsibilities, dependency, and communication patterns could all be examined within the framework of family therapy. This would be helpful, especially with the newfound insights and awareness for Sokhany from group therapy.

Level III: Cultural Empowerment

Even though Sokhany has been in the United States for many years, in many respects she is still a newcomer to the society. She is not familiar with the customs and practices in the United States and has not learned enough about the society to feel secure or comfortable. Thus, despite the years since Sokhany migrated, a mental health professional must approach her as if she just recently entered the country.

There is an immediate need for Sokhany to understand hospital regulations about spending the night with patients. In Cambodia this would be a customary practice that would not be inhibited by rules or regulations. Sokhany does not understand why she is prohibited from sleeping on the floor next to her daughter's bed. It would be important to explain the hospital rules and the rationale for these regulations. This would assist Sokhany in understanding *why* this practice is in place, rather than leaving her confused about these regulations.

Sokhany is also afraid to go outside on her own. "The men say things at me . . . . it's always those same men on the corner. I don't know what they do there all day long." For her to handle the men on the corner, there are certain things that would be helpful to understand culturally. First, an explanation about who these men are and what they are doing would be helpful. It would also be helpful for Sokhany to know what they are saying. Of equal importance is to assist her in knowing how to respond to their comments—nonverbally and verbally. Strategies for handling uncomfortable situations like this one would be very beneficial and aid Sokhany in feeling more secure in her neighborhood.

Level IV: Indigenous Healing

The torture and murder of Sokhany's husband and sons leaves her with significant psychological and spiritual malaise. Since Sokhany spent the majority of her life in Cambodia, there are deeply rooted cultural practices for death. Thus, in addition to psychotherapy, it would be highly beneficial for Sokhany to simultaneously see a monk who could facilitate customary rituals for her deceased family members. This culturally relative practice is rooted in Sokhany's belief system and would be very important in her healing.

Chapter 15

Case Study of Matilda, a 17-year-old Albanian

DESCRIPTION

Matilda is a 17-year-old female who came to the United States, 3 years ago from a small town in Albania. She migrated to the United States with her mother, father, and sister because of the civil war. Her parents were very afraid that Matilda and her sister would be taken from them and sold in Italy or somewhere else in Europe as prostitutes, which was a practice that was occurring as a result of the war. Matilda's father was particularly afraid and realized that he could not protect them.

In her town Matilda witnessed fighting and killing. She saw two men shot and killed near the main square one day, and another time was returning from the market when she saw three children shot and killed as they walked across an open field. It was also fairly common to hear about people being killed or disappearing, like the shopkeeper in the store on the road behind her house. One day he just vanished and never came to work again. Her friends and family had many stories like this and there were many versions. Some said that they escaped to another country like Italy or Switzerland, others insisted that they were taken away and killed. Matilda was never quite sure what happened to these people, but oftentimes thought about it when she was alone and lying in bed at night. A few times she tried to talk to her parents about what she heard or about why someone suddenly was not around anymore, but they just told her to not think about it and "go about her business."

When Matilda's family left Albania, her two uncles and three cousins were all fighting in the war. She worried about them, especially her one uncle with whom she was very close, and his son, who was like a big brother to her. As far as she knew they were all still alive, but having seen fighting and death close-up, Matilda knew that anything could happen at any time. Even in America, she wondered about them and wished they would write more often than once every 5 to 6 months.

Arriving in the United States, Matilda had difficulty adjusting to the culture. She did not speak English and did not really make friends at first, even though a few of the other girls did smile at her. The groups of girls here were so different and dressed with clothes that she did not own and could not afford. Also, they seemed to laugh more than her friends in Albania who did not laugh very much, although she did remember that they laughed more in Albania when she was younger, before all the fighting. She was very depressed during her first year in the United States and felt like she would never really overcome her sadness. Now 3 years later she described herself. "I am still sad on many days. I wake up in the morning thinking about all of my life so far, and how it was not so happy during the past six years." Even so, Matilda feels safer living in the United States and has begun to make plans for next year when she graduates. "I am now a senior. I have a few friends after three years and this is good. After this year, I will study to be an assistant to a dentist... I would like to do this work."

CRITICAL INCIDENT

It is near graduation and Matilda now has a few American girlfriends. She has saved enough money working as a chambermaid at a local motel to buy new clothes and a new pair of tennis shoes, although most of her money helps pay family bills and buy food. With these new clothes she feels a little less out of place, dressing more like the other girls. Her English has also improved so that she feels more comfortable at school and in the community.

Two simultaneous incidents happened that greatly affected Matilda. First, graduation was rapidly approaching and her three closest newfound friends were all going away. Two were going to college in different states and one was moving across the country with some friends and going to get a job there. Matilda had been invited, but knew her parents would never allow her to move so far away, so never even asked their permission. Friendship with these girls was very important to Matilda, and she anticipated a great loss when her friends left.

The second event that had a deep impact on Matilda was the senior prom. Each of her three friends had been invited. Matilda still did not know many boys and felt like she was very different from her classmates. When she met with her friends nowadays, they were very excited about going to the prom and talked about their plans. None of them seemed to remember that she was not invited and how that made her feel. She felt more left out than ever, and in some ways thought she had already lost her three closest friends. As prom night approached, Matilda became more reclusive. In their excitement her friends did not seem to notice. As graduation and the prom loomed, she became more reclusive, irritable, and troubled. Her parents, at a loss, requested advice from an elderly Albanian man who was the mayor of his town in the old country. He suggested that she see someone to discuss her problems, which were similar to what happened with his granddaughter.

SEQUENCE OF EVENTS

Matilda felt different even as she was getting to know her new group of friends. Sometime she recalled the deaths she had witnessed, which seemed far away from the safety of her American residential community. She once tried to talk with her friends about life in Albania, but they became bored and encouraged her to "get beyond it." Matilda remembers them saying, "Come on Matilda, that time was long ago. Now you're here. Don't think about those awful things. It's all over now." Her girlfriends preferred to talk about other things such as their hair, boys, who was unfriendly toward them, whether or not they were invited to a certain party, and frustration with their younger brothers or sisters who used their CDs or took their clothes. In one way Matilda wanted to also think these things were important, but then she would find herself worrying about her uncle and cousins fighting in the war. Whenever she started to think about them, she began to reminisce about her own life in Albania, remembering her fear of being kidnapped or raped and recalling how each day in Albania she woke up hoping that she would live to that night. Thus, as time went by in the United States Matilda grew closer with her three friends and better adjusted to the American culture. At the same time she became increasingly guilty, agitated, and upset for her growing concern with "American kinds of things," for example, how she looked, her hair, parties, make-up, and clothes. The more she felt these things, the more estranged she felt from herself and her friends. These feelings continued to grow for her and more recently came to a head.

The situation escalated as graduation day and prom night drew closer. She was very upset that she had not been invited to the prom and felt estranged from her friends. Matilda was questioning her ability to ever fit into the United States culture. At the same time she was annoyed with herself for even having those feelings, since she believed that life was much bigger than a prom. Additionally, Matilda became very angry with herself for wanting to fit in so badly and spending time with her friends talking about the day-to-day concerns they shared with each other. "How can I be thinking about someone not saying hello when my favorite uncle could die today fighting?" she would ask herself. These thoughts had increased over the past 3 years and were accentuated as graduation approached.

KEY CLINCIAL QUESTIONS

1. Ask Matilda about her friendship with her three close friends. What does this symbolize for her? What part do they play in her life? How does she feel about her friends leaving?

2. What does it mean to Matilda to not be invited to the prom What is the impact of her three friends going Why is this so profound for her?

3. Her goal to be a dental assistant—is this still her first choice?

4. It has been mentioned that Matilda feels "left out." Trace those feelings with Matilda to discover their roots—did this start during premigration, early postmigration, or later postmigration?

5. Discuss Matilda's Albanian heritage and the relationship she has with her parents and sister. What does her family mean to her?

6. Discuss with Matilda her life in Albania. What was it like to worry about being kidnapped and sold into prostitution? How was it for her to watch people suddenly disappear or be killed? What was it like for her to fear for her life on a daily basis?

7. How does Matilda manage the anxiety she has regarding her uncles and cousins who remain fighting in Albania?

8. What is important to Matilda? She struggles between accepting issues that her girlfriends find important, her life and death concerns during premigration in Albania, and her remaining family. How does she reconcile these worlds?

9. What is it like to withdraw from friends and family? What is going on for her at this time?

MULTI-LEVEL MODEL (MLM) OF PSYCHOTHERAPY INTERVENTION

Level I: Mental Health Education

The concept of psychotherapy is not familiar to Matilda or her family. Thus it would be essential to inform them about what happens in therapy. Issues such as confidentiality, privacy, the goals of therapy, and the process of talking about personal thoughts and feelings would be helpful. It may also be helpful to clarify that government has no role or relationship to what happens in counseling.

Level II: Individual, Group, and Family Therapy

It is recommended that Matilda's family participate in family therapy that is culturally sensitive. This would provide a context for Matilda's present experience and may be essential in assisting her and other family members to come to terms with premigration trauma and adjustment to the resettlement country. This would be more culturally appropriate since families in Albania provide a cultural foundation and thus offer a far better context for assisting Matilda and others to resolve their problems.

The entire family experienced the fear of Matilda and her sister being kidnapped and taken away. Her father, generally a very self-sufficient individual, was scared, creating even more fear in other members of the family. Living in this reality had a profound impact on each member of the family, and to discuss this in family therapy may prove to be highly beneficial to everyone. In addition, everyone in the family witnessed death, killing, and sudden disappearances in Albania. Since the family never discussed these issues, it would be useful to explore this premigration deep-rooted fear and trauma in family therapy. What impact does this shared experience have on how the family is functioning now?

Another essential issue for the family to examine is the relatives who continue to fight in Albania with a constant overriding threat of death. It appears that each family member carries their fear and concern about uncles, cousins, and other family members remaining in Albania in different ways. To openly discuss this in family therapy would be very helpful and decrease the isolation around these particularly important issues.

Finally, issues related to postmigration would be helpful to discuss. Matilda is upset about the upcoming prom and her friends graduating and leaving the area. It is likely that her sister and parents share similar difficulties regarding adaptation to the United States. To openly share how life events, social networks, goals, and future impact individuals in the family and the family system as a whole in a culturally sensitive manner would be important in the counseling process.

Level III: Cultural Empowerment

For Matilda, it would be helpful to discuss what typically happens when U.S. students graduate high school. For friends to move away from home at 18 is not common in Albania. Knowledge about this as normative in the United States may be beneficial. It may also be helpful to inform Matilda about common ways that friends keep in touch after they part ways in high school such as visits, e-mail, letters, and phone calls, in an attempt to provide some structure and definition to the sense of loss she is again experiencing. In addition, there should be clarification with Matilda about the requirements for becoming a dental assistant—courses and years in a postsecondary training program and prospects of finding a position once she graduates.

Level IV: Indigenous Healing

It is unclear what type of traditional healing exists in Albania, which provides an excellent case illustration of options for a psychotherapist to work across cultures with refugees. There is a need for the psychotherapist to gain information about indigenous healing that could be done in a variety of ways. One way is to access community leaders about help-seeking behavior for mental health problems in Albania. A second way is to ask the client what they would typically do if this situation were to happen at home. How would Matilda handle these problems if she still lived in Albania? Where would she seek guidance and support? A third way to find out about indigenous healing is to seek information through library or technological resources. Exploring the Internet or reading about mental health and indigenous healing in Albania would be helpful.

Chapter 16

Case Study of Toan, a 17-year-old Vietnamese

DESCRIPTION

Toan is a 17-year-old Vietnamese male who works full time in a restaurant claiming to be able to earn $16,000 annually. He attends high school and earns A's and B's in all his courses. His English has improved during his 4 years in the United States so that he no longer needs to take language classes. His teachers and school counselor describe him as very intelligent and having a "bright future." School personnel and his foster parents (Chinese American mother and European American father) were surprised when he announced that he would quit high school to earn more money since they had expected he would attend college. His foster parents became increasingly upset and strongly argued with Toan to remain in school. Finally, he reluctantly agreed, but insisted that he was "really not interested." Since that time his grades have dropped dramatically, he is frequently late to school, and more recently absent from school. Simultaneously, his relationship with his foster parents has deteriorated.

When asked why he quit school, Toan explained, "I can work much harder at a job and earn money. The money is not for me, it is to give my mother and two sisters in Vietnam. They need it." Further discussion brings out the fact that Toan is the oldest child and the only son in his biological family. He maintains regular mail contact with his Vietnamese mother and two younger sisters. His father died when Toan was 10, leaving him the "man of the house."

Toan has lived with his foster family for 3½ years. Their relationship was good up to the point when Toan quit school. His foster parents have difficulty accepting

Toan's commitment to his biological family, who in their opinion had "rejected him and sent him away." His foster parents feel they deserve Toan's allegiance after all the "hard work and love" they have given him and feel resentful and jealous toward his Vietnamese family. They are confused and concerned that Toan is not going on to college, especially given projections by his school counselor and teachers for a bright future.

CRITICAL INCIDENT

Toan stopped going to school on a regular basis. His foster father, a lawyer, and his foster mother, a secretary, leave home before Toan wakes up in the morning. They were not aware that on many mornings he stayed in bed and did not go to school. One day they were called by the school principal who informed them that Toan was absent for five straight days during the past week. In an angry confrontation that evening Toan told them he was going to quit school to work full time so he could send $2000 to his "real family." When asked what his family would do with the money, he refused to answer.

SEQUENCE OF EVENTS

Five months before school ended Toan was offered a job as a waiter by his foster mother's friend in his new Chinese restaurant. Despite his hours at the new job, Toan was still enrolled in school even though he was increasingly disinterested in his studies. He has been clear about not wanting to attend school any longer and wishes to increase his time at work to make even more money. "The tips are very good, and sometimes I can even earn $20 at one table."

His foster parents have been worried and are constantly talking about school with Toan. This has resulted in Toan's feeling misunderstood and "talked at," causing him to frequently "escape from the family" by going to his bedroom and locking his door. Sometimes he does not speak to his foster parents for 3 or 4 days. There is growing tension and mistrust at home, with Toan's foster parents believing that his Vietnamese phone conversations and laughter with friends are about them, especially when he is withdrawn and sullen around the house. Consequently, they have been setting up new house rules such as restricting Toan's phone time, which Toan feels is unfair.

KEY CLINICAL QUESTIONS

1. What does Toan believe is his obligation to his biological family?
2. What does Toan believe is his obligation to his foster family?
3. Why does he believe that his biological family requires money at this point in time?
4. Is it possible for them to wait for him to send money at a later date?
5. How has Toan dealt with his father's death?

6. Why is there tension from the foster parents toward Toan's biological family?

7. Toan is living in a biracial home in a predominantly white community. Does he experience discrimination toward himself or his foster parents? If yes, how has this affected him?

8. Explore with Toan's foster parents their reaction to his concern and feelings of obligation to his biological mother and two sisters?

9. How can the family resolve the short-term problems, for example, telephone calls with Toan's friends, quitting school versus working, poor grades, Toan's withdrawal from the family, and the foster parents becoming more demanding and restrictive?

MULTI-LEVEL MODEL (MLM) OF PSYCHOTHERAPY INTERVENTIONS

Level I: Mental Health Education

Although Toan has been in the United States for almost 4 years, he has not exhibited adjustment problems. Thus, Toan lacks experience with mental health or supportive services aimed at helping him or the family. It would be important that as counseling was introduced to assist Toan and his family, the expectations for counseling be clearly defined.

Level II: Individual, group, and family therapy

It is recommended that Toan and his family enter family therapy to address the problems they are now facing. In therapy it may be helpful to examine Toan's background in Vietnam, Vietnamese cultural values regarding family, and his continued relationship with his biological family. Toan had been the man of the house from the age of 10 when his father died, until 13 when he migrated to the United States. He is accustomed to a position of being responsible for his family, of taking care of them and continues to feel that obligation. When his foster parents challenged his decision to work and advocated that he continue with his education, it contradicted Toan's feeling of family obligation and attending to the immediate needs of his family. Discussing and understanding these issues may be highly beneficial for the entire family.

There may also be different perspectives about what it means to be a male in an American home versus a Vietnamese home. Toan may have experienced far more autonomy in Vietnam, even at a younger age, especially as it related to decisions that affect the well-being of his family. His American foster parents continue to define their role to provide long-term personal and vocational guidance, believing that time in school is an investment in Toan's future. Further clarification and understanding about this issue through therapy is important.

In addition, Toan lives in a biracial home with a Chinese American mother and European American father. The issue of being Asian and growing up in a biracial home within a predominantly white school and community would be helpful to explore in family therapy. There may be instances of prejudice or discrimination that confront Toan and his family that would be helpful to discuss.

Toan also experiences a tension in allegiance between his foster family and his biological family. His foster parents are pressuring him about his future education, believing that he must succeed educationally to have a good future. At the same time Toan maintains a sense of responsibility toward his biological mother and two sisters in Vietnam, believing that he must support them. This presents an intense conflict for Toan, who is struggling with his loyalty to his biological family in Vietnam and the demands of his foster family, which would be extremely helpful to discuss in family therapy.

Another issue for family therapy is Toan's growth and growing independence. He is at a critical turning point in his life where his 3-year role as the man of the house is finally able to be fulfilled by financially providing for his biological family. This important role is being challenged by Toan's foster parents, who are pushing him to think about longer range goals and pursue higher education, thus postponing caring for his biological family. The support by his foster parents is in direct contradiction to Toan's sense of obligation and responsibility to his biological mother and sisters, causing serious problems in his American home. It would therefore be important that Toan and his foster parents address this in family therapy, examining both long- and short-term goals as well as respect for cultural differences related to filial piety and obligation, support from his foster parents of Toan's goals, and the presence and impact of discrimination toward both Toan and his foster parents.

Level III: Cultural Empowerment

Toan is caught between his biological family obligations and pressures from his foster parents. It would be helpful for Toan to understand the degree of choice he has in choosing to work or continue with school. For example, if Toan decides to quit school, it is important for him to know the legal age that he can decide to leave school and the legal age when he can work. It would also be helpful to outline his projected longer range income at his current job versus potential earnings at another position should he finish (a) high school, (b) community college, or (c) a 4-year college. This would be instrumental in defining income with various levels of schooling and would help Toan make an informed choice.

It may also be helpful to explore with Toan any hopes he has to bring his mother and two sisters to the United States. If this is a goal, it would be beneficial to investigate costs, policies, and mechanisms to facilitate this process. Family reunification policies, the likelihood of authorization for Toan's family, requirements, and financial assistance once in the resettlement country would all be important information for Toan.

IV: Indigenous Healing

Toan's foster parents are Baptist. In Vietnam his family identified themselves as Buddhist but only attended to practices and customs on special days, leaving

Toan without a strong identification to Buddhism. Despite this, Toan grew up with a belief that when one is very sick or having problems, you visit the Buddhist monk. This is what happened when his father became ill, and Toan remembers going to the monk and watching him say prayers over his father.

Given Toan's cultural perspectives about help-seeking behaviors, it may be important to keep this in mind as an adjunct to family therapy, particularly if the therapy becomes difficult or "stuck." It is important to recognize that visiting the Buddhist monk in the nearby city might become important to Toan, especially as he struggles to find direction and answers between two different cultures and families.

Chapter 17

Case Study of Natasha, a 23-year-old Russian

DESCRIPTION

Natasha is a 23-year-old Russian female who migrated to the United States 2 years ago and has been living with family sponsors in a quiet-upper-middle-class neighborhood for the past year. The family sponsors have a 21-year-old daughter and an 18-year-son who live at home and attend a nearby college. Both parents are college educated, with the father working as a pharmacist and the mother as a sales representative. The mother has been encouraging Natasha to go out with her daughter and her friends, concerned that she spends too much time alone.

Natasha grew up in a rural area of eastern Russia. Her parents (there were no siblings) were killed in an automobile accident when she was 15 and she was taken in by another family living in her village. Natasha is reluctant to talk about that time period in Russia, but she does acknowledge that it was painful and lonely during that phase of her life. She migrated to the United States to stay with a distant aunt who lived in Colorado. Natasha explains in broken English, "One year after I arrive to this country my aunt, she leave. She go maybe New York, I not sure." Soon after she moved in with the current sponsoring family, with whom she has resided for 1 year. Until recently she appeared to be adjusting well, with her sponsoring mother describing her as "pleasant and polite." Her sponsoring father agrees, adding, "she doesn't ask for anything from us and she does everything we ask without questioning."

Natasha is in her first year of community college. Despite only a moderate understanding of English, Natasha is an A student, spending most of her time studying. Her friends at school are predominantly other Russian immigrants, although she has met several American girls through her sponsoring family's daughter. Sometimes on weekends she socializes with other students, although her sponsoring mother keeps pressuring her to go out with her daughter. Natasha had a Russian boyfriend but recently stopped "seeing him." She explained their break-up saying, "it's not so much time I have . . . my making big work in school is a must."

Recently, Natasha started to withdraw. A few times her sponsoring mother found her in her room alone crying, making both of them feel embarrassed. Natasha haltingly told her sponsoring mother, "I miss my home, and my family, and my neighborhood. It is silly to say, but I even miss the cows." Lately Natasha has had problems getting to sleep at night. "I am sometimes very afraid. The bad dreams, they come again." A few times her crying has awoken other members of the family. When asked about her crying and her dreams, she refuses to discuss them. "I no talk about it . . . no, maybe they come back to me then, I no talk about it!" It has been suggested that she see a psychotherapist and she has reluctantly agreed.

CRITICAL INCIDENT

Recently, Natasha has been more lethargic and sad, spending more and more time alone in her bedroom. Her sponsoring sister, who genuinely likes her but is tired of spending so much time coaxing and taking care of her, resents her mother's continued pressure to "take Natasha along." Even so, Natasha agreed one Saturday night to go to an "American party." The sponsoring parents were elated, believing that getting out and going to a party will be good for her. At the party Natasha knew a few of the young men and spent time talking with them. She initially enjoyed herself but gradually appeared to become more uncomfortable. She excused herself and left the house to go outside. Later that night Natasha was heard crying in her room and refused to come out or talk, repeatedly saying, "No, no, no!"

SEQUENCE OF EVENTS

Problems escalated for Natasha 2 months before when the relationship with her boyfriend ended. It was at that point that she began to withdraw more. She had not been out socially with friends for the entire 2 months at the point when she went to the party. Even so, friends (female) would call her to go out, but increasingly Natasha would cut short the phone conversations and spend more time in her room studying. As her isolation grew, her sponsoring parents became more insistent that she should go out. As the tension about Natasha staying in or going out escalated, Natasha became less communicative with her sponsoring family and spent more time in her room except for meals. Thus, acquiescing to go out with her sponsoring sister to the party was a major change in routine.

KEY CRITICAL QUESTIONS

1. How has Natasha come to terms with her family's death in the automobile accident? Has she ever discussed it with anyone? Does she think about them often?

2. What are some of the significant cultural differences between living in rural Russia and a middle-class American neighborhood? How is this for Natasha?

3. Can she speak about the time after her parents were killed? What was that like for her living with another family, not having her parents alive anymore?

4. Did Natasha have any reaction to her aunt in the United States leaving her? How did Natasha emotionally handle this experience?

5. What is it like living with her sponsoring family? Does this evoke any associations to living with another family in Russia after her parents had the accident?

6. How is community college for Natasha?

7. The loss of the relationship with her boyfriend—how has that affected her? Does it remind her of other losses in her life?

8. Is she aware that she is withdrawing? If yes, what does it feel like to be emotionally distanced from her sponsoring family and friends?

9. What is bothering Natasha about her sponsoring parent's persistence to go out more?

10. What is all the crying about? Why now?

11. What happened at the party that made her so upset? Why was she so uncomfortable?

12. What does she think is the origin of the bad dreams and difficulty sleeping?

MULTI-LEVEL MODEL (MLM) OF PSYCHOTHERAPY INTERVENTION

Level I: Mental Health Education

Understanding the cultural context for mental health from any country is important in determining how to educate a prospective client. In Russia there was a history of using mental health to accomplish political objectives as well as deal with acute mental health problems. Thus, it would be crucial that Natasha receive an explanation about mental health practice in the United States, a clear definition about confidentiality and the separation between mental health practitioners/agencies and government, and how psychotherapy works.

Level II: Individual, Group, and Family Therapy

It is recommended that Natasha participate in group therapy with other refugees in her age group who have experienced the loss of loved ones. Participating in a group where there is a shared deep loss of family or friends that is coupled with postmigration adjustment issues will poignantly illustrate that she is not alone in her deep pain. For Natasha, speaking about her parent,s death and the major impact this has had on her life in group is essential for her healing.

Their death resulted in traumatic changes in her life that can be shared by other members of the group and have a profound effect on her current feelings and behaviors. For example, it may be that her reaction to the sudden loss of her family was restimulated by ending the relationship with her boyfriend, which could be the catalyst for her withdrawal and change of mood. This was further elucidated for Natasha when she sat with the young men at the party and became increasingly uncomfortable until she finally had to excuse herself and leave. To explore these issues in group therapy would be invaluable.

It may also be helpful to investigate broader premigration issues regarding loss in group therapy. Not only did Natasha lose her family and the life-style and routines of home, but by immigrating to the United States she lost her culture, community, friends, familiar foods, and the lake. This is reflected in her heartfelt comment about even missing the cows. Natasha knows that this is "silly" but feels this as a representation for a way of life that was more familiar and comfortable. Then, after coming to the United States to live with her aunt, her aunt departed without even a clear forwarding address. Thus an exploration of loss and subsequent change in her life may be very beneficial for Natasha and likely shared in different ways by other group members.

Natasha is a very hard worker. In community college she studies intensively and receives all A's despite only a moderate command of English. Clearly, good work in college represents a longer term goal, given the hard work and effort it takes Natasha to transcend language barriers. Thus, it may be helpful to examine long-term goals for Natasha and other group members and to examine the steps that need to be taken in order to accomplish those objectives.

Another issue to explore in group psychotherapy for Natasha and other members is postmigration. How is she adjusting to her new family and life in upper-middle-class suburbia? What is this experience like for her? How does she manage it, especially given the absence of cows, which is a poignant metaphor. It may be helpful to speak with Natasha in metaphors that are important to her experience and use these in the group process, which may also be beneficial to other group members.

Finally, an important issue to discuss in group therapy relates to Natasha's current social network and her rebuffing friends. Exploring this would be critical in assisting Natasha to understand the causes of her behavior, interpersonal patterns of communication and her family and friends responses to her behavior. From what is she retreating? Bringing this to light for Natasha within a group therapy structured for refugees is an important step toward her healing.

Level III: Cultural Empowerment

Cultural empowerment for Natasha would be consistent with mental health education, clarifying the privacy of mental health and the objectives of counseling that are more personal than political.

Level IV: Indigenous Healing

Assuming that traditional healing from the rural Russian countryside are unknown to the Western therapist, it would be important to determine if there are any specific practices that would be helpful. There may be folklores in the rural Russian community or individuals within the community that would be particularly helpful. It is also possible to ask the caseworker from the agency sponsoring Russian refugees, other Russian immigrants, or inquire directly with Natasha about how people with similar experiences generally resolved these problems and worked them out "back home." Thus, it is important to utilize the cultural resources for information, including the client.

Chapter 18

Case Study of Tam, a 17-year-old Lao

DESCRIPTION

Ever since Tam, a 17-year-old Lao female, can remember, she has always wanted to be a doctor. She has spoken freely to her family about her dreams and her mother encourages her to work hard to achieve her goal. The transition to the United States has been fairly easy for Tam and her family, who have lived in the United States for 4 years. Tam has adjusted to the United States and feels very fortunate, beginning to see a future for herself.

Tam arrived in the United States with her mother, father, uncle, and two younger brothers, ages 14 and 12. Her father was killed in an industrial accident 2 years after they arrived, so the family moved in with her uncle, who was her father's brother. They all lived in a housing project that had a large number of Southeast Asian refugees. Tam's 38-year-old uncle was unemployed and spent most of his time "hanging out" at home or in the project. Her mother was an unskilled laborer in a nearby factory and worked long and exhausting hours.

In school Tam was doing extremely well. She was not only an A student but possibly the top student in her class. She is very popular and had many American, Vietnamese, and Lao friends. Her teachers described her as a "model student." She studied very hard each night but did not participate in any extra-curriculum activities. Each afternoon she rushed home from school to take care of her two brothers and help them with their homework. Three times during the last school year she went to her brothers' school in place of her mother to speak with the principal about their periodic fights and alleged stealing. Each night Tam cooked dinner for her brothers, uncle, and mother. She served everyone dinner and then waited until her mother arrived home to serve her dinner as well.

CRITICAL INCIDENT

One day after school 3 weeks before Tam was at home helping her brothers with their homework as usual. Tam's uncle came in drunk that afternoon. He grabbed Tam, forcing her to his bedroom and telling the two boys that he needed to talk to her about finances. He ordered them outside telling them to come back later to do their homework. The two boys were afraid and did what they were told. In the bedroom the uncle angrily told Tam that if it was not for him the family would not be here and that she would never achieve her dreams. He continued, yelling, "if you want to reach those high dreams you must listen to me! Do as I say! Do not question your uncle!"

At that point the uncle grabbed Tam and started to rip off her clothes. She screamed, which startled him, and managed to break away and run outside. Tam ran and hid in a nearby park, until later that evening. When she returned home her uncle had calmed down and threatened her. "If you tell anyone what happened they won't believe your story. And if you do, I will put all your family in the streets and no one will talk to you anymore and you won't have a home. Then you won't ever become a doctor. Maybe you will even be sent back to Laos."

SEQUENCE OF EVENTS

For the past 3 weeks Tam had been late to school. Not only was she late but she fell asleep during class. Her math teacher asked her if everything was alright. Tam explained to her that "one of my brothers is sick and I have to take care of him." The teacher was aware of Tam's responsibility caring for her two brothers and expressed her sympathy and hopes that her brother would soon be better.

For the past 2 weeks Tam has been coming to school late and looks uncharacteristically messy and disheveled. She does not complete her homework and avoids friends at school. One day when her teacher noticed a faint smell of alcohol on her breath, she became alarmed and confronted Tam. Tam denied any problem and ran out of the room crying.

KEY CLINICAL QUESTIONS

1. Explore with Tam what she is experiencing now related to her uncle. How would she describe the affect this has on her at home and in school?

2. What is the present communication and interaction with her uncle? How are they relating?

3. Is her mother aware of this incident or any problems at home?

4. What are the living options for Tam's family at this time?

5. What does Tam need to do to get her schoolwork back on track?

6. Who is in Tam's social network that can provide her with support?

7. Who is in Tam's mother's social network that can provide her with support if necessary?

8. How are Tam's brothers doing during the last few weeks given the problems that have manifested for Tam?

9. What agency, if any, can provide support to the family should the decision be to move out of their uncle's home?

10. What impact does the death of Tam's father have on the family?

11. Is it possible to provide psychotherapy to Tam's uncle? Is he willing?

MULTI-LEVEL MODEL (MLM) OF PSYCHOTHERAPY INTERVENTION

Level I: Mental Health Education

Tam and her family are fairly well acculturated to the United States and Tam has clear goals and aspirations. Her brother's problems in school have been adequately managed by Tam since her mother is working hard to financially support the family. Thus there has not been a need to seek professional counseling. It would therefore be essential to carefully explain the purpose of psychotherapy and to enucleate that no one is "crazy." This would ensure that no stigmas are attached and particularly that Tam does not feel that this is a major impediment to her career objectives.

Level II: Individual, Group, and Family Therapy

It is recommended that the family participate in family therapy with a culturally sensitive family therapist. This may initially involve Tam, her two brothers, and their mother in order to discuss their life in the United States and the impact of their father/husband's death on them as a family unit. This is important since it is due to his death that they are now in the predicament of living with the uncle and Tam's mother working long hours to independently support the family. In addition, the absence of the father at a critical developmental stage for the two sons may contribute to the problems they are having in school.

It would also be important in family therapy to discuss the current crisis. For Tam, at 17, to keep this a secret, in addition to the other responsibilities that she has, is not healthy. It would be important to realign family responsibilities and determine whether or not Tam's mother will assume more of a parental role in this instance. The two brothers are certainly aware that something happened that day, causing a change in their sister for the past 3 weeks, but most likely they both remain confused about the event. Thus, to have the family discuss and share this event may be an important developmental step in their growth.

It may also be important for the family therapist to gain a contextual understanding of the sexual attack directed toward Tam. Is this the first time the uncle attempted sexual abuse? What are the cultural consequences for this behavior within the Lao community? Is there shame involved in bringing this issue forward? Questions such as these are crucial before working with the family to explore feelings and reactions to this incident and arrive at decisions as to whether or not to confront the uncle, whether to remain living in his home, whether to involve the larger community, and so forth.

Decisions such as these about how to handle this very painful and disturbing event would be an important aspect of culturally responsive family therapy. What are the options? What can be done? What steps must be taken? During this phase, the psychotherapist plays a role in exploring with the family what happens to Tam given any choices they make. If the family decides to take the next steps, it is essential that the pros and cons be weighed carefully and clearly understood. For example, if the family decides to approach the uncle and discuss this with him, would they want to invite him into the therapy sessions with them, do it independently, talk with him involving other members of the community, or include a Buddhist monk or spiritualist in the discussions?

Another important issue in family therapy is related to the problems of Tam's two brothers. Is there a past history of fighting? Is there a past history of stealing? How do they describe these behaviors and their motivation for doing this? What are the associated issues to this behavior? For example, is it the absence of their mother who works long hours, the influence of their uncle, or a reaction to the absence of their father? Do they anticipate continuing future fights and stealing? Why or why not? Is there any way that the family or community could be helpful in changing this for them? What is the meaning of stealing from someone else within the Lao community?

Finally, Tam must be supported with her career goals. It is clear from her academic performance and teacher's ratings that she has great potential. It would be helpful to explore pressures and life demands on Tam. How does she manage everything, including school? What kind of support would be beneficial to her? This exploration with Tam is important in balancing her mental health with a highly demanding life.

Level III: Cultural Empowerment

If the family decides to move out of the apartment with Tam's uncle, they must know their options. An understanding of what financial support would be available for living expenses such as rent, electricity, heat, water, and telephone would be beneficial. They may not be aware that there are options for leaving, given their current financial constraints.

Level IV: Indigenous Healing

It was recommended that family therapy explore options for including Tam's uncle. One alternative is to request that a Buddhist monk assist in resolving the extended family network difficulties who could provide guidance and direction. Another method is to emply a spiritualist who may treat the uncle's evil spirit. If the family agrees, the combination of Western-based family therapy and traditional Lao healing rituals would be a powerful cross-cultural intervention.

Chapter 19

Case Study of Khaled, a 38-year-old Palestinian

DESCRIPTION

Khaled is a 38-year-old Palestinian who brought his wife and two sons, ages 13 and 11, to live in the United States near his brother's home in a major urban city. The migration to the United States was a result of a mishap during a Palestinian attack on an Israeli bus. Khaled was accidentally shot during the attack and paralyzed from the waist down. At that time he was a practicing medical doctor working in the Palestinian community. After being shot he made the decision to migrate to the United States and live closer to his brother. He has been living in the United States for the past 2 years.

Since the accident Khaled has been periodically depressed, lacking the motivation to take the required courses and study for his U.S. medical examination for licensure. Occasionally, he considers completing the additional requirements for licensure but loses interest within a few days. Despite his not being able to legally practice, a number of people in the community visit his home for treatment. When he is helping patients in his home, he always feels better. His wife, a practicing nurse, has a job in a nearby hospital. She earns enough money to support the family and has a large network of Palestinian friends who frequently visit her home on weekends and evenings, talking and laughing late into the evening. In contrast, Khaled's social network is small, and he depends on his brother for conversation and going out at night.

Khaled's eldest son is an average student in school and, like his mother, has many friends. The beginning of the school year was his first year in junior high school, a very large urban school, causing him for the first time to feel overwhelmed, afraid, and isolated. Some of the children called him names that he did not understand and led to fights. Khaled would see his son come home with facial bruises and lecture him, stating, "Never back down. If someone comes after you never turn your back or you might get hurt like your father...this world is a dangerous place. Stand up for yourself and keep your eyes looking around you so there aren't any surprises." Khaled was also concerned that his oldest son's grades were dropping and scolded him after he brought home his first report card.

CRITICAL INCIDENT

Khaled was highly agitated about his oldest son's report card that included three C's, one B, and two D's. He confronted his son who became openly agitated for the first time in his father's presence and spoke back to his father. "Father, I didn't want to come to this country in the first place. If not for your stupid accident we wouldn't be here. Why did you have to be traveling to so many communities, trying to help the sick people. And now, we are stuck here and I hate my school" Khaled became very angry at his son's outburst and began to forcefully lecture him. Instead of listening obediently, his son walked out of the living room to his bedroom, saying, "How can you lecture me? You can't even practice medicine. You act like an old man in that wheelchair!"

SEQUENCE OF EVENTS

Khaled had been more depressed recently. His wife was going out more with her friends, he was not able to provide an income for his family, his eldest son was fighting and failing exams in school, and his brother was less available than usual as he struggled to keep his business solvent. To add to these problems, his patients were coming less frequently, some claiming that there were free services with a new medical insurance. He was feeling less in control of his life and felt himself becoming more irritable and dependent on his wife and sons. During his brother's recent Sunday visit, Khaled was challenged about what he was doing. His brother confronted him. "You have potential Khaled. But you are not moving with your life. You sit and wait for an occasional patient and scold your sons. You are a doctor. Why not take the courses and the exam so you can practice. Life is not over!" All this was adding up for Khaled and, when his oldest son brought home his report card, unable to restrain himself, he angrily lectured him.

KEY CLINICAL QUESTIONS

1. What does Khaled do all day when he is not seeing patients?
2. How does Khaled feel about his wife's active social life with friends visiting, talking, and laughing until late in the evening?

3. Examine far more in depth Khaled's resistance to pursuing the medical license in the United States.

4. How does the fact that he is not the financial provider for the family affect Khaled?

5. Would Khaled like to have a larger social network?

6. How would Khaled describe his relationship with his oldest son? Is it what he wants or would he change it?

7. What is the oldest son angry about?

8. What are Khaled's projections about the future? He is losing patients and not licensed to practice medicine in the United States. What does he imagine his life will be like in 1 year, 2 years, 5 years? Explore options as he envisions them at this point in time.

9. What is it like for Khaled to be paralyzed?

10. What is it like for Khaled to leave home in a wheelchair?

MULTI-LEVEL MODEL (MLM) OF PSYCHOTHERAPY INTERVENTION

Level I: Mental Health Education

Being in the medical field and from a country where mental health only attended to seriously disturbed individuals, Khaled may have the perception that mental health is only for those with more acute emotional problems, for crazy people. He may not be aware that many people receive counseling to work on being depressed, angry, or having family difficulties that are not able to be resolved through other means, and that one does not need to be crazy to get professional help. This clarification would provide an important context for Khaled.

Once meeting with a culturally sensitive professional, it would be important to clearly delineate some of the parameters in therapy. Confidentiality would be an important issue, so Khaled was secure in knowing that this information would not go back to the community. It is important to acknowledge that Khaled has a medical degree and speak with him as a professional as the differences between medical treatment and mental health interventions are defined.

Level II: Individual, Group, and Family Therapy

The depression and anger Khaled is facing has affected the entire family. Therefore, it is recommended that family therapy be the intervention of choice. Using a systems approach, it would be helpful to realign family relationships and goals, and trace the impact of Khaled's accidental paralysis on the entire family. Feelings about their migration and communication patterns within the family that combine traditional and postmigration cultures would be helpful to explore in therapy.

One focus of family therapy would be to explore Khaled's relationship with his wife and two sons in a culturally sensitive manner. His physical handicap, inability to practice medicine, and subsequent move to another country certainly contribute to his depression and anger. Khaled's relationship with his wife is unclear especially within a culturally appropriate framework, given her continued work and active social life. How does she feel about the accident, about Khaled's depression and inactive professional life? In turn, how does Khaled feel about her supporting him and the family and her wide group of friends, who oftentimes meet at his home? The part the youngest son plays in the family is unknown since he is conspicuously absent from discussion about the family.

Another important area to explore in family therapy within the framework of Palestinian families is what is going on with Khaled's oldest son (e.g., poor grades in school, fighting at school, and anger toward his father) and how this contributes to the dynamic between son and father. There may be cross-cultural issues relevant here, with Khaled believing that the role of the father is to lecture and scold when appropriate. Simultaneously, his son is immersed in American culture through his school, which may contribute to his talking back to his father for the first time. Thus, an exploration of role expectations and communication patterns would be very important.

Level III: Cultural Empowerment

It may be important for Khaled to have information regarding medical licensure in the United States. How many classes is he required to take, what about residency requirements, how often is the examination given, and which materials would be best to study for the exam? Having an accurate picture of what is required for him to become licensed will assist Khaled in making an informed decision whether or not to pursue licensure and what steps he must take to move ahead in this process.

In addition, it would be helpful for Khaled to know about community resources for the handicapped. What benefits are available to him? Is transportation available, does he have access to support services, and is there any possible tuition assistance? Tracking this through the local Office of Handicapped Services would be beneficial resource information.

Level IV: Indigenous Healing

It may be helpful for Khaled to speak with a religious leader in the Palestinian community. This individual could provide spiritual guidance about Khaled's accident and physical disability and help him put this event and tragedy in context. In addition, he could help Khaled with issues about family, migration, and adjustment and may be an important adjunctive to family therapy.

Chapter 20

Case Study of Juanita, a 15-year-old Cuban

DESCRIPTION

Juanita is a 15-year-old Cuban female who arrived in the United States with her family 2 years ago. Before coming to the United States Juanita had been sexually abused several times by a close family friend that everyone called "Uncle." Uncle threatened Juanita not to tell anyone about their relationship, so she kept it secret. At the age of 12, when this abuse was going on, she ran away from home in Cuba. Her father searched for her and finally, late at night, found her at a friend's house. He was angry and punished her. Juanita gained a reputation of being "no good, unreliable, with her head somewhat off balance." Since that incident Juanita has had a distant relationship with her father, mother, and three sisters, keeping more to herself. Her withdrawal has only magnified the perception that she is "somewhat off balance."

In the United States Juanita found refuge when she joined a gang consisting of only girls. There she felt safe and wanted, knowing that her "sisters" would care for her and look after her. She was angry and hated men and did not want anything to do with them. In the gang Juanita spoke for the first time about the sexual abuse with her "sisters." To her surprise many of the other girls shared similar experiences. She felt like she was home with the gang. The gang would sometimes engage in robbing men who tried to pick them up, or steal clothes, jewelry, and makeup from stores, but otherwise they went to school, had average to low average grades, and were not in any trouble.

CRITICAL INCIDENT

Late one evening Juanita was out with two other gang members. They were just "hanging out" talking and somewhat bored. A car drove by and stopped in front of them. The man was interested in Juanita and wanted to know if she and any of the other girls were interested in going for a ride. Juanita asked him what he would give them. He flashed several $50 bills. The girls glanced at each other and silently agreed to take this "guy for a joy ride" as they had done a number of times before with other guys. All the girls got into the car and promised the man anything he wanted. He drove to a secluded area and parked when one of the girls pulled a knife and threatened him. Instead of handing over his money, as had always happened in the past, this man began fighting with them. The girl stabbed him and cut his stomach. "There's a lot of blood, let's get out of here," shouted one of the girls. They took his money and ran away, taking a long time to get back to the city.

All of the girls, including Juanita, had blood on their clothes. When Juanita arrived home, her father was waiting up and saw the blood. He became furious and when she would not speak with him, he decided to punish her by not allowing her out for several weeks. She had a strong reaction, at first being angry, crying, and arguing with her father. As time passed, Juanita also became sullen and depressed. Her father became increasingly concerned about her and was recommended by friends to see a psychotherapist in the local community mental health center who had a reputation of working successfully in the Cuban community.

SEQUENCE OF EVENTS

Juanita was ashamed of her relationship with Uncle in Cuba. She never told anyone in her family about what happened but felt like the memories were a disease inside of her that was growing. She could not forget what happened and repeatedly had bad dreams and flashbacks to times with Uncle. Sometimes with her friends she drank wine to forget, but she realized that this was temporary since by the next day the memories returned. Her family and father, in particular, had become stricter since being in the United States, and sometimes when he was angry would call her "loco."

Robbing men who approached her and her friends had been fun. There had been more money for eating out and buying nice things, but also she enjoyed seeing the men become afraid. She especially liked it when they did this to Cuban men who were visiting from other cities rather than the Americans. Recently they had been robbing men more often, almost twice a month. The last incident with the knife had been scary, but Juanita also was excited and enjoyed the fact that he had been hurt.

KEY CLINICAL QUESTIONS

1. Explore with Juanita her experience and deep-rooted feelings about being sexually abused.

2. What does Juanita imagine would happen if she told her parents about the sexual abuse?

3. How does Juanita feel being labeled "loco" in her family?

4. Explore what it is like to belong to the gang.

5. Ideally would Juanita want to feel a greater sense of belonging with her biological family?

6. What is Juanita angry about in addition to the sexual abuse? What would she identify as the issues regarding her anger?

7. How does Juanita view the robberies? The victims?

8. How does Juanita view the recent incident that injured the man?

9. What about stealing? Morally, does this seem acceptable to Juanita?

10. Any future dreams or goals? If yes, discuss.

11. Discuss how Juanita feels about men in general, including her father.

MULTI-LEVEL MODEL (MLM) OF PSYCHOTHERAPY INTERVENTION

Level I: Mental Health Education

Juanita is identified within her family as having emotional problems. Going to a psychotherapist may carry a negative stigma. Hence, it is essential that Juanita and her family understand the potential benefit of therapy and that people who participate in counseling are not crazy.

It would also be important that Juanita knows that what happens in therapy is confidential. This will assist her in being able to share more freely and realizing that the psychotherapist will not disclose information to her family. It is also recommended that, given the background of sexual abuse, Juanita see a female psychotherapist.

Level II: Individual, Group, and Family Therapy

It is recommended that Juanita initially enter individual therapy, followed by family therapy. Each of these interventions must be done from a culturally sensitive framework that appreciates the unique and rich characteristics of the Cuban culture. The reason for beginning with individual therapy is to help Juanita deal with the significant problems that are evident in her adjustment. It is anticipated that if individual therapy is successful that long kept secrets, such as the sexual abuse, will emerge. This is important since she is afraid to speak with her family about what happened, which has in part led them to label her as "having problems." Having her first tell her story, work through the pain and shame about the abuse, and address her "pent-up" emotions about this incident would be essential. Furthermore, this will assist Juanita in developing personal strength necessary to deal with this issue and release some of her anger and pain, important steps in the healing process.

Therapeutically, dream work may be helpful and culturally appropriate to implement as an intervention. Examining deeper unconscious issues and symbolizations of the abuse may facilitate the recollection of important details and feelings. In addition, cognitive–behavioral interventions that restructure her thoughts and beliefs regarding the abuse would be helpful, especially if she feels guilt or responsible. Tied into either of these intervention strategies would be the use of narrative therapy and storytelling, where she would have the opportunity to present and work with the story and the associated issues.

Following individual psychotherapy, it is suggested that there be family therapy. The family has joined in labeling Juanita "loco," stigmatizing her as different and problematic, beginning when she ran away from home in Cuba. There is a lack of knowledge about what happened that night and why Juanita ran away. In family therapy there could be an exploration of what running away meant to Juanita and to her family, investigating why she has turned toward her peers and feelings of not belonging in her family. It is important to note that the details of the abuse and benefit of sharing this information with her family must be weighed and decided upon within an appropriate cultural context by Juanita and her psychotherapist. Regardless, work with the family would be to strategic in reexamining communication patterns and redefining relationships in the family system.

Level III: Cultural Empowerment

The consequences of Juanita's illegal activities are important knowledge for Juanita and possibly her entire family. The stabbing of the man, hustling on the streets and robbing men, and stealing are all bordering on far more serious problems and legal complications. It would be helpful for Juanita and her family to know progressive consequences for a continuation or escalation of this behavior.

Level IV: Indigenous Healing

There may be an elderly woman in the Cuban community who may be recognized as being wise and able to assist young women in healing. If this is the case, it could be helpful for Juanita to simultaneously continue with psychotherapy and see this woman for guidance and healing, especially given the trauma of premigration abuse. She may provide a culturally sensitive context for healing that a Western therapist cannot offer.

Chapter 21

Case Study of Ru, a 16-year-old Vietnamese

DESCRIPTION

A 16-year-old Vietnamese unaccompanied minor, Ru was denied permission to move from a foster home to an apartment with some Vietnamese friends that he had just met. His sponsoring agency caseworker told him that he was too young to be living on his own and that if he should leave, he would lose his benefits and support from the sponsoring program. Although he has been in the United States for 15 months, his present placement (his third) has only been for the past 7 months. The previous two placements reported that Ru was unmanageable and "easily prone to anger and violent rages." After a careful screening, the agency chose his present placement, which is considered a "highly capable" home.

Ru had tattoos on his arms, liked to present himself as "tough," smoked cigarettes, and talked about his "good life" in Vietnam with girlfriends and money. There was little history about his family and he has no contact with anyone in Vietnam. School is of little interest to Ru, although his grades remain almost average. He likes rap music and knows contemporary bands and the schedule for the local bands' performances. His English is fair, having picked up some in Vietnam.

Ru's friendships with other Vietnamese males are sporadic and short-lived. Social relations only last a short time, usually 2 to 3 weeks until Ru "moves on" and finds other friends. It is infrequent that he brings new friends home more than two or three times. Peers report that Ru has a bad temper and has a low tolerance for frustration. He has a reputation for becoming uncontrollably angry, yelling, and sometimes even swearing at his caseworker. In the past two foster homes he was forced to leave for losing his temper, although so far that has not happened in his new foster home. He has had detention several times in school for not listening to teachers and "talking back" and has been warned that if his behavior continues in school he will face suspension.

CRITICAL INCIDENT

Approaching his 17th birthday, Ru has grown increasingly adamant about living in an apartment with newly acquired friends. Very annoyed and upset one day, Ru demanded his caseworker permit him to move to the apartment and maintain his benefits, insisting that the caseworker could "make this happen." His caseworker explained that the apartment could not be considered a foster care placement, his living situation with his foster parents would be adequate if he controlled his temper, and leaving his third foster home meant that Ru would need to find employment to be self-supportive. Ru became insistent about leaving and demanded continued financial support from the agency. As his anger grew, he began to move toward the caseworker in a threatening manner. When Ru would not calm down, the caseworker left without reaching an agreement. As he was leaving Ru yelled at him, insisting that, "I will move and receive benefits anyway, even without you, you'll see!"

SEQUENCE OF EVENTS

Ru has been in three foster homes in 15 months. His current foster home is the longest he has stayed in one placement. It appears that he has had a life of independence, beginning with gang activities in Vietnam that are represented by his tattoos. His lack of contact with anyone in Vietnam also makes him truly an unaccompanied minor who is self-reliant. His foster parents seem to be able to accommodate his need for independence and have given him a great deal of latitude. The result of Ru's autonomy is that he has not had any outbursts directed at his foster parents, which is very different from the anger he expressed toward his foster parents in the last two placements.

The sponsoring agency understands these issues, but is unsure how to address Ru's volatility and his inability to sustain relationships with peers. This is also alarming to his foster parents who have spoken several times with the caseworker and agency supervisor. There is growing concern by agency personnel and the foster parents, especially since Ru increasingly stays alone in his room on weekends listening to rap music with his door closed. Otherwise Ru's foster parents feel that he has adjusted at home and seems to "get along" even though there are some problems at school. Their one complaint is that Ru will not talk about what is going on in his life or about the past.

KEY CLINICAL QUESTIONS

1. How does Ru perceive what happened in the first two foster homes?
2. Does Ru have an idea about why he is so angry?
3. What do the tattoos signify to Ru?
4. What about Ru's family history in Vietnam? What happened to his family, especially given the cultural importance of family in Vietnam?
5. What about friendships? From Ru's perspective what is interfering with having longer term friendships?
6. How might he be able to control his self-acknowledged "bad temper?"
7. How would life be different in an apartment? Given the free reign that his foster parents give him, how would his life change if he lived in an apartment?
8. How does he see the role of the caseworker and the agency? Are they there to help him, monitor him, or regulate him?
9. Any goals or aspirations?

MULTI-LEVEL MODEL (MLM) OF PSYCHOTHERAPY INTERVENTION

Level I: Mental Health Education

Given Ru's anger, it is important for the psychotherapist to explain to Ru the reasons why he was referred for therapy. The psychotherapist must clearly communicate to Ru the role and expectations of therapy and discuss the process of working together in this format. Defining what psychotherapy is may also help eliminate the stigma attached to mental health. This will provide a foundation to work from, establishing clear expectations and clarifying the relationship and process.

Level II: Individual, Group, and Family Therapy

There is very little information about Ru's life in Vietnam. Some clues and guesses relate to gang activity and his sense of bravado and the "good life" while living there. Even though Ru has already lived in the United States for 15 months, there is almost no information about his family and relations in Vietnam, which is especially striking since he comes from a society that emphasizes family and social networks. Since the details about Ru's background remain ambiguous, it would be important to initially work with him in individual counseling to explore the roots of his anger and explosiveness. This would be especially important given Ru's avoidance of his past in Vietnam, except to project an image of "toughness."

Following individual psychotherapy, it may be helpful for Ru to participate in a psychotherapeutic group with peers that focuses on interpersonal relationships and anger management. This could either be done in the school setting or community mental health facility and would be important in reestablishing the foundation for a healthy social network, a core element in the Vietnamese culture. It would be important for Ru through group work to see that others share similar problems (universality) and to be in an environment where he can learn about social skills and controlling his impulsive anger. The combination of examining his unresolved issues related to his family and involvement in cognitive–behavioral group therapy to focus on controlling his anger and improving interpersonal skills, would be important to his growth and development at this point and better link him with his cultural roots.

Level III: Cultural Empowerment

The realities of being underage for emancipation and living in an apartment in the United States may be unknown to Ru. To help him better understand the agency decision and concerns, it would be important for Ru to have clear information about the legal and financial requirements for independent living. For example, it may be that he is not aware of landlord–tenant agreements, security and last-month rent deposits, associated expenses such as electricity, heat, telephone, and water, the cost of necessary living items such as a bed or mattress, cooking and eating utensils, lamps, and so forth. This information would be crucial for Ru to know and help him come to terms with the potential for living independently without the support from social services.

In addition, it may be helpful in therapy to clearly inform Ru about school policies and long-range consequences for the warnings he has had from school. Since he has already received detention and been warned about suspension, it would be important to explain the ramifications of being suspended. Being new to the United States school system he may have misperceptions about suspension and not know what this means in terms of his future or possibility for future expulsion. Thus it would be helpful to clarify his perceptions about the implications for continued detentions and/or suspensions.

Level IV: Indigenous Healing

The refusal to speak about his family or life in Vietnam makes Ru a good candidate for working concurrently with an elder or monk from Vietnam and participating in psychotherapy. The elder or monk may be important in addressing Ru's pain, hurt, and anger carried over from Vietnam and going beneath his toughness. Their intervention could supplement the Western psychotherapy in a culturally appropriate manner and work on these deep-rooted problems from a culturally sanctioned framework that would be more familiar to Ru.

Chapter 22

Case Study of Mustafa, a 41-year-old Somali

DESCRIPTION

Mustafa is 41-year-old refugee from Somalia who came to the United States with his wife and his younger brother 3 years ago. Life in Somalia was difficult for Mustafa. There was "civil war with people fighting everywhere, dead bodies with parts missing, and sometimes not enough food to eat so that it made the stomach hurt." His wife had complained so much about the conditions there that they finally decided to try and leave Somalia without their families. It took 2 years before he and his wife and one of his three younger brothers finally departed. Many times Mustafa remembers those years as a dream, thinking that they would never really go and leave behind his family. Yet they had, and he left thinking he may never again see his parents, two younger brothers, and his wife's family who were all left behind in Somalia. Luckily none of them were involved in the civil war so there was less danger of them dying, except by random killing. This helped Mustafa feel a little better, although he still had concerns.

Since they had arrived 3 years ago, other relatives had migrated to the United States. He had been overjoyed when his mother came to live with him, but to his great dismay, she died only 5 months after arriving at his home. This was not only a great disappointment but also a financial burden since she needed special medical attention before her death and then after she died a proper ceremony. In addition his wife's mother, two female cousins, and three nieces arrived to live with them 7 months ago. Mustafa felt a great responsibility to feed, clothe, and house them and worried that his money would not be able to support everyone.

It had been difficult for Mustafa to adjust to the United States. As much as he studied English, it was hard to learn. He also found American customs very strange and preferred to stay within the Somali community. His days were difficult and mentally taxing, with a much faster pace than he was accustomed to while trying to understand what people were saying and how everything worked. Several times people made comments to him that he did not understand. When people seemed angry or annoyed with Mustafa he became uneasy and worried.

Especially on days when people said mean things to him, Mustafa found himself thinking more about Somalia. He remembered many dreams about his home country—the furniture in his house, the smell when you walked outside, bread cooking. It was very different from America. The more Mustafa thought about these things, the more he desired to go back home even though he knew life there was difficult and sometimes even dangerous.

There had been bad luck with money. Mustafa's wife insisted that he work hard to make money so everyone could eat and the bills could be paid. She also wanted to save and bring her father, brothers, and sisters to America. Although he did not really want to, he tried to start a business for importing goods. It was only trouble. "I realized after some time that the costs for renting a store were very high. There were also many rules and regulations that were confusing. I lost money doing this." Eventually he gave up on this idea and thought about other businesses. To maintain an income while he was deciding what to do, Mustafa took a position as a building security guard 6 months ago.

CRITICAL INCIDENT

When Mustafa's mother-in-law, two cousins, and their three children came from Somalia 7 months before, things began to change. At first it was a big celebration to see them all and show them around to stores, parks, and introduce them to new friends. Everyone was enjoying their time together, but then it began to change. Mustafa wondered why they did not try to learn English or find work to help pay for food. Mustafa felt that his mother-in-law should be able to relax and remain at home but struggled to support the two cousins and children. Typically, in Somalia other members of the family contributed to food and bills, but here it was entirely up to him. When he raised this concern with his wife, she became angry and insisted that he get a better paying job.

One evening 2 weeks later his wife announced that she was going to study English at night and then find a job so "we earn enough money to live in this home." This made Mustafa angry, feeling as if she was telling him that he was not able to take care of her, her mother, cousins, and nieces. His pride was hurt and he began to worry about how he would be able to take care of everyone. In addition, he did not want her going out alone at night to English classes. "Afterall, who would cook dinner on those nights and how would she get back and forth to the class?" The thought of his wife going alone and studying English deeply affected Mustafa, who became angry and highly irritable.

SEQUENCE OF EVENTS

Life in the United States has not been easy for Mustafa. He continually struggled with culture and language. Work had been a series of continued mishaps, culminating in a failed business attempt. Money had also been a constant worry, especially supporting a growing number of family members and never having quite enough money to send any back home.

Furthermore, Mustafa greatly missed his biological family. When his mother came he was overjoyed, expecting that the others would follow. Yet, when he had high expenses for her medical bills and then her death, he realized that it would be a long time before he earned enough money to support anyone else moving to the United States or send money back to family in Somalia. During his 3 years in the United States. Mustafa found himself faced with a cycle of difficulties that he just could not seem to break.

KEY CLINICAL QUESTIONS

1.   What did Mustafa expect coming to the United States? How did he imagine his life would be after he settled down?

2.   What was life like for Mustafa while living in Somalia? How is it different than his life in the United States?

3.   What about the memories of the war? How does this affect Mustafa today?

4.   How does it affect Mustafa that the majority of his family remains in Somalia?

5.   At this point in time, what would be the ideal in terms of his relationship with his family still in Somalia?

6.   Has he properly grieved for his mother's death? Is there anything else he needs to do to be at peace with her dying?

7.   Financially, what are Mustafa's expenses? Can money be saved to help his family migrate to the United States?

8.   Does Mustafa want to visit his family in Somalia? What would it take to accomplish this?

9.   What is Mustafa's difficulty with his wife studying English? How does this relate to differences between traditional gender roles in his own culture and realities of life in the United States?

10.   What is Mustafa's overall relationship with his wife? Is this consistent with traditional gender roles back home?

MULTI-LEVEL MODEL
OF PSYCHOTHERAPY (MLM) INTERVENTION

Level I: Mental Health Education

It is recommended that Mustafa and his wife attend couples therapy. The purpose, intent, and process of couples therapy would be important to carefully explain to both of them, especially since it is not common to share personal information with strangers in their culture.

Level II: Individual, Group, and Family Therapy

Even though extended family is an important aspect of Somali life and several members of the extended family are living in their apartment, it is recommended that at this time Mustafa and his wife limit therapy to them as a couple. This is based on sensitivity to traditional roles within Somali families. The fact that Mustafa is one of two males in the home and the oldest male (he feels responsible for his younger brother) he supports his wife, his brother, two female cousins, his mother-in-law, and three nieces. To include the extended family in therapy where Mustafa is exposing his vulnerability and fallibility may cause Mustafa to lose respect and the dignity that is important in his prescribed cultural role as the oldest male in the household. Therefore, in this situation, it is suggested that counseling includes only Mustafa and his wife.

With a clear sensitivity to culture and the importance of family and extended family, it would be beneficial to reexamine the roles and relationship of Mustafa and his wife, particularly in the context of adapting to a new culture. This would relate to her desire to learn English and work and Mustafa's shame about not being able to support the growing extended family. It may also be important to examine communication patterns, particularly in light of the extended family now living with them and the hopes that more family will join them later. How they represent and share their concerns, hopes, goals, and feelings, with each other in many respects forms a basis for the household. This would be helpful to clarify and discuss.

It would also be beneficial to consider long-term goals. What are their hopes for the future? Bring more family members from Somalia, move to a bigger apartment or house or buy a car? Once clearly and mutually establishing their goals, it may be very helpful to determine a plan to move toward accomplishing those goals. How do each of them work to achieve the goals and how do they support each other? Additionally, how must life change from how it was in Somalia to move in their desired directions?

Finally, it would be beneficial to consider Mustafa's desire to return home. He reports that he is thinking about his homeland quite often and would like to return at some point. A realistic exploration would be very important, for example, does he want to go for a visit or move the family back permanently, what are the political realities and dangers for himself and his wife if he should go back, what are the costs and how would he raise the money? This information should be addressed in couples therapy, discussing his wife's feelings as well.

Level III: Cultural Empowerment

There are several areas of cultural understanding that would be important for Mustafa. First, information about health insurance would be helpful. He may not know or be aware of the pros and cons about taking a job with benefits versus not having benefits. This might be helpful in breaking the cycle of financial difficulties, especially since his extended family is currently dependent on him. Second, Mustafa has been anxious when people speak to him in angry or annoyed tones that he does not understand. To help him gain a sense of cultural mastery, it would be advantageous to discuss the situation and context for when this happened, and then offer a cultural interpretation about what is being said and why they might be making those comments. This would provide a basis for understanding what is going on in the world around him, rather then leave it to conjecture. A third area that may be profitable to explain to Mustafa regards setting up a business in the United States. The many rules and regulations that he encountered in his attempt to establish an import business made him frustrated and confused about the laws. This would provide basic information so that he could more easily decide whether or not this would be a financially worthwhile venture. The fourth area relates to the struggle with his wife's going out in the evening and studying English and eventually working. This is a threat to his pride and ability to fulfill his role as the family provider. It would be helpful to offer information about U.S. families and different gender roles within different types of families. This is not meant to persuade Mustafa or convince him to adopt cultural norms that are alien to his way of living; it is simply to present information about how other families in the new country to which he has moved financially succeed. Clearly, this has implications for adaptation to the United States and would require careful processing and discussion to determine how Mustafa and his wife would incorporate this information.

Level IV: Indigenous Healing

According to traditional healers from Somalia, Mustafa and his wife may be experiencing angry spirits that are causing his bad luck with money, sickness, problems in their relationship, and even their dispositions. This may require intervention by the "traditional doctor" or healer from the community who can work with the spirits to make life better for both of them, changing their luck and fortune. This work with the spirits complements couples therapy and may focus on such issues as the spirit of Mustafa's mother, upset relatives who are still living in Somalia, or deceased relatives or friends. Appeasing and working with these spirits in a manner that is consistent with Mustafa and his wife's belief system would be highly beneficial and supportive of the couple's work.

Chapter 23

Case Study of Nusreta, a 15-year-old Bosnian

DESCRIPTION

Nusreta is a 15-year-old Bosnian female who has been in the United States for 9 months. Her parents own a coffee shop and have demanding schedules. Nusreta has an 11-year-old brother who spends most of his time playing computer games and "thinks his older sister is really stupid and crazy."

In Bosnia, Nusreta was tortured and raped and has scars on her back and shoulders. She and her family came to the United States from the Omaraska Detention Camp, leaving behind an extended family that "might still be alive." Nusreta is confused and disoriented, sometimes forgetting where she is, what time it is, or where she is going. Sometimes her disorientation is reflected in her dressing habits; for example, she sometimes wears her pajamas under her school clothes, puts on two sweaters instead of one, or puts her shirt on backwards. She knows that "the other kids call her crazy" but shrugs it off. Nusreta frequently comments that she "wants to be happy."

Although her family and the Bosnian community accept Nusreta, they also see her as "weird and crazy." This stigma may relate to her not having many Bosnian friends, which is striking in a socially oriented culture. Since she only has a basic understanding of English and beginning level speaking ability, it has also been difficult to make friends with Americans. Even so, she has one close American female friend and one Bosnian female friend. Nusreta attends all the Bosnian parties and functions but does not feel like a part of the community so that she always remains on the sidelines "watching."

Nusreta has nightmares about "bloody people with their face banged in. Their screams wake me up just about every night . . . No, I don't get much sleep, only about, say, 3 to 4 hours a night." Nusreta has a poor appetite and does not care much about food. She admits to keeping all her feelings inside and when she speaks in her native language it is disjointed. She also has problems with her parents. "They lecture me too much, tell me what to do (laughing). I just listen. I don't really know if I hear them or not (laughing again), but they keep talking." Nusreta is indifferent toward her brother. "He's just there, sitting in front of the television." Her parents are worried about Nusreta's "crazy behavior" and want to "do the best for her."

CRITICAL INCIDENT

Nusreta's parents are getting more frustrated because they have not been able to change her "weird" behavior. They have been trying to convince her to get a haircut and dress appropriately, but to no avail. "She just won't listen. She acts like she listens, agrees and smiles when we talk with her, but she just doesn't listen or change her behavior." Nusreta's mother has tried to be patient and understanding with her but finally exploded one warm spring day. Nusreta came home wearing two heavy sweaters. Her mother approached her, as she had many times before, to tell her to remove them. As she always did, Nusreta listened passively and agreed. Her mother became angry and finally exploded. "Nusreta, it is too hot to wear two sweaters! Why are you doing this? People will think you are crazy or something! Take them off right now!" She and her husband were very distraught and decided "her crazy behaviors would have to be fixed." Although Nusreta seemed upset by her outburst, she did not say anything and would not talk about the incident.

SEQUENCE OF EVENTS

Nusreta's parents had high expectations leaving Bosnia and the detention center. They had great hopes that there would be a better life in America. The stress of the detention center made Nusreta's behaviors less noticeable; but once settled in a major city in the United States, they quickly realized that Nusreta had some bizarre behaviors that disrupted their dream of a better life. It concerned them that Nusreta took little notice of her brother and acted "strange." Over time, Nusreta's bizarre behaviors became more apparent, especially in contrast to other Bosnian youth her age. Finally, at a loss about how to reach Nusreta his parents approached the community leaders for guidance. They suggested that she see a psychotherapist who was experienced working with refugee adolescents and children.

KEY CLINICAL QUESTIONS

1. Explore with Nusreta about what happened in Bosnia. It is particularly important to discuss the trauma she experienced, but only when she is ready to disclose this information.

2. What about her extended biological family "that may still be alive." Who is in the extended family and what is their relationship to individuals in the family?

3. Any history of mental health problems in Bosnia prior to the fighting?

4. Does Nusreta or her family have a goal to get in touch with anyone who might still be alive in Bosnia?

5. Is Nusreta aware of her bizarre behavior? What meaning do these behaviors have for her?

6. How is the lack of sleep affecting Nusreta?

7. How does Nusreta feel toward her parents?

8. How does Nusreta feel about being in the United States without her extended family? Are there any symptoms of survivor's guilt?

9. How does Nusreta imagine her parents and brother feel about her?

10. Would Nusreta like to have more Bosnian friends or not?

11. Would Nusreta like to more actively participate in the social events in the Bosnian community? Why or why not?

MULTI-LEVEL MODEL (MLM) OF PSYCHOTHERAPY INTERVENTION

Level I: Mental Health Education

Psychotherapy may be confusing to Nusreta, who is already disoriented. Therefore, it would be important to carefully and clearly define for her what happens in the therapeutic process, especially given her history of torture and rape. Expectations for therapy, the role of the professional in sessions, the lack of any political or governmental association with psychotherapy, and confidentiality would be crucial to build a foundation for a therapeutic relationship. The need to communicate that mental health has no relationship with government or political processes and is not an interrogation or attempt to gather information is essential.

Level II: Individual, Group, and Family Therapy

Nusreta has many symptoms of posttraumatic stress disorder (PTSD). Initially it would be important to work with her individually to establish rapport and trust. The focus of work at the beginning of the therapeutic process would be on premigration—her life in Bosnia, memories of childhood, family interactions, special events, and the lake. After exploring her life in Bosnia prior to the fighting, it is appropriate to explore whether she is ready to discuss the more traumatic experiences during premigration and transition, for example, torture and rape. Since her dreams are frightening and disturbing, they may be a way to explore deeper issues that must be therapeutically addressed. Timing is a key issue working with her trauma, allowing Nusreta to take the lead and move at a pace that is safe and comfortable.

While working with Nusreta's trauma, the relationship to her bizarre behavior and social alienation within the Bosnian community could be introduced in the sessions. The image she projects, her internalization of that image, and resultant feelings and cognitions would be helpful to explore with Nusreta. An exploration of seeing the applicability of the concept of "dummy personality" (term attributed to Cambodians during the Pol Pot regime) as a coping strategy to survive would be helpful in better understanding and reframing her behavior.

At an appropriate time in psychotherapy after thoroughly examining premigration issues, there could be a shift to family therapy, which is consistent with the fabric of Bosnian culture. An initial focus of the family work could be on postmigration issues that includes Nusreta's behaviors. Nusreta's relationship with her parents, brother, peers, school personnel, and American and Bosnian friends would be important to discuss. This would allow her parents and brother to participate in the sessions and discuss the idealized life that her parents envisioned as well as Nusreta's expectations for family life during postmigration. It may also be beneficial for Nusreta to later join group counseling sessions in school with other refugee young women who shared similar premigration trauma. This format is culturally appropriate for Bosnians, who frequently meet socially to discuss events and issues and would allow Nusreta to explore how to live with her background and relearn about healthy interpersonal relationships.

Level III: Cultural Empowerment

Nusreta experienced torture and rape while in Bosnia and the detention center. It is likely that she has come to distrust officials and not know if people in positions of authority are reliable or trustworthy. Therefore, it is essential that Nusreta be educated about the role, responsibilities, and parameters of authority of government, agencies, and school officials. It would also be empowering for Nusreta to learn about the laws and her rights that protect her from rape, sexual abuse, and torture. This information may provide a crucial step toward feeling empowered to regain control over her life and the world around her.

Level IV: Indigenous Healing

Culturally appropriate healing in Bosnia is based on families joining together and sharing jokes and stories, although this has changed somewhat during postmigration given that atrocities were sometimes committed by neighbors in Bosnia. Given the "home orientation" of Bosnian culture, it would be appropriate to incorporate group and family therapy with extended groups within the Bosnian community at home sites. Meetings may include the expected strong Bosnian coffee ("coffee therapy") and food, in an effort to recreate a strong tradition of home as a base within the Bosnian culture. This would be particularly appropriate since within the former Yugoslavia mental health dealt with only dangerous or seriously disturbed individuals.

Chapter 24

Case Study of Faisal, a 16-year-old Iraqi

DESCRIPTION

Faisal arrived in the United States 6 years ago at the age of 10 with his mother, 4 younger siblings, and his grandparents. Faisal came from a wealthy Muslim family. His father had been a successful businessman and leader in the community in Iraq, following in the footsteps of Faisal's grandfather who was also well established and respected in their city. For generations many people had sought Faisal's family for personal and financial advice.

As the political tension had intensified in Iraq, Faisal's father was detained and held captive. The family could not find out where he was or what happened to him. As governmental pressure on the family intensified, business failed and the family savings were lost. Finally Faisal's grandparents and his mother decided that they must leave Iraq or they would surely be living in poverty and also taken as prisoners. They secretly sold everything they could and managed to obtain enough money to pay for passage out of the country for everyone, except, of course, Faisal's father. They left the country not knowing if the father was alive or dead.

Faisal's grandparents were too old to work, forcing his mother to be the sole breadwinner. Life was hard for Faisal's family in the new country, and they struggled to survive. There was the option of receiving welfare benefits, but the patriarch of the family, Faisal's grandfather, refused to let anyone apply for public assistance saying that it is shameful to receive free hand-outs. Faisal had many friends and was very popular at school and good at sports. A dream of

Faisal's had been to come to America, especially after watching the American movies and TV programs, believing that he would have wonderful opportunities in that country. While the family struggled, Faisal was trying to do well at school, hoping to be able to go to college in the future. Even so, similar to his siblings, he was finding it difficult to learn English and not getting very good grades. Faisal had very few friends, since each day after school and on weekends he worked doing odd jobs in the community to help out the financial situation at home. Life in the United States was completely different than Faisal's dream. For the first 4 years in the United States. Faisal thought constantly about his father, thinking that "if he were here things would be different . . . life would return to normal and it would be like before the war."

Three years earlier Faisal's father was located in a camp. News came to the family that he had been severely tortured and beaten. Because the family had resettled in United States, he was able to join his family after 2 years of trying to get him a visa. When he arrived it was clear that Faisal's father was not the same person he was before the war. Faisal watched him and saw how physically meek and quiet he had become, spending his days in front of the television watching war movies. Whenever he went out into the community, Faisal accompanied his father because any loud noises or sudden movement startled him. Lately Faisal had begun to feel ashamed of his father.

CRITICAL INICIDENT

One day Faisal accompanied his father to buy cigarettes. In the community, Iraqi people who had once shown his father respect in the homeland now whispered about him and smirked when he would pass by or jump at a loud noise. Earlier that week Faisal's mother had asked Faisal to quit school and get a full-time job, explaining that her sole income was no longer sufficient to support the family especially with the high medical bills and medicine for his father. As they were walking down the street, Faisal saw his schoolmates playing basketball. They needed one more person for the game and shouted to Faisal to come and join them. Faisal, who was upset and angered by his mother's request and a good basketball player, wanted to play.

Faisal told his father, "Why don't you just walk home yourself today. Our house is only one block away, and I will keep an eye on you as you walk there." The father panicked and held tightly to Faisal's shirt, begging to be taken home. His father's reaction drew the attention of his schoolmates and other people, who slowly started to gather around them. One man commented, "Look at him, he used to be an important man." A woman laughed saying, "See how he holds Faisal. What a sad case for an important man of the city." One of Faisal's peers was harsher, commenting, "It's like a baby dressed up as a man. His age is going backwards."

Although Faisal tried to calm his father, he was annoyed by his behavior and the comments by his neighbors. Faisal's father became scared, especially when he sensed Faisal's irritability and held onto Faisal more tightly, pleading with him not to leave. Faisal was very embarrassed and pushed his father away. His father fell to the ground crying, and Faisal, who was confused, angry and hurt, ran away. When Faisal finally returned home a few hours later, he found out that his father was placed in the hospital. His mother and his siblings were angry and scolded him, and his grandfather lectured him about being irresponsible. Faisal felt the world caving in around him and did not know what to do. He bolted to his room to get away, but his grandfather followed him into his room and continued to admonish him. Faisal covered his ears but could still hear his grandfather. That evening Faisal cried softly to himself through the night. He decided that he could not face anyone else after what he had done and thought it might be best if he ended his life.

Feeling hopeless and despairing, Faisal went to the medicine cabinet, knowing that his father's medicine was there. He saw the pills in the same place they had been since his father arrived in the United States. Taking the bottle into the kitchen, he poured a glass of soda and sat at the kitchen table. He emptied 20 pills into his hand and began to slowly and rhythmatically taking them, one at a time. As he was taking his third pill one of his younger sisters walked into the kitchen and screamed. His grandmother came running in, followed by the rest of the family. The pills were taken away from Faisal and the family decided that he needed help.

SEQUENCE OF EVENTS

Faisal's father had not gotten any better during the year he had been living with the family. Clearly, torture and beatings had taken their toll. As the only son, Faisal had a great deal of responsibility to care for his father, while simultaneously trying hard to earn good grades in school and contend with financial pressures in the family. He felt pulled in too many directions. When his mother asked him to quit school and contribute to the family by taking a job, Faisal felt overwhelmed and lost. His goals and hopes for a college education and good life in America were thwarted and Faisal felt that he could not live any longer.

KEY CLINICAL QUESTIONS

1. What does Faisal recall about his life in Iraq when his family was detained? What happened and what changed?
2. What was it like for Faisal when the family savings were lost?
3. Explore with Faisal what the departure from Iraq was like for him and his family?
4. What role does Islam play in the family?
5. How is it now in the United States with his mother working full time? Explore how he feels about the changes he is facing during postmigration.
6. What are Faisal's career goals? What course of studies does he imagine for himself in college? Where will this lead him?

7. What role in the family does Faisal have during the time his father was absent and then now, with his father rejoining the family in the United States? How does he feel about that role?

8. Discuss the hopelessness that led Faisal to attempt suicide. Explore in depth.

9. Given the current family situation, how might Faisal's role be constructed differently?

MULTI-LEVEL MODEL (MLM)
OF PSYCHOTHERAPY INTERVENTION

Level I: Mental Health Education

In Iraq Faisal and his family never had exposure to mental health services. In fact, they may be very cautious about personal issues given their need for secrecy departing Iraq and the detention and torture experienced by Faisal's father. Thus, it will be very important that the context and process of mental health services be carefully described to Faisal and his family to ensure clarification that it is not a government service and has no bearing on their status as refugees.

Level II: Individual, Group, and Family Therapy

It is recommended that Faisal and his family enter family therapy with the extended family, with an emphasis on a culturally sensitive intervention. Faisal's attempt at suicide, his father's torture and current state of functioning, his mother's full time work, and grandfather's insistence not to accept any financial support may be important salient factors that would warrant family therapy. It would be beneficial to examine roles and responsibilities within the family from a cultural framework. For example, with five children, who is responsible to assist their father and how is that responsibility shared? What role do the grandparents have within the family, given the condition of the father and financial obligations of the mother? What traditional responsibilities are taken away from Faisal's mother, given her full-time workload? Exploration of issues such as these would be very important, especially given the postmigration changes within a traditional Iraqi family.

It would also be helpful for family members to examine long-term goals with regards to acculturation. Faisal wants to go to college, yet family pressures are obstacles to that goal. Is the family supportive of his studying to improve his grades and further his education? If yes, how can they assist him in that process? If no, what are the alternatives? What about long-term expectations for his sisters? His mother? How does the family see the future?

During this time of great stress in the family, it is no surprise that Faisal tried to overdose on pills. Interestingly, he did this at the kitchen table, in a place he was sure to be noticed. Even so, it is a cry for help. It would be helpful for the family to realize, through family therapy, that Faisal's despair needs careful attention. Exploration of the depth of Faisal and other family members' hopelessness is important, generating support and care, especially during this time of continued adjustment.

Finally, it is essential that Faisal's father get mental health care to overcome 3 years of torture and beatings and his symptoms of posttraumatic stress disorder (PTSD). There are mental health professionals specifically trained in this area who would be invaluable in helping him deal with this deeply painful experience and assist the family with understanding and accepting the prognosis for treatment of PTSD. Family support helping the father to resolve this trauma is instrumental in healing and postmigration adjustment.

Level III: Cultural Empowerment

A major struggle for the family is finances. It is recommended that the family learn about financial support services available to them and discuss the ramifications of accepting this support. This would be particularly significant given the grandfather's rejection for support and the subsequent pressure that is placed on Faisal's mother. For example, welfare, phone, electric, or heating bill support may be discussed as temporary assistance, until there is enough financial stability to be self-supportive. Furthermore, an exploration about how Faisal can contribute to the family financially and also continue his studies such as attending night school, working only part time and continuing to attend day school, may be beneficial.

Level IV: Indigenous Healing

Historically in Iraq individuals who have mental health problems usually go untreated by professionals. Those with more evident mental health problems are viewed as scary and being possessed by evil. Since there are not facilities for the mentally ill, they stay within the community and are given food by the community members. Since Faisal and his family are Muslims, they may place great faith in a well-respected sheik in their community who has worked with many victims of war. The sheik could provide a special ceremony using the Koran as a basis for the healing. This may be acknowledged by the family as a culturally appropriate means to address the current problems in the family and be an invaluable intervention in conjunction with family therapy.

Conclusion

Counseling and psychotherapy with refugees is highly complex and requires unique cross-cultural perspectives. To effectively work with refugees to attain a sense of mental health and well-being, we have proposed the Multi-Level Model (MLM) of counseling and psychotherapy, a four-level cross-cultural intervention approach that integrates traditional Western psychotherapy with indigenous healing methods, cultural empowerment, and psychoeducational training. The MLM was conceived by Bemak, Chung, and Bornemann in the mid 1990s based on their collective work with refugees from around the world. The model was expanded by Bemak and Chung in previous periodicals and book chapters and further developed in this book. It is based on their continued work with refugees from different countries and regions of the world and is distinctive in that it may be applied across cultures, taking into account cultural dimensions that are applicable to the psychological well-being for different refugee groups. The model is unique in that it is geared specifically toward working with refugee populations and takes into account premigration and past trauma, cultural belief systems, worldviews, acculturation, psychosocial adaptation, the experiences of racism, discrimination and oppression in the resettlement country, social justice and the influence of resettlement policy on mental health. The MLM provides a holistic framework that conceptualizes a fluid and integrated strategy to meet the multifaceted needs of the refugee population.

Part III

Global Perspectives
on Refugees

Introduction

Significant global changes have impacted the psychosocial adjustment of refugees around the world. Environmental disasters, social upheavals, political fighting, wars, and intercultural and religious conflicts are causing numbers of people to flee their cities, towns, villages, and countries, sometimes into new countries and other times within their own countries as described previously in this book. The majority of these people are refugees for the first time in their lives. Global agreements that were made 50 years ago are debatable and open for interpretation in a 21st century context, generating discussion and disagreements about global and economic responsibility for refugees.

The psychosocial adjustment of refugees is a highly complex issue given political, economic, and multisectoral interests and priorities within diverse cultural and national settings. Historical origins of various countries come into play as they consider current policies and their own national receptivity to the plight of today's refugees. Additional issues such as the fact that one-fifth of the world's population lives in abject poverty (Desjarlais, Eisenberg, Good, & Kleinman, 1995), predictions of environmental disaster (Quammen, 1998), the continuation of 36 current worldwide wars and conflicts, violence, racism, and substance abuse (Bemak & Hanna, 1998), or the clearly articulated goals and actions of terrorists contribute to issues that affect the mental health and relocation of refugees.

To more specifically address what is going on in various parts of the world, this section will examine the situation of refugee resettlement from the perspective of six countries in different parts of the world. Since each country determines its own policies and procedures for working with refugees who are admitted to its nation, this section offers a unique viewpoint that examines the policies, procedures, and practices within these countries that have bearing on work with refugees. Five colleagues from around the world were invited to share ideas about their work and experiences in those countries. The last chapter in this book was written by the first two authors given their past work with Afghan refugees and the first author's visit to that country. Included in this section are two countries from Africa, one from Central Asia, two from Europe, and one from the Pacific Rim. Five of these countries have accepted refugees from different parts of the world, while the sixth country, Afghanistan, is currently facing mass migration due to war and is the country with the largest number of refugees for the past 10 years. The chapters will provide an overview of the culture, national policies that guide the work done by mental health professionals with refugees, help-seeking behaviors within a cultural context, belief systems about health and wellness, and current national practices as they relate to the psychosocial adjustment and mental health of refugees.

REFERENCES

Bemak, F., & Hanna, F.J. (1998). The twenty-first century counselor: An emerging role in changing times. *International Journal for the Advancement of Counselling, 20,* 211–218.

Desjarlais, R., Eisenberg, L., Good, B., & Kleinman, A. (1995). *World mental health: Problems and priorities in low income countries.* New York: Oxford University Press.

Quammen, D. (1998, October). Planet of weeds. *Harper's Magazine, 297,* 57–69.

Chapter 25

Norway: A "Welfare Society" for Refugees?—National Issues in Refugee Mental Health

Edvard Hauff

Norway is a small country with 4.5 million inhabitants; the number of asylum seekers and resettled refugees is also fairly small. But it is rich in natural resources, and the income from the petroleum sector gives the country the possibility to develop the "welfare society" further—an ideology that has been dominating the country since the World War II. It is might thus interesting to consider how such a rich and politically stable nation addresses issues relevant to the mental health of the refugees resettling there. Using a study of the mental health of Vietnamese refugees who resettled in Norway in the 1980s as the point of departure, I will in particular focus on two issues: the access of refugees to mental health services and the opportunity to find meaningful activities in the new country.

STATISTICS

One in 10 Norwegians has immigrant background if we use a wide definition (born abroad or having at least one parent who was born abroad). Approximately 50% of the immigrants come from Africa, Latin America, Asia, and Turkey. There are 65,000 persons with refugee backgrounds in the country. The number of asylum seekers was 10,842 persons in 2000. This figure includes more than 4000 persons from Yugoslavia, the majority of whom were Albanians from Kosovo who already had temporary protection in Norway. The other major countries from which the asylum seekers originate are Somalia, Afghanistan, Iraq, Iran, Pakistan, Romania, Russia, Slovakia, and Bosnia–Herzegovina. Only 1.2% of the asylum seekers were granted asylum in 2000. In addition, normally 30 to 40% are given residency permit due to humanitarian causes. Furthermore, Norway has a quota of 1500 refugees each year who are resettled here in collaboration with the United Nations High Commission on Refugees (UNHCR). In 2001 half of these places will go to refugees from the Middle East, 300 to refugees from African countries, and 200 to refugees from former Yugoslavia.

HISTORICAL BACKGROUND

During the first half of the 20th century Norwegian authorities tried to prevent immigration of persons they regarded as undesirable, in particular gypsies, but also immigrants with Jewish background. There was a strong assimilation pressure toward the immigrants who settled here. After World War II and the signing of the Geneva Convention, the Norwegian refugee policy gradually became more systematic and active, both nationally and internationally. An increased labor immigration in the early 1970s contributed to the formulation of an general immigration policy where the objectives were integration, equal opportunities, and participation in the society. But at the same time there was a general halt in issuing new working permits—a situation that is now changing. Thus, the majority of immigrants resettling in Norway today are refugees or persons in refugee-like situations.

Norway was one of the countries where the mental health of refugees received early attention, in particular through the work of Eitinger with the displaced persons in Europe after World War II. Eitinger himself came to Norway as a refugee from Czechoslovakia before the war and was later deported to the concentration camps in Germany. He published his doctoral dissertation on the psychiatric state of postwar refugees in Norway in 1958 (Eitinger, 1958). Later Eitinger and Strøm (1973) studied the health, including the mental health, of Norwegian concentration camp survivors. These early studies stimulated further studies of traumatic stress, the consequences of torture as well as of forced migration both in Norway and in other countries, and helped to lay the groundwork for the comparatively early European research—and to some extent also clinical—focus on the psychiatric consequences of catastrophic life events [preceding the more recent North American posttraumatic stress disorder (PTSD) tradition].

In spite of these early studies, the Norwegian health care system was relatively unprepared to address the mental health needs of the "newer" refugees groups who started to arrive in small numbers from countries outside Europe in the mid-1970s. Few Norwegian mental health care professionals had special competence in transcultural clinical work, and there were no specialized services for refugees or torture survivors. However, Amnesty International was stepping up its work against torture internationally, and an Amnesty group of psychiatrists was formed in 1981. One of its aims was to identify psychiatric sequels after torture among Chilean refugees in Norway (Fossum, Hauff, Malt, & Eitinger, 1982). Refugees themselves, resettlement workers, and mental health professionals started to point out the needs to establish services targeting the psychosocial needs of the refugees in the country.

DEVELOPMENT OF REFUGEE MENTAL HEALTH SERVICES

Since the organization of mental health services for refugees in Norway may be somewhat different from many other countries, I will describe briefly how these services developed.

In the community cohort study of Vietnamese refugees we found that among the 22% of the refugees who had a psychiatric disorder after 3 years in Norway, none were in contact with public mental health services, and 8 out of 10 had no contact with a primary care physician either. However, 1 out of 2 requested psychosocial assistance when this was offered (Hauff & Vaglum, 1997).

Thus, the experiences from conducting this study confirmed the need to address this issue more systematically, and after having worked as a psychiatrist in a refugee camp in the Philippines, I took the initiative to establish a small national psychosocial team within the public mental health services. This team was active from 1986 to 1990, and the objectives were to develop clinical methods, train health personnel, propose services, and provide health education and promotion. Denmark had recently established a rehabilitation center for refugees, but the Norwegian Ministry for Health and Social Affairs chose to address the wider mental health needs of the refugees in the country. However, at least half of the patients seen by the team therapists had been tortured (Hauff, Lavik, Dahl, & Sveaass, 1989; Dahl, Hauff, Sveaass, & Lavik, 1989). The team also identified extensive training needs in refugee mental health care among mental health professionals.

The experiences with the small national psychosocial team for refugees indicated that a more permanent center should be established to function as a national resource center in this field. The Psychosocial Centre for Refugees was established as a university center in 1990 in collaboration with the University of Oslo, The Municipality of Oslo, and the Ministry of Health and Social Affairs. The center is now a part of the Department of Psychiatry but has its own board with representatives from different faculties. The center runs a small outpatient clinic for traumatized refugees (Lavik, Hauff, Skrondal, & Solberg, 1996) provides courses and supervision for health personnel in the field of refugee mental health, especially in the health regions adjacent to the capital, conducts research (mainly clinical) and participates in several international projects and programs (e.g. in Latin America and Cambodia). The center also publishes its own journal in Norwegian, *Linjer*.

Recently, four small regional psychosocial teams for refugees have been established, covering the whole country. These teams are either part of a psychiatric outpatient department or part of the primary health care services. These teams have more or less the same functions regionally as the university center but with less emphasis on research.

PROBLEMS IN SERVICE DEVELOPMENT

The model described above is consistent with the public health care model in Norway. The intention is that the national center and the regional teams should supervise and train personnel in the psychiatric services in the regions, while the psychiatric services should be responsible for these functions in relation to the primary health care and social services. But the optimal functioning of this system depends on the ability to establish sufficient competence and capacity in the general psychiatric services, to be able to supervise and receive referrals from the primary health care. Experience has shown that it is possible to develop such a competence to a certain extent. However, frequently the first-line services are not receiving the required expert assistance, mostly due to the turnover of the professional staff in community mental health centers and other relevant departments, as well as limitations in the capacity to receive referrals (Major, 2000). The primary health care is responsible for the health care in the reception centers for asylum seekers. Thus, when their competency and interest for refugee mental health issues is limited, the assistance to the reception centers is likely to be insufficient.

Norway has an equity-oriented health care policy (Sosial-og helsedepartementet, 1997). Obviously, this is an advantage in helping minority groups gain access to appropriate health services. But, unintended inefficiency in the public health sector is a phenomenon with which many countries have been struggling. This is also the case for Norway, in spite of the strong economic situation in the country since the oil boom started. In fact, one aspect of this is a slow rate of implementation of new initiatives in the public health care.

An example from Norway may illustrate this problem. The government has recently decided to prioritize mental health care and intends to spend an additional US$3.2 billion over an 8-year period. Thus Norway is in a different position than many other countries, which tend to decrease the expenditure on mental health care (Hauff, 1999). The plans also include further service provision for refugees and ethnic minority groups. Already in a white paper from 1996 (Sosial-og helsedepartementet, 1997) the government proposed to establish a national "competency unit" for physical and mental health care for persons with immigration background. But 5 years later (at the time of this writing) the Ministry of Health had not proceeded further than to confirm the intention to establish this unit (Kommunal-og arbeidsdepartementet, 1997). Furthermore, in another white paper (Sosial-og helsedepartementet, 1997) the government proposed to build up special competency in transcultural psychiatry in a number of clinical psychiatric departments, but this development has not materialized yet either. Hopefully, ethnic minority groups will have stronger lobbying capacity in the future and thus be able to influence the implementation of similar health initiatives in a positive direction.

Such inefficiency may have a stronger impact in countries where there is a strong emphasis on public health services since private health providers or non-governmental organizations probably are less likely to try to complement the public services than in countries with a more privatized health care system. Furthermore, the ethnic minority groups, which could lobby for greater equity and further development of minority-oriented health services, are probably weaker than in other countries with a longer history of larger immigration movement. On the other hand, the fairly strong presence of the public sector field in the health care field in Norway has probably led to more systematic public mental health services for refugees in Norway than in several other countries, as described above (van Willigen, 1992). The academic sector has also responded positively to the challenge and incorporated refugee mental health as a prioritized field of study, and the fact that the University of Oslo has taken on this responsibility has probably had a positive impact upon the quality of the efforts of competency building nationwide.

EMPLOYMENT AND MEANINGFUL ACTIVITY

Clinical experience and research findings indicate that employment and other meaningful activities are essential factors for the quality of life of anyone, and not the least recently resettled refugees (Schwarzer, Johnson, & Hahn, 1994; Beiser, Johnson, & Turner, 1993; Lie Sveaass, & Eilertsen, 2000). Commonly, newly arrived refugees are much more concerned about their employment and educational opportunities than their access to health and mental health services. Thus, from a preventive and rehabilitative point of view, one might expect that the refugees' integration in the labor market was a highly prioritized objective for the immigration authorities. One might expect that the conditions were favorable in this respect in a country such as Norway with a low unemployment rate.

In the community cohort study of the Vietnamese refugees mentioned above (Hauff & Vaglum, 1997), we found that the refugees were poorly integrated into the labor market after their first 3 years in the country, and that the losses and the war trauma to which the refugees had been exposed appeared to have an impact on their career choice and was associated with lower integration into the labor market. There were no indications that they had identified any specific fields of opportunity in which they actively were pursuing their careers (unlike the electronics industry in the United States). The Norwegian resettlement policy was at that time, as it is now, to disperse the refugees to municipalities all over the country. This policy probably diminishes the refugees' opportunities to establish social network, which could facilitate job finding, entrepreneurship, and intraethnic employment.

Have these structural barriers against social and labor market integration become less pronounced with time? We do not have good comparative data, but there are indications that the situation has not changed markedly.

We were interested in how important unemployment and lack of meaningful activity was for refugees who were seeking specialized mental health services. In a study of the outpatients treated at the Psychosocial Centre for Refugees, University of Oslo (Lavik et al., 1996), it was found that 42.3% of the men and 26.7% of the women were unemployed or without participation in any educational or vocational training program at the time of referral. The high proportion of unemployed men in the sample was considered as a risk factor because it implies inactivity and the feeling of "uselessness." To analyze the relationship between the general level of psychosocial function and the impact of sociodemographic factors, traumatization, and exile, a multiple regression analysis was carried out with the general level of psychosocial functioning [the Global Assessment of Functioning (GAF) scores in the *Diagnostic and Statistical Manual*, Fourth edition, (DSM-IV) system] as the dependent variable. Among the predictor variables included, only the variable "unemployment/no school" had a highly significant association with the GAF scores. It was estimated that the effect of being unemployed or out of school is an expected reduction of 6.4 points on the GAF scale (a 100-point scale), controlled for the other predictors. This finding indicates that unemployment and inactivity is a destructive context for psychosocial function in exile.

However, how is the situation for refugees who are not in a help-seeking position related to the mental health services? Official Norwegian statistics show that the registered unemployment rate for immigrants in Norway still was fairly high in February 2001, with 7.3%, while the unemployment rate for the general population was considerably lower at 2.8%. Immigrants from African countries have the highest unemployment rate with 13.4%. Immigrants from Asia and eastern Europe also had high rates, 9.9 and 9.6%, respectively. On the other hand, the rate for immigrants from western Europe was only a few decimals higher than for the entire population. These relative differences appear to be independent of the economic trends in the country, but the absolute level depends on these trends (Østby, 2001). Refugees and other immigrants continue to represent a high proportion of the participants in public-sector job creation programs. They accounted for 32.0% of all persons covered by such schemes and included mostly nonwestern immigrants. However, it is questionable to what extent such schemes are able to make any considerable change in the unemployment rates. However, there are positive changes over time. The percentage of Vietnamese persons who were employed increased with the time of residence in the country, and there was an increase from 29 to 43% over a 2-year period. Among Somali refugees the increase was from 21 to 27%.

This underemployment of refugees and other immigrants is not only due to limited Norwegian language skills. Skepticism among employers to nonwestern immigrants and underutilization of the immigrants' competency are apparently greater problems, including insufficient and ineffective certification procedures for the formal education they have undertaken before arrival in Norway (Vassenden, 1997). In a sociological study of refugees in Oslo, Djuve and Hagen

(1995) found that the refugees position in the labor market was characterized by (a) difficulties in obtaining employment, (b) limited access to segments of the labor market, mainly in the service industry, where the demand for qualifications is low, (c) the terms of employment are loose, (d) they feel overqualified, and (e) there is a large difference in employment rates among the different nationality groups.

Asylum seekers are experiencing additional difficulties due to the long periods they have to remain in reception centers while their application for asylum is being processed. The average length of stay in these centers in the beginning of 2001 was approximately 13 months, although the immigration authorities' aim is that no one should stay there longer than 6 months after they have a permit to stay in Norway. The combination of lack of access to employment, financial problems, and insufficient psychosocial support has been found to have rather serious consequences for the asylum seekers' health and quality of life (Lauritsen & Berg,1999).

However, some efforts to change this situation are being made. In 1998 the Ministry of Labor and Administration issued a plan of action to recruit persons with immigrant background to the public sector. For example, asylum seekers, when there is no doubt about their identity, can now obtain work permits during the period they stay in the reception centers, and governmental institutions are obliged to interview at least one applicant with immigrant background when vacant positions are to be filled. But the effect of these measures are not yet apparent, and the changes in attitudes among the employers in the private sector appear to be slow.

The government is particularly concerned about the importance of assisting the refugees and other immigrants to obtain employment during the first 2 to 3 years after arrival in the country. Thus the government encourages the municipalities to establish special introduction programs for immigrants in relation to the labor market. The main components in these programs are: assessment of previous education and work experience, individual qualification plans, and close follow-up of these plans. It remains to be seen how effective these programs will be to ensure integration of the immigrants in the labor force. Such efforts are not only important from the individual immigrant's points of view but also for the national economy, due to the projected shortage of labor in the future. Hopefully, this situation will further stimulate the public and private sectors' efforts to integrate refugees and other immigrants in the labor force in the future, where they can obtain employment that is in accordance with their education and interests.

However, the research findings from Norway and other countries (e.g., Lavik et al., 1996) clearly show that there is a number of resettled refugees who are so traumatized by catastrophic events before or during the flight, that it is not sufficient to provide employment. These survivors also need individualized long-term rehabilitative services, both from a medical and a vocational perspective. If they are not able to take up paid employment after a period of rehabilitation, they often need assistance to obtain the disability pensions to which they are entitled in this country. There is still a need for innovative approaches to identify and start to assist refugees with long-term rehabilitation needs much earlier after resettlement than what is being done in this country at present.

CONCLUSIONS

Rich welfare societies may have several problems regarding resettlement and integration of refugees, which are not necessarily solved by a strong national economy or low unemployment. We have examined some of the problematic issues experienced by refugees and asylum seekers in Norway, particularly in the field of refugee mental health services and integration in the labor market and the opportunity to obtain meaningful employment.

It has been possible to establish and maintain a nationwide specialized refugee mental health care system that functions as an adjunct to the psychiatric and general medical care as a part of the national public health care model. Furthermore, the field of refugee mental health has been strengthened as a relevant academic field. However, general system-related problems—for example, bureaucratic inefficiency and rigidity—pose a threat to the optimal functioning of such a model.

But refugee mental health care in a public health perspective is more than provision of services. It also includes preventive interventions and a focus on the refugees' quality of life and opportunities for a meaningful existence in the country of resettlement. In this context we have identified the barriers against employment as a long-lasting structural problem that is of major importance from a mental health point of view. The government has recently introduced some additional measures to try to remove these barriers. It remains to be seen how effective they will be. Norway is gradually changing into a more pluralistic society, also ethnically, and this may gradually contribute to more positive attitudes toward immigrants among employers. Such a change in attitudes, combined with a political commitment and continued public funding of the type of interventions described above, is probably necessary to ensure that refugees and other immigrants find meaningful activities and be integrated into the labor force in their new country.

REFERENCES

Beiser, M., Johnson, P., & Turner, R. (1993). Unemployment, underemployment and depressive affect among Southeast Asian refugees. *Psychological Medicine, 23*, 731–743.

Dahl, C., Hauff, E., Sveaass, N., & Lavik, N. (1989). Klinisk erfaring med behandlingstrengende flyktninger. *Tidsskrift for Den Norske Lægeforening, 109*, 1871–1874.

Djuve, A., & Hagen, K. (1995). *"Skaff meg en jobb!" Levekaar blant flyktninger i Oslo.* Oslo: Forskningsstiftelsen FAFO.

Eitinger, L. (1958). *Psykiatriske undersøkelser blant flyktninger i Norge.* Oslo: Universitetsforlaget.

Eitinger, L., & Strøm, A. (1973). *Mortality and morbidity after stress. A follow-up investigation of Norwegian concentration camp survivors.* Oslo: Universitetsforlaget.

Fossum, A., Hauff, E., Malt, U., & Eitinger, L. (1982), Psykiske og sosiale følger av tortur. En pilotundersøkelse. *Tidsskrift for Den Norske Lægeforening, 108,* 325–328.

Hauff, E. (1999). Transcultural perspectives of the management of mental health care: Challenges in Europe and in low-income countries. In J. Guimon & N. Sartorius, (Eds.), *Manage or Perish* (pp. 95–100). New York: Kluwer Academic/Plenum.

Hauff, E., Lavik, N.J., Dahl, C-I., & Sveaass, N. (1989). Psykososiale problemer blant flyktninger i Norge. *Tidsskrift for Den Norske Lægeforening, 109,* 1867–1870.

Hauff, E., & Vaglum, P. (1997). Physician utilization among refugees with psychiatric disorders: A need for "outreach" interventions? *Journal of Refugee Studies, 10,* 154–164.

Kommunal-og arbeidsdepartementet. (1997). St Meld nr 17 (1996–97). *Om innvandring og det flerkulturelle Norge.* Oslo: KAD.

Lauritsen B., & Berg, B. (1999). *Mellom håp og lengsel - å leve i asylmottak.* Trondheim: SINTEF Teknologiledelse IFIM.

Lavik, N., Hauff, E., Skrondal, A., & Solberg, O. (1996). Mental disorder among refugees and the impact of persecution and exile: Some findings from an out-patient population. *British Journal of Psychiatry, 169*(6), 726–732.

Lie, B., Sveaass, N., & Eilertsen, S. (2000). Family, activity and stress reaction in exile. In N. Sveaass (Ed.), *Restructuring meaning after uprooting and violence: Psychological interventions in refugee receiving and in post-conflict societies* (pp. 1–19). Oslo: Institute of Psychology, Faculty of Social Sciences, University of Oslo.

Major, E. (2000). Psykiatrisk/psykologisk arbeid med flyktninger og asylsøkere. *Tidsskrift for Den Norske Lægeforening, 120,* 3420–3423

Østby, L. (2001). Hvorfor fokusere på innvandrerne? *Samfunnsspeilet, 2,* 2–14.

Schwarzer, R., Jerusalem, M., & Hahn, A. (1994). Unemployment, social support and health complaints. A longitudinal study of stress in East German refugees. *Journal of Community and Applied Social Psychology, 4,* 31–35.

Sosial- og helsedepartementet. (1997). St Meld nr 25 (1996–97). *Åpenhet og helhet. Om psykiske lidelser og tjenestetilbudene.* Oslo: SHD.

van Willigen, L. (1992). Organization of care and rehabilitation services for victims of torture and other forms of organized violence: A review of current issues. In M. Basoglu (Ed.), *Torture and its consequences: Current treatment approaches* (pp. 277–298). New York: Cambridge University Press.

Vassenden, K. (Ed.) (1997). *Innvandrere i Norge. Hvem er de, hva gjør de og hvordan lever de?* Oslo/Kongsvinger: Statistisk sentralbyrå.

Chapter 26

Swedish Perspective on Refugee Adjustment, Resettlement, Acculturation, and Mental Health

Solvig Ekblad

Research on recent immigration reveals that immigrants keep an extensive transnational network on social community and related issues (for a review, see Mollica, 2001). Schiller (1999) states that "to adopt transnational migration as the research paradigm is to change the unity of analysis; persons in sending and receiving societies became participants in a single social unit" (p. 99).

INTRODUCTION

During the last 20 years, migration waves to Sweden have experienced changes in many respects. In recent decades, Sweden is characterized as a country changing from being homogenous to becoming a multicultural society. Since World War II Sweden has received waves of labor and refugee migrants, and today almost 12% of the population are foreign born. They are part of the more general phenomenon of globalization, so that economic crisis or conflicts in one country affect very distant societies such as Sweden. Migrations are not homogeneous; they are constituted by different human groups: asylum seekers, displaced persons, refugee quota, qualified workers, and economic immigrants.

Refugees who flee because of war or political or religious persecution are of particular concern to mental health professionals. They "may have additional psychological burdens and potential risk factors for mental illness not encountered in non-refugee immigrants or migrants" (Ekblad, Kohn, & Jansson, 1998, p. 42). Traumatic stress such as cognitive/emotional reactions to external stressors are often due to sociocultural displacement that are not adequately dealt with through traditional socio-cultural coping mechanisms. If psychological stress is not attended to, it can become persistent and disabling, limiting an individual's capacity to restructure his or her life into the host society and instead increase social isolation and passivity. In turn, the person may become a burden to him or herself, family, community, or country. In addition to acculturation, a further challenge for those newly arrived refugees in need of mental health care may be the attitudes toward the mentally ill and unfamiliar mental health systems. Similarly, mental health professionals may have limited knowledge of the immigrant's language, culture, or attitudes about mental illness. This requires a knowledge and understanding of risk and buffer factors for mental illness during premigration, migration, and postmigration (for an overview, see Ekblad et al. 1998).

Many issues are common for immigrants, asylum seekers, and refugees and to the service systems that address a wide spectrum of needs. Among them is the care for mental health needs and the development of comprehensive services that act upon a wide range of health determinants. It is particularly important to address the ability of this group to access the mental health systems. Simultaneously, there is an important need to network with service providers. Essential issues must focus on holistic, community-based approaches (child and gender-sensitive, nonstigmatizing, nondiscriminatory, and culturally appropriate) as well as evidence-based accessible services that can be effectively implemented and that provide a framework to achieve increased consensus in operational models, strategies, and programs to improve mental health and human rights among newcomers. There are four main issues (a) accessibility to services, (b) morbidity, (c) mental health, and (d) the priority of basic mental health needs, which is relevant to health planning. The somatic and mental health of refugees and immigrants are closely interconnected.

NATIONAL POLICY

This issue is getting a higher priority in Swedish political agendas, and the European Union is preparing a common policy on asylum and has recently established the European Refugee Fund to support the efforts made by member states to grant appropriate reception conditions to refugees and displaced persons (Bardsley, 1999).

ASYLUM PROCESS

There is general increased interest in meeting the needs of migrants, who are faced with poorer levels of health and more social and health risks, to help them get integrated into Swedish society. The Swedish Migration Board processes applications as quickly as possible and decides whether the applicants will be allowed to remain in-country. The process is considered confidential to maintain privacy. Migration Board officers investigate the reasons and justification for each refugee applicant to determine whether or not he or she will be allowed to stay in Sweden.

SOCIAL AND ECONOMIC CONDITIONS

Every one seeking asylum in Sweden receives what is called an SIV card. It must be carried at all times. This includes situations such as signing for daily benefits or housing benefits, visiting a doctor, nurse, or dentist, collecting prescriptions at a chemist shop, and other various situations where it must be demonstrated that the person is seeking asylum in Sweden.

STRUCTURES IN PLACE TO INTEGRATE
ALL ASYLUM-SEEKERS OVER THE AGE OF 16
AND THOSE WITH PERMISSION TO STAY

Organized activities can consist of a certain kind of work experience at/or outside the reception center and may include one of the following activities:

*   Family-based activity: The adults are responsible, together with the staff, for planning and conducting activities.
*   Compulsory school for children and studies for young persons aged 16 to 18.
*   Swedish language instruction for adults: Most adult asylum seekers have the opportunity of attending Swedish language lessons and general instruction about life in Sweden.
*   Work: If the asylum case takes more than 4 months to decide, the applicant can work in Sweden.
*   Health checks and medical care: The applicant is offered a free health examination. In this examination medical samples will be taken and the person will have the opportunity of talking to medical staff.

The National Integration Office's task is, among other things, to work for the improvement of the conditions for newly arrived immigrants, with regards to the possibility of economic self-support and participation in society. In 1997, the Integration Office published guidelines on how the municipalities should work to assist integration through individualized introduction plans. The purpose of the introduction for newly-arrived refugees and other people who are in need of protection is to provide the individual with the prerequisites needed to be economically independent and to be part of Swedish society. The document states, among other things, that any health problems experienced by adults or children who are newly arrived should be acknowledged and, if need be, adhered to through health care and/or rehabilitating/habilitating activities (Integrationsverket, 1997). In April 2001, the Integration Office produced a document that outlined the guidelines for the introduction of newly-arrived refugees and other newly arrived immigrants. The aim, as stated in the document, is to provide the refugee and other newly arrived immigrants individually with the prerequisites to be self-sufficient and participate in the Swedish society.

HEALTH AND MEDICAL CARE

Under the Health and Medical Services Act, immediate health and medical care must be offered to a person currently staying within the county, even if that person is a nonresident. The same applies regarding immediate dental care under the Dental Care Act. Asylum seekers and other foreign citizens who have applied for residence permits in Sweden are not registered as residents. Thus, county councils (or the equivalent) are under a limited obligation to provide health and medical care for these groups of people, similar to the policies for temporary aliens. As permission is obtained for residence permits and settlement as a registered resident in a municipality, the county council (or the equivalent) requires similar obligations of this person as is required of Swedish citizens.

Under the Communicable Diseases Act, all examination, treatment, and care (medication included) necessary for the control of disease in connection with an epidemic is free of charge for the patient within the scope of county council (or the equivalent) health and medical care, as long as the patient is health-insured under the National Insurance Act. Under the State Compensation (refugee reception, etc.) Ordinance, county councils and municipalities receive economic compensation from the state in accordance with certain principles.

If the adult person is taken ill during the waiting period, he or she is entitled to emergency medical care and emergency dental care. The person is required to pay a personal charge for every visit to a doctor at a health center or to a nurse, while asylum-seeking children are entitled to medical and dental care on the same terms as other children in Sweden. Even so, there is no charge for maternity care, preventive child and mother care, and care under the Swedish Communicable Diseases Act. Dental care is free of charge for children under 18 (Migrationsverket, 2000). If personal expenses are high, the person may apply for medical care through a special grant.

HEALTH INFORMATION AND FAMILY PLANNING

Upon arrival in Sweden asylum seekers/refugees are given information on health matters and a general introduction to health and medical services in Sweden. Information should also be supplied concerning contraception, the availability of gynecological health checks, and Swedish abortion law (Allmänna råd, 1995)

INTERPRETING SERVICES

Any person who needs an interpreter when meeting social and health care staff or other officials has such a right.

MENTAL HEALTH CARE UTILIZATION

To date there are few national studies concerning utilization of mental health care among immigrant groups. Ferrada-Noli (1996) noted in an epidemiological study on suicide that there was a significant overall overrepresentation of immigrants in the total number of suicides and cases of undetermined suicide and accident. The same author also found a co-variation between suicide and immigrant status, unfavorable socioeconomic conditions, and lack of psychiatric care. Johansson (1997) showed that ethnicity was an independent risk factor for suicide and for high psychiatric admission rates with regard to migration, health, and suicide. Bayard-Burfield (1999) found that among patients in Lund University Hospital, there was a higher risk of attempted suicide among foreign-born than among Swedish-born individuals.

Diderichsen and Varde (1996) found in Stockholm county that migrants from non-Scandinavian countries consumed lower psychiatric care utilization rates than the rest of the county's population. In a register study in the County of Stockholm, Ekblad, Oxenstierna, and Akpinar (1998) found a diverse pattern of psychiatric mental health care utilization regarding different groups and genders. The study concluded that there are challenges within health care in meeting mental health needs among the migrant population and that there may be a potential underutilization of mental health care among some groups in the migrant population. This may be connected with how people view of illness.

Bäärnhielm (2000) highlighted how Turkish and Swedish-born women gave their illness different meaning than that constructed by the caregiver. "Different interpretations of illness meaning by patient and caregiver constitute a situation of different realities according to the significance and social reality of the illness" (Bäärnhielm, 2000, p. 4). Bäärnhielm and Ekblad (2000) performed a qualitative study conducted with the aim of exploring structures of illness meaning among somatizing Turkish-born migrant women living in a poor and low-status suburb of Stockholm in contact with local health care services. The Turkish women rarely accepted or valued psychiatric attribution as a tool for recovery, nor was it helpful in linking bodily symptoms to emotional distress. The results of the study point to the mutual need of exploring meaning in the clinical encounter to help patients make sense out of different perspectives of illness and healing. Bäärnhielm's (2000) results

point to a need for enhanced knowledge about how people make sense of: illness, clinical encounters, different perspectives of illness and healing and the role of the social context in this with regard to both mental health care delivery and mental health promotion in multicultural settings. In conducting such research special consideration should be shown to people in a migration context as migration entails exposure to the stressful situation of being uprooted, dislocated and relocated. For clinical care, results indicate a need to explore meaning between caregiver and patient. (p.4)

A recent study of patients by Lindencrona, Ekblad, and Charry (2001) focused on the circumstances of and the treatment provided for patients attending the clinics. Collaboration with other professionals involved with the patient was also conducted. The study was performed at a community mental health center south of Stockholm with a patient population consisting mainly of immigrants. The circumstances of many of the new 670 patients attending the clinic in 1998–1999 are alarming. Various needs (social, psychological, and medical) within the group were not met. The group experiencing the most difficulties appears to be the newly arrived traumatized patients, who often have major symptoms as well as experiencing the poorest circumstances, such as lack of work and insufficient knowledge of the Swedish language. This group was young and often in a situation in which they had to attempt to combine family life, including young children, with trying to establish themselves in a new society. This process may be even more difficult and correlated with earlier trauma. To facilitate the provision of good care for everyone in the catchment area, it was necessary for the clinic to find new strategies to strengthen the patients and meet all their needs. The clinic's organization must be constructed as able to ensure that the newly arrived persons are assessed from a holistic perspective. Assessments must be based on the three different perspectives for psychiatric care (biological, social, and psychological). Lindencrona, Johansson, Blight, and Ekblad's model (revised from Silove, 1999) described patient needs through the concepts of attachment, security, identity/roles, human rights, and existential meaning. These could be used as a base for a wider assessment of the patients' circumstances as well as the needs for intervention.

SPECIAL CENTER/CLINICS FOR TRAUMATIZED SURVIVORS

In Stockholm there is a center for tortured refugees (Red Cross Centre) and a center for tortured and war-wounded refugees, a refugee medical center. Also, at present in Sweden there are eight refugee psychiatric clinics and six special clinics for children and adults, eight of which are open to asylum seekers. Presently, there are no comprehensive studies of an evaluation of the assessment, treatment, and staff facilities at these clinics. However, lack of money and staff makes it difficult to improve services for these patient groups.

LESSONS LEARNED FOR MENTAL HEALTH PRACTICE

There are several lessons to be learned from the Swedish experience that may be generalized beyond national borders. They are as follows:

- An assessment of the patient's personal background and level of acculturation will alert a sensitive staff to potential cultural conflicts with regards to treatment. It is also fruitful to identify culturally appropriate interventions.
- Mental health services should be based on international consensus of best-practice models for the care of refugees (e.g., evidence-based knowledge).

- Communication: Patient's idioms of distress may rely on a complex system of metaphors and proverbs. This may create miscommunication, early termination of treatment, nonuse of mental health service, or visits to indigenous healers.

- Once clients trust the staff, a helping alliance can be developed and maintained and may be more important than solving problems. This contact may be destroyed when a staff member is on holiday or on leave if there is no one else available to trust, thus creating an increase in illness and disability.

- Interventions and context may create an external loci of control in the individual or group. Therefore, mental health staff need to incorporate people other than just the identified patient or client, in both the construction and resolution of problems and also, where relevant, in the actual processes of helping.

- Length of treatment; short-term and directive or long-term and psychodynamic care should be viewed from a person, event(s), and environmental context.

- Issues of temporality: Making and keeping appointments at fixed times or starting and ending sessions promptly might be a source of difficulty.

INEQUALITIES IN MENTAL HEALTH CARE AND SOCIAL SERVICE UTILIZATION

It has long been known that immigrant people in any society may have difficulty understanding and accessing care. For instance, behavioral and cognitive therapies are obviously more suited than psychodynamic approaches to the Arab population (Al-Kreawi & Graham, 2000). In addition, cultural beliefs and values may influence perceptions of need for care, particularly mental health care. Another universal factor is the stigmatization of mental health issues as well as the perception of privacy about such issues as well as the desire to hide such complaints. Mental health programs that stimulate mechanisms of adaptation and foster self-help to minimize helplessness are particularly welcome. Thus, barriers among migrants to seek mental health treatment may be connected with:

- Help-seeking behavior
- Mistrust
- Stigmas
- Cost
- Clinician bias

Furthermore, some cultures may use traditional medicine or religious/traditional ceremonies for treatment and are less familiar with western mental health interventions. Western approaches tend to emphasize the individual and minimize the importance of the sociocultural context and social networks. This is nicely stated as follows: "The group gives the individual protection and security, a feeling of belonging and identity, as well as emotional and practical support during crises. A drawback is the diminished sense of 'self.' The fate of an individual with ambitions or values of the collective, is likely to create isolation or even ostracism" (Al-Kreawi & Graham, 2000, p. 13).

CONCLUSION

More preventive measures that include better reception conditions in a gender perspective for asylum seekers and other migrant population groups are needed. Organizations involved in employment assistance to recognized refugees and other migrant groups should be encouraged to consider the particular gender needs of immigrants.

In spite of the increase of knowledge among health professionals in the field of migration and mental health issues, there are many barriers to apply this knowledge and to improve reception policy and mental health programs. In part, such barriers reflect failures of communication between scientists, service providers, and policymakers. These barriers also reflect basic realities in the delivery of needed services for migrant groups (Jaranson, Forbes-Martin, & Ekblad, 2001). Improvement requires actions at several different levels (e.g., individual, family, organizational, community, policy). Multicultural issues should be given a priority in training, research, and service efforts in the field of mental health promotion.

It is clear that there is a need for cross-cultural research to enhance our understanding of psychopathology. Three ways to do this were identified by Canino, Lewis-Fernandez, and Bravo (1997). First, cross-cultural comparisons can be useful for the development of hypotheses about the possible etiology of particular disorders. Second, cross-cultural studies can help us to distinguish between etiological factors that are more susceptible to cultural and contextual influences and those that are more related to biological factors. Third, the identification of risk and protective factors associated with the development of specific disorders can have important implications for prevention. The basic challenge is how to develop a mental health research approach that searches for equivalents of the categories of the dominant classification systems across different cultures while at the same time being flexible enough to register significant local differences in health and illness.

REFERENCES

Al-Krenawi, A., & Graham, J. (2000). Culturally sensitive social work practice with Arab clients in mental health settings. *Health & Social Work, 1*, 9–22.

Allmänna råd från Socialstyrelsen. (1995). *Hälso- och sjukvård för asylsökande och flyktingar.* Socialstyrelsen 1995:4.

Bäärnhielm, S. (2000). *Clinical encounters with different illness realities. Qualitative studies of somatization and illness meaning among Swedish and Turkish. born women encountering local health care services in Western Stockholm.* Unpublished master's thesis, Karolinska Institutet, Stockholm, Sweden.

Bäärnhielm, S., & Ekblad, S. (2000). Turkish migrant women encountering health care in Stockholm. A qualitative study of somatization and illness meaning. *Culture, Medicine and Psychiatry, 24*, 431–452.

Bardsley, M. (1999). *Project Mégapoles: A network for public health within the capital cities/regions. Health in Europe's capitals: similarities and differences.* Luxembourgh: European Commission.

Bayard-Burfield, L. (1999). Migration and mental health. Epidemiological studies of immigrants in Sweden. *Dissertation Abstracts International, 60*, 336. (University of Lund, 1990).

Canino, G., Lewis-Fernandez, R., & Bravo, M. (1997). Methodological challenges in cross-cultural mental health research. *Transcultural Psychiatry, 2*, 163–184.

Diderichsen, F., & Varde, E. (1996). Konsten att fördela resurser efter behov. Stockholmsmodellens kriterier. *Läkartidningen, 93*, 3677–3683.

Ekblad, S., Kohn, R., & Jansson, B. (1998). Psychological and clinical aspects of migration and mental health. In S. Okpaku (Ed.), *Clinical methods in transcultural psychiatry* (pp. 42–66). Washington, DC/London: American Psychiatric Association Press.

Ekblad, S., Oxenstierna, G., & Akpinar, A. (1998). *Invandrarbakgrundens betydelse för sjukvård och socialförsäkring. En folkhälsorapport för Stockholms län.* Stockholm: invandrarenheten, IPM; Stockholms universitet, Stockholms läns landsting och Karolinska institutet/Edsbruk: Akademitryck AB.

Ferrada-Noli, M. (1996). Post-traumatic stress disorder and suicidal behavior in immigrants to Sweden. *Dissertation Abstracts International, 50*, 0735. (Karolinska Instituent, 1996).

Integrationsverket. (1997). Retrieved January 1, 2001, from http://www.integrationsverket.se/nystart.html, 2001-01-09.

Jaranson, J., Forbes Martin, S., & Ekblad, S. (2001). *Refugee mental health: issues for the new millenium.* Unpublished manuscript.

Johansson, L. M. (1997). *Migration, mental health and suicide. An epidemiological, psychiatric and cross-cultural study.* Unpublished doctoral dissertation, Karolinska Institutet, Solna, Sweden.

Lindencrona, F., Ekblad, S., & Charry, J. (2001). Kartläggning av levnadsomständigheter, behandlingskontakter och samverkansinsatser för nybesökspatienter på Fittja psykiatriska öppenvårdsmottagning 1998–1999. Institutet för Psykosocial Medicin (IPM), Avdelningen för stressforskning, Karolinska Institutet, WHO:s Psykosociala Center, Stockholm, Sweden. *Stressforskningsrapporter nr 296.*

Lindencrona, F., Johansson, Blight, K., and Ekblad, S. (2002). Theory and choice of method in studying health promoting initiatives from a transcultural perspective (in Swedish with an abstract in English). *Nordisk Psykologi, 54*, 7–26.

Migrationsverket. (2000). Retrieved July 19, 2001, from *http://www.migrationsverket.se/ Facts* about . . . . . . *refugee reception.*

Mollica, R. (2001). Responding to migration and upheaval. In G. Thornicroft & G. Szmukler (Eds.), *Textbook of Community Psychiatry* (pp. 439–451). Oxford: University Press.

Schiller, N. (1999). Transmigrations and nationstates: Something old and Something new in the US immigrant experience. In C. Hirschman, P. Kasinitz, & J. DeWind

(Eds.) *The handbook of international migration* (pp 94–119). New York: Russel Sage Foundation.

Silove, D. (1999). The psyhosocial effects of torture, mass human rights violations, and refugee trauma—toward an integrated conceptual framework. *Journal of Nervous and Mental Disease, 187*(4), 200–207.

Chapter 27

Southern Sudanese Refugees:
In Exile Forever?

Nancy Baron

HISTORY OF THE REFUGEE PROBLEM

The southern Sudanese refugees living in northern Uganda share the psychosocial consequences of long-term exile with 20 million refugees living in foreign lands around the world and 20 million more internally displaced within their own countries (Desjarlais, Eisenberg, Good, & Kleinman, 1995). In 1988 and again in 1994, waves of thousands of refugees fled from Sudan into northern Uganda. They fled a war between the Muslim Sudanese government and a Christian rebel group called the Sudanese People's Liberation Army (SPLA).

Such events are not new to this corner of Africa since Sudanese refugees also entered Uganda in the 1960s, and the now-hospitable Ugandans fled their country's war and were welcomed guests into southern Sudan in the 1970s. At present the SPLA controls those areas of southern Sudan that were once the homes of the refugees. Over the years, some refugees have returned home but 156,374 refugees (UNHCR, 1999) continue to wait. Even though the SPLA encourages people to return, the ongoing threat by the Sudanese government and the minimal education and health care available in their war-torn country discourages repatriation. Peace talks and agreements are not long-lasting so a return home is not eminent.

Upon arrival in Uganda, the refugees were moved into transit camps with cramped substandard living conditions and full dependency for food, shelter, water, sanitation, and health care on the United Nations High Commission for Refugees (UNHCR). Over the years, as it became obvious that the refugees' return home was not eminent, the plan was revised. The Ugandan government generously agreed for the refugees to move onto arable unused farmland. Landowners were eager for the refugees to be their tenants because the land was unused due to rocks, lack of roads, physical isolation, no schools, no medical care, and, worst of all, active Ugandan rebel activity. The refugees and their UN caretakers took on the task of developing this land, and most of the refugees were moved from transit camps into *settlement sites*.

The UNHCR and its partners refocused their activities to encourage refugee "self-reliance" and integration so that refugees could grow their own crops and feed themselves. It was thought by the international authorities that the Sudanese, people with some of the same tribes, religion, and languages as the northern Ugandans, could be integrated with their Ugandan neighbors, sharing land, health care, and educational facilities and joining together to develop the area. The plan is fine in principle but not as easy to implement. Though from common backgrounds, they are still different people, and the local Ugandan neighbors often feel threatened by the settlement of the Sudanese, who outnumber them in some counties.

Resources in these northern areas are limited, so sharing is difficult when there is not enough for even the local people. Self-reliance is also not only a physical activity requiring hard work by the refugees; it also requires mental and emotional change. Years of refugee life have promoted a "learned helplessness" (Seligman, 1975) and many feel entitled to support. After years of dependency, the switch is complicated, especially when self-reliance is attached to the refugees' recognition that the soil now given for farming is given by people believing their return home is not eminent. They fear they will be forgotten by the international authorities. Yet, the refugees also recognize that after years of dependence on an unreliable aid system that the independent ability to survive might be best. However, this part of Africa is not always cooperative. Despite many efforts by nongovernmental organizations (NGOs) and the Ugandan government, the early years of self-reliance with irregular rains, locusts, and crop failures has left many refugees struggling to stay alive. Added to that is the ongoing activity from Ugandan rebels who periodically raid the camps for food and to abduct young men and women.

The psychosocial issues related to the lives of these refugees began with survival, and for many have never moved far beyond this. For the women, daily life is filled with drawing water, cutting firewood, farming, pounding grains, cooking, bathing, nursing the youngest baby, and eating. There is little energy left for much else. For the men, daily life is often without meaningful activity. With little land to farm, only a part of the year, there are many hours, days, and weeks with nothing to do. Strong efforts are made to send children to school; yet the few dollars it may cost per year is often too much for a family to afford. Youth are eager for secondary education and advancement; yet there are few opportunities.

Therefore, the psychosocial problems of these people is often directly related to their daily survival.

The Transcultural Psychosocial Organization (TPO) is an international NGO specializing in the provision of psychosocial and mental health assistance in countries during or after conflict. Its assistance to the southern Sudanese refugees and Ugandan citizens living in northern Uganda began in 1994 and continues today. This chapter will discuss the changing psychosocial problems of these long-term refugees and the efforts to implement sustainable community-based psychosocial and mental health interventions.

CHANGES OVER TIME IN THE PSYCHOSOCIAL PROBLEMS OF REFUGEES

Initially lost lives, homes, properties, and experiences of horror filled the minds and hearts of the refugees. Memories of the trauma of their displacement were soon replaced, however, with the ongoing misery of daily refugee life living in poverty with little hope for improvement or a return home. While living in exile, day by day they experience the erosion of their identities living as guests, on someone else's land, in some one else's country, confronted by someone else's culture and values, as well as ambivalent hospitality. They are caught in a cycle of violence in which they feel powerless, victims of a war that is supposed to be for their benefit yet without a voice (Baron, in press).

Over time, the loss of the independent ability to survive becomes most important. Prior to exile, most Sudanese were farmers and independently cared for their families; now they feel helpless and often humiliated. Having material possessions, culturally demonstrates the success of the family; therefore, the loss of properties is profoundly felt. Cattle represent wealth and are used to pay for dowries and the performance of rituals. Most of the cattle were either stolen or died, and so the wealth needed to perform rituals for funerals, weddings, and conflict resolution is no longer possible, which causes much distress and familial conflict. Traditionally, most Sudanese men are polygamous, and families try to have as many children as possible to enlarge the numbers of their extended family and clan. Without a dowry, arranging for wives is difficult; and without wives there is the serious risk of not having children. Lost land is not only an issue for survival, but land also provides a stable homestead necessary for the rituals of the family, clan, and tribe.

Ancestors are buried on a family's land, and the Sudanese want to live among the spirits of their ancestors and be buried with them. Additionally, the unavailability of the usual methods of problem solving leaves a vacuum. Community, clan, and tribal elders are relied on to make decisions and establish law and order. As refugees, this system is disorganized due to the premature death of many adults and estrangement of the natural communities of clans and tribes, which always lived in close proximity and are now split apart.

The initial displacement caused social changes, which caused distress and disruption. This did not, however, lead to severe symptoms that warranted mental health treatment. It is noted that the development of chronic and severe mental health symptoms in a refugee population is the "exception rather than the rule." (McFarlane & De Girolamo, 1996). Though relatively few people experienced extreme symptoms immediately after their displacement, at one time or another most Sudanese refugees felt miserable and reported experiencing some mental health symptoms in various degrees of severity and complained of some loss in ability to function. The complaints included: feelings of fear and anxiety, physical pain (head, neck, back, chest, stomach, joints), shortness of breath and tightness in the chest, loss of energy and motivation, change in temperament, estrangement from friends and family, disturbed sleep or nightmares, inability to make decisions, concentrate, or remember, lost faith or spirituality, inability to work, loss of interest in care of family and self, and change in interest in sex, food, or pleasure. Most refugees were unaware of the normal emotional and physical stress reactions that could follow displacement. Some were distressed by their feelings of stress and became further distressed by the fear of not understanding their symptoms. Speaking of emotional distress is not culturally acceptable; so, as a result, it is not surprising that some developed psychosomatic aches and pains. They feared that these pains were associated with life-threatening disease or injury and felt further stressed when health professionals refused them treatment (Baron, in press).

There was no standard response to the initial distress. Levels of intensity of trauma and levels of intensity of distress were not clearly related. A rape or a family death or loss of property could all cause low or high levels of distress seemingly dependent on the individual and family protective factors and capacity to cope. Some people responded without a problem to the initial displacement and had symptoms of stress later; others had symptoms at the beginning that later disappeared. Victims reacted to trauma in accordance with the social, cultural, or political meaning it had for them, their families, and their communities.

Traumas provoke change or problems for an individual but also influence the overall tone, personality, or behavior of a family or community. This is especially relevant to the Sudanese, who rarely act alone and who believe that life is strongly influenced by family and community. Sudanese communities often share experiences of violence, and in reaction to these traumatic events not only do individuals suffer and change but people report that the overall personality of the family and community change. Some report that as an overall group they are now less trusting and more fearful of each other and have less motivation to help each other. Feelings of hopelessness and helplessness pervade some families and communities. Some blame their neighbors or other tribes and want revenge or to remain distant from them. Families and communities report changes in culture, traditions, faith, and spirituality due to their shared experiences. Some communities strengthen their belief in God and/or spirits; others believe less. Some believe that they cause the traumatic events to occur due to their lack of adherence to traditional rituals or lack of faith while others feel it is God's will (Baron, in press).

As the years in exile progress, there remains a wide disparity in response. Though many refugees continually feel miserable about their ongoing status, the ability to cope seems to differ. Some cope adequately and create a new life while others are unable to reorganize and restabilize their lives. Some refugees had previous psychosocial problems that are exacerbated while others have new psychosocial problems provoked by their displacement and exile.

Even though the entire population suffered from traumatic experiences prior to their displacement, once in exile most cope. This does not mean that they do not feel depressed and despairing and have nightmares and fears. They did at the beginning and some still do. Yet, in a reasonable amount of time after their displacement they were doing their daily chores, playing with their children, making new babies, and occasionally laughing. In other words, coping. A range of factors seems to provide protective functions that seem to minimize stress, assist coping, and prevent posttraumatic stress disorder (PTSD).

The refugees' mechanisms for coping are challenged, however, as the cumulative stress continues to grow as the years in exile progress. After years in exile, the cumulative effects of the stress of their living situation seem to outweigh the memories of the initial traumatization.

For refugees, traumatization is usually not a specific traumatic event in the sense of an isolated incident or a set of events that have left painful scars. More often, it is an enduring, cumulative process that continues during exile because of distinct new events, both in the native county and in the country of exile. It is a chain of traumatic stressful experiences that confront the refugee with utter helplessness and interfere with her or his personal development over an extended period of time. (Van Der Veer, 1995, p. 152)

PRESENT PSYCHOSOCIAL PROBLEMS

Now more than 12 years into exile, the problems most disturbing to these refugees include:

Loss of Hope

After years in exile, many refugees feel that Uganda may be their home for an extended time. Recognizing this causes many to feel anxious, depressed, stressed, and to lose hope. Seligman (1975) reported that a low level of perceived control over their lives resulted in high levels of frustration and chronic depression in refugees.

Poverty

First, as refugees dependent on handouts of insufficient food and now as subsistence farmers with small plots of land, these southern Sudanese are some of the world's poorest people. Relative poverty in Europe or America where there are social welfare nets to assist people is very different from the poverty of Africa where starvation and disease pervade. For refugees it is believed that low socio-economic status is a major risk factor for failure to adapt, cope, and achieve well-being in the new living environment (Brody, 1994).

Overwhelming Family Responsibilities

The Sudanese feel strong responsibility for the care and maintenance of their nuclear and extended families. Premature death due to war, acquired immunodeficiency syndrome (AIDS), and lack of good health care is prevalent. The living adults are burdened by these deaths and take responsibility for the care and education of all related adults and children. It is not unusual for an adult to have the full financial responsibility for up to 40 relatives.

Vulnerable Populations

The vulnerable populations (including the physically disabled, mentally ill, mentally retarded, abandoned or orphaned children, chronically ill, elderly without families, and widows without families) struggle to cope within the settlements. With substandard living conditions and the need for caretakers to spend large amounts of time struggling with daily survival tasks such as fetching water and wood, the vulnerable can become a burden to their families and communities (Desjarlais et al., 1995).

New Traumatic Experiences

Many of the refugees do not feel safe in the settlement environment that was set up for their protection. The continuing rebel insecurity triggers the fears caused by the original exile. Every incident of insecurity, even though it only directly affects a small portion of the population, has a strong ripple effect throughout the extended refugee community. Many live in a heightened state of hypervigilance that seems to increase stress-related and psychosomatic illness.

Suicide

Increased risk of suicide may be related to an apparent elevated rate of depression among refugees (Orley, 1994). In 1999 in this refugee population, 17 adults (10 males/7 females) committed suicide or 11.3 suicides per 100,000 people (an average number according to world standards). Within this population in 1999, only adults committed suicide. If we count only the adult population, it becomes 25.2 suicides per 100,000 adults (Baron & Jurugo, in press). Compared to known worldwide statistics, this result, in a small adult population, is potentially one of the highest known rates in the world (Desjarlais et al., 1995).

Alcohol Use

Generally, refugees report that the incidence of alcohol overuse throughout the settlements is on the increase. In particular, it is reported to affect men of all ages including the young and the elderly. These are groups who often feel particularly disenfranchised and without hope for their futures. It is a cyclical problem made more difficult because the women, with little means to make a living, brew alcohol within the camps to earn money to feed their families. This readily available cheap alcohol is drunk by the men. The increase in alcohol use seems to be a causal factor of other problems, that is, domestic violence, marriage break-ups, and child abuse or neglect.

Loss of Culture—Changing morality

The elders complain of a loss of culture and despair that the youth are not respecting or adhering to the traditions. There is an increase in youth pregnancy. In Sudan, the usual community response to a youthful pregnancy would be marriage. However, in exile due to lack of resources the young men often have no means to pay the dowry so many families prohibit the young couple from marrying. Increased numbers of young men, over 18 years of age, who impregnate underage girls are imprisoned for defilement. The family will refuse the marriage, even if the sex was consensual and the couple within a couple of years of age, if the man has no dowry payment and have him charged with a crime and imprisoned. The hope is that his family will raise funds for a dowry to have him released from prison.

The cumulative effect of all of these factors causes symptoms of distress of various levels of intensity throughout the refugee population. In Sudan, traditional methods of helping were used to assist people with any problem. The current problems are a challenge to these traditional helping methods.

TRADITIONAL HELPING METHODS

Prior to displacement, the refugees lived in traditional rural communities and had little contact with the contemporary world. The communities retain strong traditional beliefs that explain the causes of the "misfortunes" of war, premature death, sickness, conflicts and the like, which can be seen in the following list.

Traditional Beliefs That Explain the Cause of Misfortune

Cause	Examples
Spirits	Meeting a spirit of the dead while awake.
	The spirit of a dead person comes to you in your sleep.
	Not visiting the burial place of a dead family member.
Unperformed Rituals	The proper rituals are not performed.
	Someone dies away from home and the proper ritual of bringing a stone or soil from a river or stream, in the direction of where the person died, is not followed.

Someone is not buried in the proper way: on the left side for a female, on the right side for a male.

Certain big trees that were the previous site of rituals cannot be chopped.

Your mother dies and you do not pay a cow to your uncle.

After the death of a family member, the rest of the family does not discuss the cause or slaughter a bull.

Upon killing an animal, elders are selected to eat the most important parts including the testes, kidney, and liver.

If the parts are destroyed, so the elders cannot eat it, the cook or his family may have misfortune.

Curses   In anger or spite, one person can bewitch or put a curse on another.

Buying charms from a witch doctor, it is possible that the charm can backfire and turn on you.

Fighting with another person in a stream or lake.

You murder someone and do not lick the blood. (Baron, in press)

For centuries, families internally managed all problems through the help of their extended family members, traditional healers, elders, community, and church leaders. In Sudan, most rural villages had no government legal system so the elder clan groups were expected to mediate conflicts and provide punishment for offenses against family or community. Because of exile, many clans are split apart due to death and dislocation. The placement of refugees into settlement sites by authorities was random, thereby, further splitting the clans and tribes. A western idea to improve tribal relations was to randomly mix everyone together. This choice had repercussions so that the usual elder councils are no longer available. Also, in African communities, clan members care for their vulnerable members without question. In the present settings a neighbor of a different clan or tribe is not going to easily change generations of tradition and assist in caring for an unknown neighbor's blind mother or retarded child, especially not when the traditional beliefs are that the disability might be caused by angry spirits.

Historically, traditional healers were the mainstay of treatment for mental health and psychosocial problems. Healers believe that these problems are caused by spirits. The spirits become angry and punish people when they are neglected and/or traditional rituals are not performed. Resolution always involves performing rituals. The traditional healers continue to treat those people who believe in them, especially for disorders explained as spirit possession and curses. However, the healers are not effective in treating problems of refugee life and poor living conditions or severe mental illness, mental retardation, or epilepsy. Traditional healers are also expensive, and many people have no financial means to pay a healer or pay for rituals. A U.S. $15 goat for slaughter is a major expense.

Many people now follow the tenets of the Christian church, so they no longer believe in the value of healers. The church in the Sudan teaches that mental illnesses and other misfortunes are caused by evil spirits who harm people without strong beliefs in the church. It teaches people to believe strongly in Christian tradition, and then pray to overcome misfortune. Some people are hesitant to give up the traditional beliefs despite the teachings of the church and integrate traditional rituals including animal slaughter with prayer to cover all the possibilities to appease God, spirits, and ancestors in order to find relief.

TPO–UGANDA PSYCHOLOGICAL AND MENTAL HEALTH PROGRAM

Prior to determining if a program should be initiated, TPO explored the traditional methods of helping to determine its effectiveness and if there are any gaps in services. The strength of individual resilience, support of family and community, and traditional methods of problem solving and healing allow most of the Sudanese to cope with their refugee status; however, an array of symptoms are not easily managed by traditional methods. TPO–Uganda is designed to assist those refugees who have psychosocial or mental health problems that are not resolved through traditional helping methods.

The overriding philosophy of the TPO–Uganda program has remained the same from the start. The program is designed to empower the refugee population to treat the unmet psychosocial and mental health problems of their members utilizing a community-based culturally appropriate approach. In the context of the Sudanese culture, TPO assists individuals to find relief from their distress and resolution of their problems within the structure of their families and communities

It is often assumed that the problems of refugees will be because of the traumas suffered because of war and violence. Over the years, TPO found that in actuality the refugees seek help for problems due to a wide array of social issues that may be secondary consequences of the displacement as well as mental illness and epilepsy; see the following list:

Requests for Assistance

Help a family find a confused, naked man who ran into the bush talking to himself and threatening to harm anyone in his way.

Assist a family after the rebels abducted their daughter and stole the family's food supply while the family's children are starving.

Calm a violent quarrel between a drunken man and his wives.

Mediate a dispute between neighbors due to one believing the other "cursed" the family.

Find a home for a mother and her retarded child after being abandoned by her husband and family.

Speak to a parent who is not paying a child's school fees.

Advocate to the United Nation's for a community whose seeds for planting did not germinate.

Rush to a home where a child is dying and help the family secure medical care.

Help a depressed widow with seven children and no extended family.

Assist a suicidal childless woman.

Assist a man charged with defilement locked in prison without a trial.

Provide assistance to a person suffering from the cultural stigma placed on people with epilepsy.

PROGRAM GOALS

TPO has a series of curative and preventive psychosocial and mental health interventions that aim to strengthen communities, families, and individuals so they can develop mechanisms for long-lasting sustainable self-help. The overall goals of the TPO–Uganda program include:

- Culturally sensitive community-based interventions utilizing indigenous "helpers."
- Provision of curative psychosocial and mental health assistance through mid- and long-term supportive problem-solving assistance.
- Prevention of psychosocial and mental health problems through crisis intervention, psychosocial education, and community, youth and child activities.
- Increase community awareness and sensitization of psychosocial and mental health issues to assist in preventing problems and empowering communities and families to help their needy members.
- Encourage empowerment of individuals to help themselves within the context of family.
- Work cooperatively with all community, NGO, or government leaders and helpers.
- Promote human rights, peace, and reconciliation.

CHANGING COMMUNITY ATTITUDES

Though southern Sudan has no history of treatment for the mentally ill, the country of Uganda does. It has one psychiatric hospital and a school of psychiatry and psychiatric nursing. However, when TPO began, treatment was only available in the cities and not accessible to the refugee or national populations in the rural areas of the north. The role of psychosocial and mental health care needed to evolve in order to be accepted within the traditional structures. Bringing in educated outsiders to the rural communities was not believed to be an effective way to introduce new ideas and change community attitudes. To establish a sustainable system of self-help, it was most important that this evolve from inside the communities. This has required a process to change attitudes through comprehensive community education to introduce new ideas about the cause and possible treatment of problems, and then proving the effectiveness of treatment through successful case examples.

Indigenous people needed to be trained to provide effective preventive and curative psychosocial and mental health services. Convincing volunteers to participate in this initial process was not possible so the first step was to select, hire, and train an indigenous staff of paid "counselors." Prior to working with TPO, most had little contemporary knowledge about psychosocial and mental health identification and treatment and were only aware of traditional methods of healing. For example, during training one staff person reported: "I remember when I was young. A relative became mentally ill. He was locked in the house and the meat of an elephant was burned. The smoke successfully chased away the demons." Training was needed to help the staff integrate traditional beliefs with useful western ideas. Maintenance of some of the traditional beliefs were necessary; however, those that prevented effective helping and violated human rights needed to be changed. For example, ostracizing, neglecting, and abusing people with epilepsy because it is believed that they are cursed rather than providing western medication is damaging.

CASCADE OF TRAINING APPROACH

A "cascade of training" approach was utilized and the counselors were only the beginning of the cascade. Once trained, they educated community leaders, traditional healers, health workers, and teachers who then educated community members. The cascade then reached throughout the communities and referrals came forward for treatment (Baron, in press; Hobfoll & de Vries, 1995). Ugandan nurses then became willing to work in the rural areas with the financial support of TPO and the security of working alongside indigenous people. Effective treatment sold the effectiveness of the interventions, and the cascade of training led to a cascade of referrals and opportunities to assist the population. To become an entirely sustainable service, eventually indigenous people were not only counselors but became the program managers and trainers of trainers.

This effective service then interested the Ugandan Ministries of Health, Education and Social Affairs, and TPO was invited to provide training and technical assistance to them. Now 7 years after beginning its operation, TPO is working with the government to integrate some of its services into the national government ministries, which will provide ongoing treatment to the national and refugee population. The indigenous staff will become a local NGO and continue to provide programming, training, and technical assistance.

PSYCHOSOCIAL AND MENTAL HEALTH INTERVENTIONS

TPO interventions utilize a family- and community-focused approach, similar to the Multi-Level Model (MLM) of psychotherapy developed by Bemak and Chung (2002). An individual's problems are understood within the context of family and community; and support and resolution is found within the family and the community.

A model describing levels of intervention (Green et al., 2001) is used to explain the TPO interventions. Different levels of program interventions are

Figure 27.1
Psychosocial and Mental Health Intervention Levels

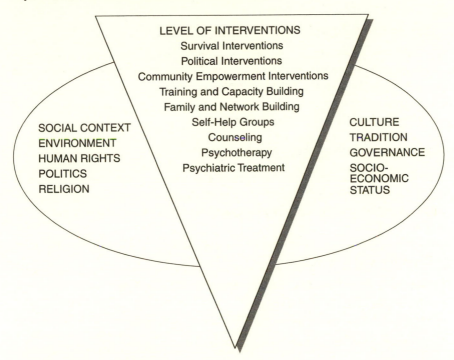

LEVEL OF INTERVENTIONS
Survival Interventions
Political Interventions
Community Empowerment Interventions
Training and Capacity Building
Family and Network Building
Self-Help Groups
Counseling
Psychotherapy
Psychiatric Treatment

SOCIAL CONTEXT
ENVIRONMENT
HUMAN RIGHTS
POLITICS
RELIGION

CULTURE
TRADITION
GOVERNANCE
SOCIO-
ECONOMIC
STATUS

Source: From Baron, Jensen, & de Jong (in press).

divided into nine categories. The division is arbitrary and categories are interconnected. They are presented in descending order with the interventions needed
for the most people written first and requiring the least trained staff and go down
to the smallest need but require the most trained staff. Within each category, it is
specified if it is a preventive or curative intervention. Lists of examples of some
of the types of programs presently implemented by TPO–Uganda are outlined
within each category. Each of these interventions is influenced by the context
and many existing community and societal factors including those regarding
human rights, governance, politics, environment, culture, traditions, socioeconomic status, and religion (See Figure 27.1)

SURVIVAL INTERVENTIONS (PREVENTIVE)

All helping efforts need to first ensure survival. The lack of adequate survival
tools, that is, not enough food or medical care, can cause extreme emotional
stress and can result in symptoms of distress. Types of interventions providing for survival have an impact on emotional well-being. Methods used can

either promote normalcy and empower people or promote helplessness and dependency.

Examples of Interventions

- Training of United Nations and other aid organizations to understand the importance of integrating concepts about positive mental health and empowerment rather than promote dependency and learned helplessness.
- Referral to available resources in the community since many people do not know what services exist or how to access them.

POLITICAL (PREVENTIVE/CURATIVE)

Political interventions promote human rights, peace, democratization, conflict resolution, and reconciliation. They are critically important since wars and violence are perpetuated by hatred and aggression within the same communities that hold the victims.

Examples of Interventions

- Advocacy for human rights, refugee rights, and children's rights
- Training of staff about human rights
- Psychosocial and mental health assistance to inmates in prisons
- Community building and peace and reconciliation activities

A history of tensions between tribes in southern Sudan continues within the settlements. Children and youth continue to be taught fear and hatred of other tribes as has been taught for centuries. TPO promotes activities to try to change attitudes. Sport leagues between tribes that hate each other yet do not really know each other are organized. It seems more difficult for children, youth, and adults to maintain hateful stereotypes when they have positive experiences.

COMMUNITY EMPOWERMENT ACTIVITIES (PREVENTIVE/CURATIVE)

These interventions promote community empowerment and self-help. Communities often have skills for helping that are not utilized for people with psychosocial and mental health problems due to a lack of appropriate knowledge. These interventions encourage communities to help themselves and to help their most vulnerable members. These interventions promote the recreation of normalcy within daily life.

Examples of Interventions

- Community participation in psychosocial helping workshops

To be effective, community education needs to flood the entire community. Thus, TPO developed a community education approach that reaches throughout the communities. Community Participation in Psychosocial Helping (CPPH) workshops target community leaders. Its overall goal is to increase community sensitization and awareness and mobilize leaders to help their vulnerable members and activate their communities to help themselves and know when and how to make referrals to TPO and other aid organizations. In 1998 and 1999, counselors held 360 training sessions in which they trained more than 8000 community leaders, religious leaders, teachers, health workers, youth leaders, women leaders, traditional healers, government officials, and NGO workers. Building awareness promotes the referral of people with problems to the available services but also provides a "preventive" function. Educating people about potential problems can prevent their occurrence or exacerbation. For example, alcohol education can prevent youth and children from becoming abusers, knowledge about treatment for high fever can prevent brain damage, and understanding of stress can minimize psychosomatic complaints.

CRISIS INTERVENTION

TPO counselors are members of the communities they assist and live in the refugee settlements. Thus, they are available to respond immediately to any crisis. According to the refugee communities, TPO's quick response has the effect of immediately calming the victim and community, supporting the victim and family, assisting in quick referral for assistance, and activating community and family support for the victim.

Large numbers of suicide attempts and deaths prompted TPO to begin a suicide prevention initiative. TPO staff continually facilitates workshops to educate government, UN, and NGO staff and health workers. A team of community leaders in each settlement was trained as a community crisis intervention team (CCIT) that responds to each crises and when needed requests the further assistance of TPO. The CCIT and TPO co-lead special workshops for community members to explain suicide risk and encourage prompt assertive community response.

Suicide Prevention

A 15-year-old girl became pregnant by an "older" man. The mother became "hysterical" and attempted to hang herself. The CCIT intervened and prevented the suicide. The mother then went on a hunger strike. The TPO Counselor was informed by the CCIT and worked with the team to provide counseling to the mother and daughter.

TRAINING AND CAPACITY BUILDING OF HELPERS (PREVENTIVE/CURATIVE)

Training and capacity building is essential for all psychosocial and mental health helpers. A cascade approach is used to build knowledge and skills at all levels of helping.

Examples of Interventions

- Training an indigenous staff as paid "counselors."
- Awareness raising and skill development of the host government officials
- Awareness raising of the home government officials
- Training of health workers, teachers, and UN and NGO staff.

FAMILY AND NETWORK BUILDING (CURATIVE)

The TPO counselors utilize a family- and community-focused approach. Interventions promote the family and/or a network of supporters to help their members who are vulnerable or have psychosocial and mental health problems.

Case Example

A woman asks the TPO counselor for assistance. Her husband deserted her and their seven children to go to live with a young woman who will become his second wife. In this culture, wives are considered the property of the man's family since they pay a dowry for her, and her children are, therefore, their responsibility. It is acceptable to take a second wife but important to arrange to provide for both equally. The TPO counselor helps to arrange a meeting between the wife and the husband's family in order to organize for the care of the first wife and her children. Arrangements are made within the family meeting, which satisfy everyone. Despite this, the woman feels angry and sad and the counselor initiates counseling with the couple.

SELF-HELP GROUPS (CURATIVE)

Self-help groups are a sustainable method that promote people with similar problems to help each other rather than depend on the help of a helping person.

Examples of Interventions

TPO groups are both preventive and curative:

- Curative groups include support groups for alcohol abusers, widows, mothers of retarded children, children who experienced recent traumas, ex-rebels, returned abductees, families of unreturned abductees, and mothers of children at malnutrition centers.
- Preventive groups include psychosocial education on alcohol and epilepsy for communities, as well as sports leagues, drama groups and traditional dance for children and youth.

COUNSELING (CURATIVE)

The purpose of "counseling" is to assist individuals, families, or groups to resolve problems and relieve emotional distress through talking in a supportive, confidential environment. The process of counseling differs according to the context and culture.

Examples of Interventions

TPO counselors are taught the basics of counseling using an 11 step approach (Baron, in press). TPO counselors are known within their communities for the understanding, compassion, and support they offer to their clients. They work with an individual and his or her family to empower them using an action-oriented problem-solving approach. The step approach is from Baron (in press).

Eleven Spiral Steps for Psychosocial Helping

Step 1: Direct all help toward self-help by empowering the person within the context of his or her family and community.

Step 2: Involve a network of potential support including family, friends, or community in the helping process.

Step 3: Build and maintain a trusting relationship between the person asking for help, his or her family or support network, and the helper. (This is a prerequisite for all helping and continuous process).

Step 4: Listen attentively to all the involved people (continuous process).

Step 5: Probe all of the necessary information (continuous process).

Step 6: Encourage expression of all feeling by all the involved people (continuous process).

Step 7: Offer compassion, empathy, emotional comfort, and support to all without bias (continuous process).

Step 8: Assess the problems (important to build initial plan of action and to update throughout the process of helping).

Step 9: Develop a plan of action with all of the involved people in compliance with context, culture, and capacity (important to start the process of helping and to update throughout process of helping).

Step 10: Step-by-step implementation of the plan of action toward problem solving.

Step 11: Ending the helping relationship when the process is completed and evaluate the effect of helping.

PSYCHOTHERAPY (CURATIVE)

The ability to provide psychotherapy requires extensive training and supervision, and this expertise is not available in northern Uganda.

PSYCHIATRIC TREATMENT (CURATIVE)

In the African countries "psychiatric treatment" often includes the mentally ill, people with epilepsy, and mental retardation. These people can become a serious drain on the family's ability to survive. The family's meager resources are often consumed in search of care, and enormous time and energy are diverted from other domains of life (Desjarlais et al., 1995). The disabled person can become a burden and out of necessity neglected. A dignified quality of life is an international human right. Mental health care is relatively inexpensive; in Uganda medication costs an average of $9 a month for the most seriously mentally ill and half a dollar for people with epilepsy. With proper treatment, many of those who were once a burden on their families can become productive.

Examples of Interventions

- For the treatment of the mentally ill, TPO–Uganda provides a combination of psychotropic medication and community- or family-based psychosocial education and interventions. Ugandan psychiatric nurses are trained in community mental health care and facilitate mobile mental health clinics in the rural areas.
- TPO advocates to the Uganda health ministry, United Nations, and aid donors to understand the importance of treatment for the mentally ill.
- TPO provides extensive sensitization and awareness workshops within the communities to promote referral of mental health cases.
- Within the refugee population the incidence of epilepsy is high due to illness, fever, infection, accidents, and injuries. Prevalence of epilepsy is as high as 3.7 to 4.9% in Africa and Asia (Adamolekkun, 1995). Communities fear people with epilepsy; and due to their seizures, people suffer many accidents particularly falling into fires or drowning. Since the health centers did not treat people with epilepsy, TPO provided drug treatment as well as education and support for the person, family, and community. TPO led seminars for health center staff and now after 7 years, the health centers will takeover all epilepsy medical treatment.
- Families frequently bring their retarded children to TPO desperately searching for assistance. Many of the children appear to have brain damage, which seems to have occurred after high fevers; frequently they also have ongoing convulsions. Since the problems for a retarded child and the family are many, most of the families have been to traditional healers and spent a great deal of money trying to find a cure for their children. Some of the children are neglected, and few retarded youth or adults are found within the settlements. Fathers often desert the mother of a retarded child, believing she is cursed and fearful that she will give birth to more retarded children. Communities often shun the family and child; therefore, many are locked away so no one can see them. Single mothers often have to leave the retarded child unattended in a hut all day in order to tend their fields. TPO counselors provide a range of services from emotional support to families, education about mental retardation, encouragement to families to provide love, compassion, and care to the child, and training to show parents how to educate their children and teach them basic self-help skills. Ongoing support and education groups for parents are held in some settlements. Since

many parents complain that the care of this child restricts them from being able to care for the rest of the family, TPO initiated a special income generation project in which each retarded child is given a goat. As the goats multiply, they can be sold for income.

EFFECTIVENESS OF INTERVENTIONS

The needs of the refugees within the poverty of rural Africa and the never-ending cycle of war can appear overwhelming. TPO activities sometimes seem small compared to what is needed. TPO cannot make peace and help the refugees return home, it has no food to feed the hungry, no money for schools, no training and employment opportunities for the masses; none of the basics. Sometimes TPO wonders about the depth of what it can provide. Yet, when you speak to the refugees assisted by TPO, they have no doubt. They say that TPO workers listen to them, talk to them, care about them, and are advocates for them. In their world, a world of people who feel forgotten by the world, this listening and caring is highly appreciated and felt to be effective.

The following description is from Baron (in press).

A Day in the Life of a Counselor

The counselor awakens in the home of her family within the refugee settlements. After preparing breakfast, she sends her older children to school and turns over the care of her baby to her sixteen year old niece.

It rained during the night so the roads are muddy and she drives her motorbike over the slippery, rutted roads to her field office. She arrives at 8:30 A.M. to a find a client's mother waiting for her. The mother is frantic. Her son refused to take his medication for the past couple of days and has relapsed. He was shouting and running about all night and in the morning threatened to harm a neighbor. The counselor tries to calm the mother and gets the details of what has happened to determine the seriousness of the problem.

Using her radio hand set the counselor contacts the large field office and speaks to her supervisor. She explains the situation and it is agreed that she will try to stabilize the family until a psychiatric nurse can arrive. The settlement is about an hour drive from the field office. The nurse is responsible for a clinic that day and must be found at another location. With bad roads, it may be afternoon before she arrives.

The counselor accompanies the mother to her home. Neighbors report that the man ran into the bush. The counselor meets to camp chairman and some of the man's relatives. They arrange to go and look for him and will report to the counselor when he is found.

The counselor returns to her office and spends 30 minutes completing her case notes from yesterday. She then begins the filed visits arranged for that day. She drives by motorbike to a client's home about 30 minutes away. The client is a woman who was raped by rebels in an attack to the settlement last week. Immediately after the incident, the counselor went to the settlement and found the victims. She assessed their need and decided to offer some supportive counseling to this woman and her family. The woman cries and talks of the incident and her feelings and her husband's reactions. The counselor meets with the couple together and discusses their feelings. The husband is fearful that his wife might have contracted AIDS and refuses to have sexual relations with her. The wife feels frightened that he might leave her. The counselor encourages them to talk and tries to assist their problem solving. There is no easily available testing for AIDS, but the counselor agrees to try to arrange testing. She teaches them about condom use and leaves after two hours.

The counselor drives half an hour to the home of a family with a four year old retarded child. The child is severely retarded and unable to sit. Last week the counselor and father talked about how to build a seat for the child since the mother was burdened by having to carry the child on her back. The counselor was pleased to see the father had followed through. The child was sitting and the mother able to perform her chores. The parents talk to the counselor about their eldest daughter. She wants to marry but the boy's family is hesitant due to the retarded child. They fear that retardation is a family trait that will be passed to future grandchildren. The counselor explains that since the child's brain damage appeared after having a high fever it is not hereditary. The family invites the camp chairman to discuss the problem. It is agreed that a meeting with the boy's family will be held to discuss the problem. A local traditional healer will also be consulted and invited to the meeting to discuss ways to prepare the family so that the marriage can take place.

The counselor returns to the home of the mentally ill man. He is found and some of the relatives are sitting with him inside a hut. He is shouting and appears to be delusional. The counselor uses her hand set to call the field office and learns that the nurse is on her way. When the nurse arrives, he meets the client and assesses the problem. He decides to medicate him with a quick acting psychotropic injection. The counselor and nurse speak with the family and develop a plan for maintaining the client safely at home. The nurse and counselor will return the next day to follow-up on their treatment.

It is now 6 P.M. and the sun is setting so the nurse and counselor return to their homes.

REFERENCES

Adamolekun, B. The aetiologies of epilepsy in tropical Africa. *Tropical & Geographical Medicine, 47*(3), 115–117.

Baron, N. (in press). Community based psychosocial and mental health interventions for southern Sudanese refugees living in long term exile in Uganda. In J. de Jong (Ed.), *War and violence: Public mental health in the socio-cultural context*. New York: Plenum.

Baron. N., Jensen, S., & de Jong, J. (in press). The mental health of refugees and internally displaced people. In J. Fairbanks, M. Friedman, J. de Jong, B. Green, & S. Solomon (Eds), *Psychosocial policy and practice in social and Humanitarian crises: Report to the United Nations*. New York: United Nations.

Baron, N., & Jurugo, E. (in press). *Comparing worldwide suicide rates to a refugee population*. Manuscript submitted for publication.

Bemak, F., & Chung, R. C-Y. (2002). Counseling and psychotherapy with refugees. In P.B. Pedersen, J.G. Draguns, W.J. Lonner, & Lonner, & J.E. Trimble (Eds.), *Counseling across cultures* (5th ed., pp. 209–232). Thousands Oaks, CA: Sage.

Brody, E. (1994). The mental health and well-being of refugees: Issues and directions. In A. Marsella, T. Borneman, S. Ekblad, & J. Orley (Eds.), *Amidst peril and pain: The mental health and well-being of the world's refugees* (pp. 57–69). Washington, DC: American Psychological Association.

Desjarlais, R., Eisenberg, L., Good. B., & Kleinman, A. (1995). *World mental health problems and priorities in low-income countries*. New York: Oxford University Press.

Green, B., Friedman, M., de Jong, J., Solomon, S., Keane, T., Fairbank, J., Donelan, B., & Frey-Wouters, E. (Eds.). (2001). *Trauma in war and peace: Prevention, Practice, and policy.* New York: Kluwer Academics/Plenum.

Hobfoll, S., & de Vries, M. (Eds.). (1995). *Extreme stress and communities: Impact and intervention.* Dordrecht: Kluwer Academic.

McFarlane, A., & De Girolamo, G. (1996). The nature of traumatic stressors and the epidemiology of posttraumatic reactions. In B. van der Kolk, A. McFarlane, & L. Weisaeth (Eds.), *Traumatic stress: The effects of overwhelming experience on mind, body and society* (pp.129–155). New York: Guilford.

Orley, J. (1994). Psychological disorders among refuges: Some clinical and epidemiological considerations. In A. Marsella, T. Borneman, S. Ekblad, & J. Orley (Eds.), *Amidst peril and pain: The mental health and well-being of the world's refugees* (pp. 193–207). Washington, DC: American Psychological Association.

Seligman, M. (1975). *Helplessness: On depression, development and death.* San Francisco: Freeman.

UNHCR (United Nations High Commission on Refugees). (1999). *Uganda statistics and self-reliance strategy literature.* Kampala, Uganda: Author.

Van der Veer, G. (1995). Psychotherapeutic work with refugees. In R. Kleber, C. Figley, & B. Gersons (Eds.), *Beyond trauma: Cultural and societal dynamics* (pp. 151–168). New York: Plenum.

Chapter 28

Cultural Problems for Western Counselors Working with Ethiopian Refugees

Lewis Aptekar

INTRODUCTION

I am a clinical psychologist and Professor of Counselor Education at California's San Jose State University, I train counselors to work in the schools and social service agencies of Silicon Valley. My research interest focuses on mental health, what it is, and how it survives in cases of trauma and extreme poverty. These interests have taken me from the excesses of the Silicon Valley where even the relative wants of people fade in comparison to the absolute needs of much of the world's population. I have been in the stark hovels called homes by the street children in many countries of Latin America and Africa. I have seen the suffering caused by the loss from environmental disasters. And, I am far too aware of the long enduring pains caused by the traumas of war.

The Transcultural Psychosocial Organization (TPO) of the Free University of Amsterdam and a World Health Organization (WHO) Collaborative Center had been working on a cross-cultural study to assess the prevalence and types of mental disorders among war-traumatized populations. They wanted to find out if there were cultural differences that led to increased or reduced incidences of mental disorders. In addition, they wanted to find ways to support and build upon existing and successful coping strategies. The TPO believed that the existing

(Western) taxonomy of psychosocial responses to war trauma were unclear and inadequate. Its research plan called for an epidemiological survey with the long-term aim of adapting interventions to the evaluated needs of the population. It also included training a core group of people in mental health so that they, in turn, would be able to train nonprofessionals to provide mental health services in communities where trauma was prevalent. Between the research and training emphases, the project's goals and mine seemed a perfect fit.

The Ethiopian project was to press harder for answers than I could then imagine. I was forced into a spiritual life long ago cemented over by the secularity of my profession. The apparently simple question—does mental health have a spiritual component?—was not the only question that punched me in the solar plexus, leaving me as unprotected as a babe in the woods. I was forced to deal with the relative wealth of being a U.S. citizen in the face of the overwhelming poverty of some people in other parts of the world. (I had in my pocket the money to pay for the medicine or food that would keep death at bay.) I was made to view my own actions. The worst of it was that I could not help but judge myself.

FROM THE NOTES: TO GIVE OR NOT TO GIVE

Today, our first client was a middle-aged woman, Hiwat, dressed in shambles and without shoes. Her tent was so exposed to the elements that her bed, which was made of raised earth, had begun to erode onto the mud floor. A week or so ago she had been to a natural healer who gave her "something to drink." She said that two large "things" came out of her stomach, one through her anus and the other from her uterus. One of them came out in one piece and the other in smaller pieces. She felt better now, she said. Curiously, in spite of this, she seemed oriented to time, place, and person and appeared to have no delusions.

She had just come back from begging and showed us a plate full of *injera*. (*Injera* is the local flat bread made from *teff*, an endemic grain). She also had received some coins and had paid 10 cents to buy a small amount of Chile pepper. What she would eat today was used *injera* and Chile peppers. I gave her 10 birr (about 7 birr per U.S. Dollar). She was so pleased that she cried, and, to hold back my tears, I gave her 20 birr more. She was so amazed that she fell to her knees and thanked God while kissing my hands in appreciation. From them on, each time I saw her, she continued to ask for help.

As I was walking to the next tent, a young man, David, came up to me whose right hand was bandaged with what appeared to be a discarded rag. He unwrapped it to reveal an acutely infected burn that covered his whole hand. He gave me the prescription for three medications given to him by the doctor. I sent one of my helpers to the pharmacy to get an estimate of the cost. My actions meant that I had committed myself to helping him.

I passed the tent of a friend, Yodit, that was no larger than the size of a small closet. She was sitting alone in the back of her space, her mouth open with fever,

and when she saw me all she seemed to have energy for was to unbend her arm
so she could put her hand out for food.

I made my way into the tent of a 14-year-old orphan girl who was continuing
to waste away since the first time I saw her about 2 months ago. Although I had
talked to her three times, she still had not yet lifted her long curled eyelashes to
meet my eyes. Today her arms were covered with suppurating sores, which were
freshly greased from a jar of medicine that lay in her lap like a sleeping cat. Her
face, had lost its muscle tone, and her eyes had taken on a distant gaze. If it were
possible to see death in someone's face, than this would be its image. When I
asked her what she needed she said, "food and medicine."

I worked for nearly 2 years in Kaliti, a refugee camp outside of Addis Ababa,
as a mental health expert for a WHO-supported project. In addition to my professional skills, being Western meant that people in the camp thought I had a lot of
money. Although the parameters of my wealth were probably substantially exag-
gerated in their eyes, it is sufficient to say that I had enough to improve, if not
save, many people's lives. On the other hand, what I did have, even if I was to
give it all, would never solve all of their problems. The question was how to act,
given my newfound status as a professional, with a great deal of wealth working
in a very impoverished setting.

I did not have an easy answer indeed; much of what transpired throughout this
assignment was in great part my attempt to figure out my moral and professional
response. If I could accept that the people in Kaliti were not suffering as much as
I would have given their circumstances, I could excuse myself for not giving. So
I asked myself, was it possible for people to get accustomed to suffering? Did
losing one's children in a country where children commonly died mean that parents suffered less than a parent, like myself, whose expectation for my children
is health and longevity did?

These and other cross-cultural counseling questions, abstractly presented in
books, became for me (and for other Westerners) a stark reality in the field
(Schrift, 1997; Kleinman, 1980). As a result, one by one Western helpers had
their reasons for not offering material assistance. One told me that she could not
help the people in Kaliti because she was working on a research project and that
giving money would jeopardize the validity of her study. Another said he could
not give because it would only reinforce the stereotype of white people giving to
black people. Another did not want to assist because he felt that the people
would only waste the money, using it to buy *qat* or alcohol instead of what they
"really needed." Others withheld assistance because they thought that the community leaders were corrupt and would take it, or part of it.

When the program started, we had the idea that we could offer mental health
services, and some practical help such as access to a nurse, but that we were not
going to supply material aid. This was appropriate to the Western notion of
avoiding dual relationships. Yet, when we got to know Hiwat, David, Yodit, and
the others, we had to examine the arbitrary line we drew between material aid
and mental health assistance. The more we stuck to the line of offering only
Western-oriented mental health assistance the more the people in the camp

tried to kindle away at our position and find a way to get help for their pressing material needs. They did this by continually chipping away at what we promised, taking any small affirmative gesture as a clear and enduring promise.

THE IMPORTANCE OF MENTAL HEALTH IN HUMANITARIAN AID

In such dire circumstance, what, if any, is the value of counseling? Is it really a fool's errand, a laughable enterprise, given their other priorities? That is what at least one person told me early on in our project. We were at a party when a man in charge of a large international aid office asked me about the nature of my work. When I explained that we were starting a mental health program, he, to be frank, laughed in my face. He said that if he were giving money for aid to Ethiopia, mental health would be far down on the list, certainly behind immunizations, shelter, sanitation, primary health care, and so forth. His list went on for an uncomfortable amount of time. Although I was substantially taken back, I could not dismiss his point. The people's poverty was so striking that their mental health could easily be viewed as an addendum.

It is, of course, naive to believe in serendipitous events, but that seemingly chance encounter proved, over the course of my stay, to be a central point around which my concerns for what we were doing floated. We, as Western-trained counselors, had all inherited what I saw as an ethnocentric scale of values derived by Abraham Maslow, the American psychologist, who defined the basic needs of humans as food and shelter while citing community and spirituality as higher needs (Maslow, 1968). I have come to believe that all these needs are basic, and that, without the so-called higher ones, people who have to compete for the lower needs would never manage, at least not in places like Kaliti where the fight is for very real stakes. Mental health was what differentiated the competition in securing what was necessary to survive. Without mental health, whatever aid was given allowed only temporary respite. With each continued round of assistance people without adequate mental health took a seat further in the back, and in places like Kaliti there was not much room for people at the lower end of the line.

I could have (and probably should have) responded to the aid expert at the party by saying that a single person with a major mental disorder was a significant financial drain on his or her family and community. In addition, the costs and problems of caring for such a person in a developing country were often catastrophic to the whole family. Just because people in developing countries were more likely to be involved in manual labor (and not highly skilled work requiring higher order cognitive skills) did not mean that the mentally ill were less important on the scale of managing family or community welfare. In fact, not only were the mentally ill not able to contribute to the family income, but they caused family members to lose time on their own work in order to care for them. Moreover, their families had to come up with such day-to-day expenses as the additional costs of medical care, the repair of objects broken, and other needs of the mentally ill. And, this is only talking about persons with classic mental disorders. When one considers the lost productivity linked to alcohol, drug abuse, and dependence, the costs are even higher.

I should have told the man at the party right then that differences in mental health (because of emotional and/or cognitive disabilities) often made the difference between those people who would receive essential services and those who would not. In Kaliti, getting what Abraham Maslow referred to as the necessary needs, that is, food and shelter, was a competitive effort requiring both psychic energy and mental alertness. The winners were the most mentally healthy. There was a crucial circularity: mental health decreased as basic needs went unfulfilled; and basic needs were not met because of poor mental health. As time wore on, it became more and more apparent that the level of a person's mental health was what separated those who succumbed from those who survived.

Among the people in Kaliti it was quite easy to see differences with regard to their will to live, as well as in their faith in what the future held in store, and in their degree of fear of everyday life. These are markers for people working in the field of mental health. It was a pity that when donor agencies were making their choices about how to spend their limited funds (or, for that matter, when they were seeking funding from the Western governments or international aid organizations), they had such a hard time convincing people to give money for mental health. My work proved that this is shortsighted. The physical well-being of the displaced, ultimately the question of who will live and who will die, is dependent upon mental health.

This is not to advocate separate mental health clinics or individual counseling for the mentally ill; I am calling for an understanding that community and spirituality and mental health are basic needs. To increase the will to live of a community such as Kaliti means not only giving its members food, shelter, and health. It is equally as basic to help the community stand up for what it needs, to oppose those who are not being forthright about what they should be getting, and to learn to help each other move beyond their dire circumstances. Without food, shelter, and medical care, it is impossible for the community to succeed; but even with these services, success is not likely.

Without realizing it, many aid programs are complexly intertwined with mental health. Counselors, for example, should be able to show that the typical employment projects involving training are uplifting, *while* the people are enrolled in them. But without work to be found *after* the program finishes, the people's well-being in Kaliti fell even further because their expectations were allowed to rise beyond reality. The result was that their mental health, their motivation, and ability to sustain optimism declined.

Even in choosing which aid programs to fund the mental health counselor has much to offer. Because securing work in Ethiopia depended upon who one knew and one's ability to get their favor, it was probably wiser to work on resolving the health care problems than trying to train the displaced for work (unless it meant introducing them to people who would hire them). Improving health actually earned larger yields from the investment dollar than money spent on employment training, and the reason for this was in no small part due to the fact that better physical health led to more sustained mental health than job training without employment.

LEARNING ABOUT CULTURALLY APPROPRIATE COUNSELING FROM DAILY LIFE IN THE STREETS

For a Westerner working in Ethiopia it was impossible to pass a day without being asked for material assistance. At almost every traffic light there were several beggars, any of whom had more than ample reason to be given alms— ex-soldiers without legs or mothers with blind or deformed children. But more than numbers was the fact that beggars with disabilities did not discreetly hide their digitless hands or misarranged feet; instead they seemed to purposely expose them. One unforgettable man stood at military attention in front of the High Court. He was dressed in a dark suit with a tie, but his pant's zipper remained open, exposing testicles the size of small watermelons.

To explain the flaunting of disability I went back to the most important Ethiopian Orthodox legal document, the *Fetha Nagast* (the Law of Kings), written in the 17th century and still used for ecclesiastical law today. It contained several rules pertaining to the responsibility of giving to the unfortunate. One rule stated that by giving a person was earning the support of God. The more a person gave, the more likely he or she was to gain God's favorable attention.

Because the Ethiopian Orthodox Church taught that the act of giving to beggars placed the giver in good standing with God, meeting a beggar on the streets and giving alms was in effect being in church and paying religious tribute. The more obvious one's deformity meant that the more opportunity there was for the able bodied to be generous.

Over the long history of Ethiopia, this relationship spread from begging from people with disabilities to the more general relationships between people of different status. One Western woman who worked in our program related a story of a healthy and nondestitute Ethiopian teenager who had asked her for assistance to go to school. The young man prepared a list of books, priced them, and then asked our colleague to buy him the books. When she said no, the teenager asked her for library privileges in the university library. When our colleague said no again, the teenager asked her for a chair to study at home, and when she said no, he asked for a light to see by. Finally, our colleague, at wit's edge, told him to prepare a written proposal of everything he wanted. The teenager refused to do this and continued to ask in person for other things. While our colleague felt she had redrawn the line of professional propriety far beyond what was appropriate and wrote the boy off as exasperating inappropriate, it was possible to understand the boy's refusal to write his requests in less pejorative terms. For him, putting his requests on paper meant that he could not prostrate himself, not show his inferior status to her, and therefore he would no culturally legitimate his claim.

The culturally acceptable fact that allowed people of lower status to ask in a religious context for assistance from people of higher status with the expectation that the latter had a responsibility for giving led to a serious professional conundrum for Westerners. From their cultural perspective they asked because they thought we Westerner counselors were educated people and therefore of high status, and, by giving to them, we could show our thanks to God for our well-being. When our professional stance dictated a refusal, they felt we were not living up to our responsibility, so they became more persistent, trying even harder to help us, which in fact made us angrier and less likely to help. Our professional secular neutrality moved the interchange from the religious to the secular so that when the beggar asked a religious question, and the answer was secular, we were seen not just as stingy but also as blasphemous.

THE NEXT QUESTION: THE LOGISTICS OF HELPING

Even if a Westerner settled on the moral, professional, and cultural problems associated with giving material assistance, which to be honest, I did in the affirmative, another set of questions loomed up: how to solve the logistical problems of giving help. In my case, I had to deal with the following: Should I give to only some people and face the challenge of favoritism, or should I give to the camp committee expecting that at least some of the money would be siphoned off for "administrative fees"? In either case, and not unimportantly, how would I stop giving after I started?

On one of my revisits to the camp (my first assignment lasted for almost 2 years, which was followed by several return visits over the next 2 years); I was given some $200 from an American friend. He had seen my videotape about the dire circumstances of the people in the camp and wanted to help. I gave some of it out to particular groups in need, one of which was a group of about 120 orphaned adolescents. I called a meeting with them to do this, but even before it started there was jockeying for position. One young man claimed to be an orphan but was not on the list we had made. He kept demanding that I give him something. There were two members of our camp's sports team who had broken their legs while playing in a game. They stayed in the tent and kept asking me for money. One lady who had a partial paralysis, probably due to a stroke, waited in the rain asking for transport money to go to the doctor.

After facing these problems I went into a private tent with four of my assistants to figure out to whom to give the money. I told my helpers that I had been given a fixed amount of money to spend and asked them to make the decisions about how to give it away.

First to enter was Asnake, a 21-year-old war-orphaned boy who was working as a waiter earning 100 birr per month. He had missed the meeting I had with the orphans because of work, and so he had missed 50 birr I gave to the other orphans. Today he was offered only 20 birr.

Next came a man in his thirties wearing a red University of Indiana sweatshirt. He came in with a prescription for an antibiotic. He looked healthy. He was not given any money. Next was an indigent woman who was given 5 birr for food. Then, a woman breastfeeding a baby was also given 5 birr for food.

One old man who had been very helpful in seeing that others in the camp got their Food for Work grain bullied his way in by using his staff to clear his way. He was given 10 birr for food. As it was put into his hand, he said that this was far more generous than necessary, enough for two people. With tears in his eyes he bowed to kiss my knee.

About this time a young man with mental health problems showed up, standing in the doorway blocking the way for others to enter and refusing to leave unless we gave him money. He said he needed money for school and for transport, then showed us his clavicle, which was protruding, and said it was dislocated and he demanded money to go to the doctor. He was refused help and told that the day before he was given money to visit the psychiatric hospital but did not go. He refused to leave. Finally one helper gave him a birr, but this was not enough. He still refused to budge. The stand off lasted several minutes before he was offered another birr. Finally, he left, but only for a short time. He returned twice more causing us to spend less time with the others.

A young man who lost an arm when he stepped on a mine came in next looking for money for transport to a job prospect. He was refused. Then it was a woman who wanted money for transport to visit her children who were being fostered in Addis. She was refused. We continued seeing people and making judgments about their claims for a couple of hours. Of course, as word got out that we were giving money, the crowd rather than diminishing grew. Each person had a case, but eventually we ran out of money, leaving many people still queuing.

As we left the tent, many people said we had previously promised to see them (and in fact this was true for some of them). They all felt they deserved help, and certainly they felt they needed it. What determined who actually got the money was not pretty to examine. Furthermore, I had to consider that the most needy were not even able to get out of bed to ask. It was just logistically impossible to give each of them what they wanted. They would have to accept that we were helpless in meeting all of their demands. They had to understand that not everyone was going to be helped. To try to get to this point across, I tried to understand how Ethiopians viewed mental health and counseling and related that to Western views.

UNDERSTANDING THE ETHIOPIAN POSITION ON COUNSELING

It was estimated that 2.6 million adults and 3 million children suffered from psychiatric disorders in Ethiopia (Ayaya & Aboud, 1993). Normally, their first attempt at cure would be to pray for the good spirits to spit on the evil spirits. If this did not bring relief, the next step was to go to the church for spiritual guidance. If that failed, then it was common to go to natural healers.

There were several types of healers, *zar* spirits, wizards, shamans, and others. Cures included drinking holy water, divination of leaves, eating ash without water, beating and burning, animal sacrifices, and the application of animal blood. In all cases, the therapeutic goal was to relieve the person of the effects of the demons and to teach the sufferer how to accommodate the possessing spirits.

Without judging these remedies, I found it worthwhile to list the differences between them and what we used in the West. For example, take the physical setting where treatment took place. In Ethiopia mental health services were provided in the church or in an area designated for its spiritual value. In the West mental health services were provided in the doctor's office or other types of professional and sectarian spaces.

There were many other comparisons. When Ethiopians went to a traditional healer for psychological problems, they supplicated themselves to God or to other forms of the supernatural. In the West a client formed a professional alliance with a healer, and expected healing to come from secular theories based on natural science principles.

In Ethiopia the client had no power in the counseling relationship and trusted his weakness to the all-powerful priest or traditional healer, while in the West counseling was conceived as a reasoned dialog between counselor and client.

The Western client expected that therapy would include occasional emotional arousal, but mostly the Western client expected to have controlled verbal recollections of past and current events. Among traditional Ethiopians clients expected to be taken over by spiritual possession. In the West the client was expected to learn to react to social situations differently, or to control his or her behavior, or to make cognitive changes. Ethiopian clients expect to be told what to do, which was often done in an elaborate ceremony.

A healer in Ethiopia went through training and passed through the rites of passage within a religious context. This was different than attending graduate school. While the Ethiopian's training called for accepting the unknown, the Westerner is trained to find rationale truth. The Ethiopian healer was more likely to receive insight into the clinical process from prayer than at academic conferences.

Even the idioms used in clinical communication show the same distinction. In the West they were primarily verbal and rationale, while in Ethiopia they were composed of a special semiotic language, one of trance and possession (of riders controlling horses). Likewise, the explanatory models of causation, which in the West were environmental and physical, were in Ethiopia spiritual and animistic. In short, the philosophy behind mental health services in the West was secular humanism and the therapy democratic. In Ethiopia the philosophy was religious and the practice authoritarian (see Kleinman, 1988 for more information on how to compare the causes of mental health problems and therapies across cultures).

ETHIOPIANS GIVING TO ETHIOPIANS, PUBLIC HEALTH COUNSELING

Even from the time of the arrival of the first Europeans in the 19th century, the Amhara of high status sponsored yearly feasts (*giber*) for the indigent. They also had clubs (*sembete*) whose purpose was to give to the poor. According to historians (see Iliffe, 1987; Pankhurst, 1990 for more details), by giving the wealthy helped the people of low socioeconomic status feel that they would be taken care of by the rich and powerful and thus more likely to feel indebted to them, which made them more valuable. As an old Ethiopian saying goes, "The poor served a purpose by enabling others to be charitable," (Iliffe, 1987, p. 25).

There is a significant body of research in anthropology on gifts; which in essence says that the reason for giving ranges on a continuum form altruistic "pure gifts" to "real barter," meaning that people gave with the idea that they would get something later in return. There is also considerable information about the exchange of gifts, which is thought to have the function of maintaining social obligations. Whether the gift is given altruistically or in self-interest remains open to debate and is quite possibly unsolvable (see Malinowski, 1926; Parry, 1985; Schrift, 1997 for more information) but that it increased social solidarity seemed valid in Ethiopia.

While reciprocity was central to social affairs, it had particular boundaries. There was reciprocity for family and within religious institutions, but there were rarely gifts from the state or from civic organizations for the general welfare. This explained why we experienced generosity on the one hand and the lack of it on the other. While it was common for a family to share their last morsels with one another, the government felt that the 3 kg of wheat per day each displaced family received from the Food for Work (FFW) program was too much. This was in the face of the fact that the grain was not a gift from the government; it came from foreign donors who gave it as international aid. In fact, the Ethiopian government from Haile Selassie's time to the present periodically told foreign donors that they could not just give assistance. Foreign governments would have to pay an import tax on their donations before their aid could enter the country, thus robbing its own citizens of what in the end often turned out to be their lives.

When I was meeting with the orphans to give them the donated money, a man came in saying his sister was deathly ill. She was taking medicine for anemia, and as a result there was no money for food. I told him I would come by before I left. Then I told Guiday, an orphan boy, who I had known quite well to loan him 5 birr and then get 6 birr back later. (He would have the money because he was going to get 50 birr). Everyone laughed at the idea that I should ask Guiday to loan the man money. Yet, it made perfect sense to me. I tried to explain to the orphans that Guiday had come into some money from a gift I was able to give him, which he did not need immediately: so why should he not become a banker and help someone who needed it now while earning a little for himself? Would this not also possibly help them become more involved in the camp?

I was hoping that after my 2 years of counseling, this group of young people, who were at the bottom of the scale even in Kaliti, because they had no family, and who were dependent upon the goodwill of others, might see themselves as being benefactors. As we went over this, it occurred to me that these war orphans were characters in Plato's Republic. Plato warned that the strength of the family (and of religious groups) worked against the well-being of the civic government. The stronger the family, the more unlikely it would be that those in need without family would suffer. Indeed, later when one young orphan, Soloman was dying of AIDS (acquired immunodeficency syndrome) he pleaded to have someone kill him. All he needed he said was a single injection. He reasoned that since he had no family he would die a lonely death.

SOME ASPECTS OF OUR COUNSELING PROGRAM

The goals of our community mental health program were to get people active in solving their problems and to have them become good citizens toward each other. Each of which seemed obvious to the Westerner, but foreign to the Ethiopian culture, where it was common to accept God's will rather than to challenge circumstances. Given our major cultural and professional differences, what could we Western counselors do? The first problems we had were forming a therapeutic alliance and identifying the client. It was our idea to treat the whole camp as an individual client in crisis. Eventually, Westerner counselors working with children and families in particularly difficulty circumstances in the developing world would have to accept the fact that there are always more problems than can be solved and not enough material resources and personnel to meet the basic needs. In short there is no other choice but to work with the whole, although this did not necessarily mean that individuals should be ignored.

We did very little one-on-one interviewing and utilized none of the more modern techniques currently in vogue with Western clients suffering from posttraumatic stress disorder (PTSD), such as relaxation training and eye movement desensitization (Shaprio, 1995), which we found to be culturally inappropriate and too costly. Nor did we have a great deal of success with active listening skills (Rogers, 1980) because lecturing in a loud voice was more of a culturally appropriate way of expressing concern (and, thereby, of being heard). About the only Western theory that we used was a variation of reality therapy (Glasser, 1998). The cognitive model helped us to get people to accept their situation (Meichenbaum, 1977; Rotter, 1982).

Working with the camp as client had to be mitigated by the fact that not everyone in the camp needed the same mental health plan. In Kaliti there were the physically ill who were emotionally strong. On the other hand, there were the physically weak and dying who were not emotionally coping. In these latter cases, the lack of health care smacked the effort of empowerment and the efforts of group counseling in the face. (Nevertheless, we learned that paying regular visits, listening, and touching was valuable in helping these people come to accept their fate).

In some cases their mental disorders were made more difficult because of their physical illnesses. In the case of AIDS the community shunned these people because they feared that they were contagious. To some extent the same could be said of those with leprosy and epilepsy. There were also the more clearly defined psychiatric patients. In these cases, psychotropic medication was needed. Our job was to see that they took their medicine and that the dose was appropriate. Added to these groups of people were the many who were not ill themselves but who had to treat and deal with the loss of their loved ones who were ill. Grief was, in fact, as rampant as lack of health. In dealing with these stressors, we could rely on the mechanisms within the culture that helped people with grieving and supported those in mourning [for further discussion see Aptekar (in press), Aptekar & Giel (in press), and Aptekar & Stocklin (1996)].

In the face of all the difficulties, we had to remember that there were those who were very resilient. One was Mama Zewde, who had buried three children since being displaced but who still was able to dance in public ceremonies. Another was Ato Abdu, a one-legged-man, who fostered an orphaned girl with leprosy. There was Mulu's stepfather who spent his days with Mulu's 2-year-old hemipoligic daughter on his lap, smiling; and the elderly lonely Lumlum who found pleasure from fostering the orphaned Frazier. And there was resilience in the motivation to succeed of the high school students who studied, in my camp helpers, and in a surprising number of other young people. They needed public recognition for what they had done, not only for themselves but so the community might be aware of what they had done and others might see the possibilities. In the case of the young people, they needed opportunities to move on with their lives. Indeed, in the case of the youth, the community did relax its restrictions and allowed them more freedom to move into the secular culture, which was one reason why they fared as well as they did (see Aptekar, Paardekooper, & Kuebli, 2000).

These people were very different from those who were simply unable to function, like Abana, the woman with eight children she could not feed. She could only survive by getting assistance because not much skill building could be done with her or others like her, because of their low functioning abilities. Some groups in Kaliti simply needed advice and opportunity. We were able to help them by opening doors, by training them in presenting themselves to government officials who might help them, and by encouraging them to move forward in getting what they deserved. Just knowing that their claims were legitimate and that the process of rebuilding their lives was possible was important to them.

With regard to forming a therapeutic relationship, I had learned from my work with clients in crisis that it was often valuable to allow clients in crisis to become temporarily dependent on the counseling relationship. Rather then fostering independence immediately, even though that was an ultimate goal, many people in the camp still needed support. Most of the displaced people in Kaliti were not able to see that, what had appeared to be a never-ending low, was, in fact, only a far too long lull in yet a still long life to be lived. They were not yet ready to fight their own demons. By being able to rely on us in the short term, they were building their forces to fight their problems in the long term.

Furthermore, I learned that it was during the time of crisis that therapeutic outcomes were lost or won. If the counselor could extend care that exceeded the client's expectations, the person in crisis was ready to join in on a therapeutic relationship, perhaps more so than at any other time. In no small amount this was because people in crisis felt the full value of extra care. The difficulties we experienced in working out a relationship of trust with the camp and the constant bickering over what and if we would give material assistance, was, in fact, symptomatic of their difficulty in facing the crises in which they lived. The people of the camp could use the strength provided by a crisis counseling relationship, one that would allow them, in the short run, to be dependent and to see that we cared about them beyond the ordinary. In the long run, this would help them regain their ability to master their environment and go far in having them trust us and thus join in a therapeutic relationship with us.

But trust is not easily won in a situation such as Kaliti. We had some hard facts to face. We were not able to just slide up to their children (their lack of hygiene and aggressive demands were often overwhelming). We had, during the course of the program, allowed the camp to be used in promotional efforts without being able to offer the people material assistance. Obviously, we could not continue along this path and receive their trust or reach our objectives. However, we had some things going for us. Two things separated me from the other people working in Kaliti: my tenacity and longevity. I came to the camp for the long haul and it was not easy to get me not to come.

I can add a third factor that helped; I liked being with them in the camp—or at least most of them. To the people in Kaliti it was apparent who liked being in Kaliti and who was just putting in their time in order to earn some points toward getting a better job, or a certificate, or something else. I found sitting in their tents, drinking coffee with them, and listening to them a source of enjoyment. It was rewarding to be able to get to know them on a personal level. This gave me personal satisfaction and professional credence.

As much as I saw them as tragic survivors, I also felt them to be my teachers. I believed I could learn from them how to survive tragedy and live without unnecessary material comforts. They came to know that in my having things to learn from them, they could take in what I had to offer them, particularly in terms of ideas about improving their mental health. This brought me a degree of acceptance that came to be the base upon which we approached each other.

We moved forward when we realized that it was enough to be able to work closely with their everyday issues of food and illness. It was not solving their dire situation that counted; it was working on them that counted. Helping them sometimes meant no more than holding the hand of the sick and dying, thereby reinforcing the fact that human life had value, that all their lives were valuable. No matter how miserable their material existence had become, we showed them through daily concern that they were worthy of care.

Sometimes just very basic factors loomed larger than we had imagined. For example, I cannot overstate how important adequate information is for mental health. Just by helping people in the camp know more of what the government was offering, what other resources were available to them, and, finally, to know which information was accurate and which was not made them feel as if their problems could be more manageable.

FINAL REFLECTIONS

The ideas I am presenting here have evolved throughout my work in Kaliti (which indeed rested upon my former work in somewhat similar situations). Still they represent much agonizing, frustration, and plenty of new humility. What I came to understand in Kaliti was that therapeutic technique did not have to rely on the basic idea of individual counseling in the Western tradition, talking about what brought the person sadness. What I learned in Kaliti was to act as a person with integrity who puts himself in the middle of wretchedness. I tried to create a special spiritual place, where people could retreat, to find meaning and hope in the midst of misery. When I encouraged the young people to have fun so they could replace the childhood they had lost, I was trying to set an example for the community to follow. When I sat with them in their tents slowly drinking coffee recalling the small pleasantries that life still provided for them, I wanted to let them know that enjoyment was still possible. In short I tried to create a space that gave them all some reprieve.

To do this I found it necessary to go against the grain of common Western practice, that a counselor should not be overinvolved with his clients (Remley & Herlihy, 2001). A model for me, in this regard was Rene, a Dutch attorney who gave up his profession in order to help street children in Brazil. He became "too" involved, according to the authorities, with the way the children were being treated by these authorities, that he was forced to leave Brazil with 24 hours notice. He then took up residence in Maputo (where he still resides), carrying out one of the more interesting and effective programs for street children.

He developed a level of respect for the children that went beyond the ordinary and that worked toward lifting up their self-esteem, which, in turn, made the children more capable of coping with their lives. What was unique about his program was that he did not accept the standard procedures, which had always been accepted without question. He pointed out that what was seen as legitimate care for the children was in fact far below standards. By his challenging what was the standard fare, the children felt that they were children not simply "street kids."

I can remember when he and I and several other people were on an official visit to what was considered an outstanding program for street children in sub-Saharan Africa, Lusaka, Zambia. While we watched, the children were being fed some thin meat stew, sloppily ladled out from two institutionally sized pots by an elder street boy. Everyone looked on approvingly, commenting on how well the kids were eating; Rene alone complained. He announced publicly that this food was fit only for dogs, and, more importantly, that the scene reminded him more of a prison camp than a family. Of course, he was right, but none of us had seen this until he pointed it out. We had universally judged the kids, because they were poor street children, as subhuman and thus deserving to eat as if they were dogs who should be grateful for whatever scraps that were offered.

Rene, however, in his own work, bought the animals for his children "on the hoof," and taught the kids how to butcher them. In addition, each child had a plate and utensils and ate with dignity. Not only did he feed them better (and more cheaply, as it turned out), he was also aware of the symbolic nature of eating. His kids ate like a family, not like chickens stuffed into industrial feeders. As a consequence, they assumed the dignity of family members rather than surly combativeness of dogs boarded at a kennel.

CONCLUSION

Early in the program, we learned that Sister Mary, a Catholic from the Italian Comboni order, the order that specialized in working with "outcasts," had been providing a feeding program for the indigent in the neighborhood for several years. The first time I met her, in a rather long-winded account of her work, Sister Mary told me that it was difficult to work in Ethiopia because at a fundamental level one could never finish the job. Usually when people said that it was difficult to work in Ethiopia, they meant that it was difficult to work with the government. Or, we had heard from people trying to counsel in the camp, that it was difficult to work in Ethiopia because the people never stopped asking for help; no matter what they were given they were never satisfied. After dismissing these possibilities I thought what Sister Mary meant was that the problems were far greater than the resources to solve them, and in one way she did mean that. Later I learned that she really wanted to say was that God's work was never done.

I remember leaving Sister Mary's compound one day. There was a young Oromo woman from Kaliti with a 10-month-old girl waiting to see her. The little girl had been completely burned over her face. A soiled white piece of cotton cloth was wrapped around her head, like she had a toothache so that it was still possible to see a gag inducing red pimple, the size of an apple, protruding from the cornea of one eye. As the woman reached out to say hello to Sister Mary, I could see that the fingers of her hands were burned to the stubs. Sister Mary welcomed her in her arms and complained to the girl's mother that the child had a runny nose.

Sister Mary had developed her modus operandi, one that was filled with caveats, judgments, exceptions, and broken rules. In short a system devised, probably as subconsciously as consciously, to keep her going. She had continued by finding a way to ignore the incurable obvious and embrace the barest of possibilities.

As for myself, I was never able to accept the significant degree of lauding I received from many people in the camp (and most Westerners upon my return home), who assumed I was a martyr, working selflessly for the well-being of the poor. While it is true that for many people the main draw of humanitarian aid and psychosocial counseling in this context is the desire to be a savior to the poor, it was only partially true for me. After I came back to American, many people expressed a kind of reverent stance toward what I had done, as if I had gained stature by slumming the worst of circumstances. But knowing my more complex motivations for slumming, which because it was beyond normal experience had for me its own draw, I was not able to gather satisfaction from their solicitations.

Acute conditions were common in Kaliti, the depths of which were rarely encountered in the West. I was able to measure the degree of physical suffering by the stages of bargaining the sick made, at least this is how I can explain it to my Western colleagues. In the West most of us have been sick enough to know that there is a stage where we wished only to be left alone. We also have another familiar stage, a time when we talk to ourselves about our past behaviors ready to make amends if only we can recover from the illness. There is even another depth familiar in the West, that of praying to God to end the illness. Maybe there are some Westerners who are so sick that they have experienced the next step, pleading with God to end their lives. Here, like with my friend Soloman, illness finally reaches the place where the body does not respond to anything outside of itself, where it is impossible to lift one's head or even offer a smile of gratitude. At this place even the psyche shuts down to zero, already having offered itself to the winds of despair and finding no response. In my case being exposed to these kinds of earthly realities was certainly a part of my attraction, perhaps more than I wanted to let on, even to myself.

But this was only part of it; there was also the fact that I found myself in the here-to-fore unimaginable position of being a wealthy philanthropist. I was able to put myself in a common man's dream, "if you won the lottery, how would you use it for the betterment of humanity"? When I took *this* opportunity, I found it an immense burden, but correspondingly, a rare opportunity to mix professionalism with a spiritual life.

REFERENCES

Aptekar, L. (in press). The changing developmental dynamics of "children in particularly difficult circumstances": Examples of street and war traumatized children. In U. Gielen. & J. Roopnarine (Eds.), *Childhood and adolescence in cross-cultural perspective*. Westport, CT: Greenwood.

Aptekar, L., & Giel, R. (in press). Walks in Kaliti, life in a shelter. In J. de Jong (Ed.), *Trauma war and violence: Public mental health in the socio-cultural context*. New York: Plenum-Kluwer.

Aptekar, L., Paardekooper, B., & Kuebli, J. (2000). Adolescence and youth among displaced Ethiopians: A case study in Kaliti camp. *International Journal of Group Tensions, 29*(1–2), 101–135.

Aptekar, L., & Stocklin, D. (1996). Growing up in particularly difficult circumstances: A cross-cultural perspective. In J. Berry, P.R. Dasen, & T.S. Saraswathi (Eds.), *Handbook of cross-cultural psychology (2nd ed.). Vol. 2: Basic processes and development psychology* (pp. 377–412). Boston: Allyn & Bacon.

Ayaya, M., & Aboud, F. (1993). Mental ilness. In H. Kloos & A. Zein (Eds.), *The ecology of health and disease in Ethiopia* (pp. 493–506). Boulder, CO: Westview.

Glasser, W. (1998). *Choice theory: A new psychology of personal freedom.* New York: HarperCollins.

Iliffe, J. (1987). *The African poor: A history.* Cambridge: Cambridge University Press.

Kleinman, A. (1980). *Patients and healers in the context of culture.* Berkeley, CA: University of California Press.

Kleinman, A. (1988). *Rethinking psychiatry.* New York: Free Press.

Maslow, A. (1968). *Toward a psychology of being.* (2nd ed.). New York: Harper & Row.

Malinowski, B. (1926). *Argonauts of the Western Pacific.* London: Routledge & Kegan Paul.

Meichenbaum, D. (1977). *Cognitive behavior modification.* New York: Plenum.

Pankhurst, R. (1990). *A social history of Ethiopia.* Addis Ababa: Institute of Ethiopian Studies.

Parry, J. (1985). The gift, the Indian gift, and the "Indian gift." *Man, 21*(3), 453–473.

Remley, T., & Herlihy, B. (2001). *Ethical, legal, and professional issues in counseling.* Upper Saddle River, NJ: Merrill Prentice Hall.

Rogers, C. (1980). *A way of being.* Boston: Houghton Mifflin.

Rotter, J. (1982). *The development and applications of social learning theory: Selected papers.* New York: Praeger.

Schrift, A. (Ed.) (1997). *The logic of the gift: Toward an ethic of generosity.* New York: Routledge.

Shapiro, F. (1995). *Eye movement desensitization and reprocessing.* New York: Guilford.

Chapter 29

Global Perspectives on Refugee Mental Health: Reflections from "Down Under"

Alan Chapman

INTRODUCTION

New Zealand began its formal humanitarian commitment to provide sanctuary for refugees in response to the major dislocations of people in Europe during World War II. Since 1944, New Zealand has resettled approximately 25,000 refugees and displaced persons (NZIS, 2001).

The provision of specialist services to assist these settlers cope with the traumatic experiences they had endured has a somewhat more recent history. Not until a national conference in 1987 highlighted this issue of refugee trauma (Abbott, 1989) did efforts become focused, albeit the needs being obvious to those who were already involved. A further 10 years passed before the first dedicated mental health service for refugees was developed. Even now the existence of specialized torture and trauma support agencies is limited to two major centers of resettlement.

Wellington Refugees as Survivors (RAS) Centre is one of these agencies. We commenced our work in 1997 with a staff comprised of full- and part-time professional counselors/psychotherapists and a part-time psychiatrist. The clients we have seen in our agency are mainly from the Horn of Africa countries and the Middle East.

Consequently, our experience of delivering services to this client group is relatively new, is still evolving, and is developing in some interesting ways. Our journey has been interesting in that it has challenged our initial expectations and has been developed against a background of a host culture that has a well-developed response to the issues of biculturalism rather than multiculturalism.

THE NEW ZEALAND REFUGEE
RESETTLEMENT EXPERIENCE

Like many countries whose history includes colonization, New Zealand has been settled over the centuries by "migrant" groups. From the earliest settlements established by Maori (circa AD 1100–1300) to the first European arrivals (1600–1700) (Sinclair, 1959) and later conquestorial "takeovers," New Zealand has been the final destination of those needing to find sanctuary for a variety of reasons. Frequently the reasons were economic, but often people came to avoid social or political persecution.

Following World War II, initially refugees were Polish children and their guardians. In subsequent years many other people displaced from Europe arrived. As theaters of human tragedy have continued throughout the 20th century, New Zealand has continued to be responsive (see Table 29.1), within the bounds of what politicians perceive to be appropriate to our resources. More recently the nationalities resettled have become more diverse, although the numbers continue to be limited to an annual quota (see Table 29.2). A critical aspect of the process by which the quota is selected is that the New Zealand government allows the

Table 29.1
Major Nationalities of Refugees Resettled in New Zealand (1944–2000)

1944	Polish children and their guardians
1949–1952	Displaced Europeans
1956–1958	Hungarians
1962–1971	Chinese (in Hong Kong and Indonesia)
1965	Russian Christians, "Old Believers" from China
1968–1971	Czechoslovaks
1972–1973	Asian Ugandans
1974–1981	Chileans
1974–1991	Eastern Europeans (Polish, Czechoslovaks, Hungarians, Bulgarians, Romanian, Yugoslavs, Soviets)
1975–2000	Indochinese: Vietnamese, Cambodian, and Laotian
1979–2000	Iranian
1988–2000	Iraqi
1992–2000	Bosnian, Somali, Sri Lankan, Ethiopian, Sudanese
1999–2000	Afghani
2000	Burmese

Source: From NZIS (2001, April). Copyright 2001 by New Zealand Immigration Service. Reprinted with permission of author.

Table 29.2
Number of Arrivals in New Zealand under the Refugee Resettlement Program by Nationality and Fiscal Year (1994–1995 to 1999–2000)

Nationality	1994–1995	1995–1996	1996–1997	1997–1998	1998–1999	1999–2000
Afghani	—	—	—	—	41	26
Bosnian	21	4	4	3	—	—
Burundian	—	13	—	17	—	20
Congolese	—	13	—	17	—	20
Eritrean	—	21	—	10	47	26
Ethiopian	50	130	72	151	199	131
Iranian	6	—	24	70	39	2
Iraqi	318	136	266	241	130	52
Laotian	—	5	62	—	—	36
Somali	39	299	21	137	212	207
Sri Lankan	21	25	12	3	—	7
Sudanese	8	—	14	10	33	70
Vietnamese	341	116	23	8	—	60
Yugoslav	—	—	3	—	—	27
Other	18	31	26	27	22	26
Total	**822**	**780**	**527**	**677**	**726**	**716**

Source: From NZIS (2001, April) Copyright 2001 by New Zealand Immigration Service. Reprinted with permission of author.

Office of the High Commissioner for Refugees to determine the annual intake population, comprised of those refugees "targeted (as being) in greatest need of resettlement" (NZIS, 2001).

THE NEW ZEALAND SETTING—OUR BICULTURAL JOURNEY

The honoring of complex and controversial legal obligations and the evolution of biculturalism has had an important impact on the development of New Zealand society over recent decades. It has involved a journey in which the colonizers have attempted to reconcile its differences with those colonized, the indigenous Maori people. This has involved an acknowledgment of past travesties, an acceptance of difference, and the institutionalization of a process for reconciliation.

Since the arrival of European settlers, there has been the long slow transition from policies of conquest, segregation, assimilation, integration, and, finally, to partnership. This means that there is much in New Zealand institutional structures, laws, and awareness that can accommodate the differences presented by refugees. This is not to suggest that New Zealand society is free from prejudice and intolerance. It does, however, speak to the stage of the "journey" that New Zealand has reached and the enhanced possibilities for successful resettlement outcomes for refugees today.

CURRENT WORK WITH REFUGEES IN NEW ZEALAND

The experience of working with refugees today is influenced by a number of key factors. The combination of these factors is what has determined the clinical/therapeutic approach that our agency has evolved in its short history. The key factors are:

- Range of ethnic groups that have been included in the annual quota
- Culturally determined attitudes to trauma and to problem solving
- Family, rather than individualistic, focus of the client communities
- Government policies for the reunification of families
- Skills and attitudes of the agency's (RAS) staff

As is obvious from the information contained in Tables 29.1 and 29.2, New Zealand has settled small numbers of a diverse range of refugee communities. New Zealand's geographical isolation further complicates the ability of people to keep contact with their families and familiar social networks. Not only does the distance and the perceived (as well as the real) barriers that such distance presents exacerbate the loss of contact, but the relatively small size of the communities in New Zealand presents significant social difficulties. There are insufficient fellow community members to offer mutual support, familiarity (such as opportunities to converse in one's native tongue), the continuance of social practices (such as marriage prospects), and community leadership (from elders, healers, spiritual leaders). Consequently, there is a greater reliance on the host country's largesse and a forced dependency on support agencies. This runs at odds with the goal of reempowerment, which is so important to those who have been so disempowered.

Aristotle (2001a) develops these observations when he notes, from his Australian experience, that:

Separation from or loss of family members is a common consequence of the refugee experience. Refugee communities, meanwhile, may be limited in their capacity to convey the protective effects of personal relationships and social support. This may be due variously to the emergent nature of communities, the collective consequences of exposure to trauma and torture, and divisions within communities, often stemming from conflict in the country of origin. (p. 6)

If this is the reality for refugees settling in Australia, with the numbers that it accepts, then it is even more influential for those settling in New Zealand.

CULTURE AND MENTAL HEALTH PRACTICES
FOR NEW ZEALAND REFUGEES

Much has been written about culture and its impact on the delivery of mental health services, especially to traumatized refugees [for discussion see Bemak, Chung, & Bornemann (1996), Bracken, Giller, & Summerfield (1997), Cariceo

(1998), and Tribe (1999)]. Our work has reinforced all the fallacies that arise from assuming that "Western" psychological paradigms are universally applicable. The underlying tenets of much psychological theory and practice assume the existence of concepts of self and a reliance on degrees of introspection. When these are not part of one's worldview, they are next to useless for the clinicians working cross culturally.

Adams and Gilbert's (1998) review of the literature relating to those factors that create barriers to counseling with cultural minorities identified a number of pertinent matters. These comprised the workers' training and experience, communication styles, rules and conventions, values, cultural biases, and power. Reference is also made to Sue and Zane's (1987) findings on service appropriateness. A high drop-out rate (50%) after the first session among ethnic minority groups reflects the "talking past each other" experience (i.e., a mismatch between client and worker's expectations).

This is consistent with our early experience with clients. While we commenced our work with clients assuming that we would be "trauma therapists," we have been taught very clearly by our clients that they require different skills from us. Typically, clients do not present with the need to "resolve" their torture and trauma experiences. The clients we see are more likely to indicate that those are matters from their past and they have no wish to revisit such issues. In fact, any attempt to explore their trauma story is met with strong resistance stemming from a fear of being flooded by horrific memories; the same memories that usually feature so prominently in their regular and distressing nightmares. Mollica (1989) has long since questioned the presumption that ventilation of thoughts and feelings is appropriate for all. Blackwell (1989) has suggested that the imposition of a host community's dominant therapeutic ideology risks repeating the processes of colonization. Consequently, we at RAS are more likely to be asked to assist with other matters that are perceived to be the causes of their current difficulties.

FAMILY REUNIFICATION

Maslow (1954) long ago proposed the existence of a hierarchy of human needs. Satisfaction of needs, and progress up the hierarchy, was dependent on sufficient satisfaction of lower order needs. This theory has relevance to the expectations that clients have of us as "supporters." Frequently the requests we have for assistance relate to either basic needs (such as housing, welfare income, or employment) or family reunification. It may well be that we never touch on the trauma history. If we do, it is likely to be either as part of satisfying family reunification application requirements for immigration or after a client has been engaged with the service for 3 to 6 months. By that stage they have found no other means of alleviating the pain of their overpowering symptoms and developed sufficient trust in the worker to risk disclosure.

As has already been noted, focusing on the family of clients coming from "collectivist" cultures presents enormous challenges to the policies and capacities of host countries. Cotton (2001) notes that "once the definition of family is extended beyond the standard Western concept of the 'nuclear' family, then reunification requests can quickly spiral upwards, soon becoming potentially impossible to contain" (p. 1).

FAMILY REUNIFICATION POLICIES AND IMPLICATIONS FOR REFUGEES

Policies permitting family reunification are, therefore, restrictive and complex. Our clients, however, have such an overwhelming obligation to family that this becomes the entire concentration of their resettlement energies, despite the distress of their own circumstances. For most refugees their absent family members are living in the same circumstances that they themselves left. The awareness of the perils in which family members are living is a further catalyst driving the resettled refugee to seek any opportunity to fulfill his or her family obligations.

Under the provisions of New Zealand Immigration Service (NZIS) policy, one possible means of achieving entry for family is through application on humanitarian grounds. This policy permits the presentation of a case based on grounds of serious emotional or physical harm threatening either the New Zealand resident or his or her family member still living in another country. For the category of serious emotional harm, the verification process requires a report from a psychiatrist attesting to the degree of emotional harm being endured. The supporting evidence required is quite specific and the threshold for "serious" is high.

This policy has a number of contentious and ubiquitous implications. The perverse incentive of the policy is for applicants to present as seriously impaired as is possible. The greater the emotional impairment the better the chance of having a humanitarian application accepted. The requirement that only psychiatrists can complete such reports, while aimed at ensuring a level of reliability, puts an enormous financial pressure on applicants, for the following reasons. An agency such as ours, with 8 hours per week of psychiatry time, is unable to meet the demands for such reports. This means that those wishing to apply under these provisions must seek reports from psychiatrists in the private sector. The cost of such a report is high, involving 3 to 4 hours of clinical time. This places a huge financial burden on people who are predominantly surviving on welfare benefit incomes, sending money to family overseas, paying application fees for the immigration application, and then, if they are successful, the airfares for the family members, as well as support after they arrive.

It appears that, despite the obvious hurdles presented by this policy, a large number of our clients are prepared to endure the hardships required to submit an application, frequently amidst extreme pressure from the waiting family. Cotton (2001) reflects that:

Many resettled refugees receive pleading or accusing letters or calls from relatives wishing to join them in their new country. There is often little understanding or belief, among remaining family members, about the difficulties faced by newly settled refugees. Many refugees come from societies in which bribery and corruption is rife. It is difficult (both for newly arrived and remaining family members) to believe that there is usually no way "around" or "through the system." (p. 1)

The need to explore every opportunity is exacerbated by the knowledge that some applications are successful, usually in what are seen to be the "same circumstances." Unsuccessful applicants are thus perceived, or perceive themselves, as not having tried hard enough. And so the pressures mount and the mental health risks increase.

SERVICE DELIVERY ISSUES

The funding that supports our nongovernmental organization comes from Vote: Health, central government's budget for public health services. The requirements for public mental health expenditure are that services are to be delivered to those most in need, currently determined to be the 3% of the population with the most severe mental health disorders, as defined by the *Diagnostic and Statistical Manuals*, fourth edition (DSM IV) or the *International Classification of Diseases*, tenth edtion (ICD 10). While torture and trauma victims have little difficulty "complying" with this specification, the risk of medicalization of client services is high. Given what has already been shown above as the inadequacies of such a culturally bound approach, this presents us with an ongoing ethical dilemma.

Aristotle (2001b) states that: "A sound conceptual framework is important in ensuring that services are primarily determined by the needs of the individual and community as opposed to personal or professional preference of people engaged to provide services . . . a framework which promotes a systemic and holistic approach is highly desirable when working with refugees and survivors of torture" (p. 2). To this can be added the dictates of policymakers and funders.

This thinking is very much behind the service configurations that we have developed. Initially this came from the manner in which we were established. Local community groups, who already worked with refugees and migrants, were eager for clients to have access to appropriate services to support those who were exposed to traumatic experiences. Some of these agencies (an interpreting service, ESOL [English Speakers of other Languages] tutors, and a resettlement service) already shared offices. Two parallel processes then came together—a community-based lobby group was successful in obtaining funding for the establishment of trauma treatment services and funding was also obtained for the creation of an expanded "one-stop-shop," the Multicultural Services Centre (MSC), of agencies providing services to refugees and migrants.

This was a philosophically driven plan to ensure that resettling refugees and migrants could get easier access to a range of complementary services. An original hope of having a primary health care service as part of this MSC lost out when the logistics and costs became prohibitive.

SERVICE DELIVERY MODEL

While this provided a solution to the debate that Aristotle (2001a) describes as polarizing the relative merits of a medical or clinical based model of operation as opposed to a more community-based operation, it still left us to learn about the model of service delivery that clients would find most acceptable. The major influence on this evolution was the shared attitudes among the inaugural staff. This team placed a higher priority on client-centered services than adherence to a particular therapeutic model.

Although the founding staff training backgrounds were mixed—psychology and social work predominated—there was common belief in the need to deliver services in culturally appropriate ways. This was made easier by the staff's own cultural expertise and the specialist skills that this team contributed. From the beginning the variety of training backgrounds has become ever more diverse. The agency's "style" has been developed with input from staff trained in Bosnia, Greece, New Zealand, United Kingdom, United States, Colombia, Cambodia, Australia, and France.

The challenge has been to find some framework on which to "hang" the various factors that contribute to the context of our work. Specifically, the relevant factors have been:

- Expectations of stakeholders, namely clients, funders, and allied health/welfare agencies
- Skills, attitudes, and knowledges of the staff
- Predominant problems with which clients present, for example, family reunification needs
- Resource constraints (staff numbers are small, currently 4.5 FTEs [Full Time Equivalent])
- New Zealand's immigration policies
- Reliance on overseas research and models of service delivery

When it became clear that our clinical training needed to supplement rather than direct our interventions, the place for Maslow's model to inform our practice approach was evident. A social work model was also relevant. This combines "a dual focus on (a) the empowerment of clients (be they individuals, families groups or communities) to find their own solutions, and (b) to learn from the experience of clients" and "to inform the society at large about the injustices in its midst, and to engage in action to change the structure of society that create and perpetuate injustice" (NZASW, 1993, p. 1). This was a comfortable fit with our experience of working with clients who had little experience of "counseling" or put little value on the act of sharing intimate feelings with people who were not family members, elders, or spiritual leaders.

In our search for a conceptual framework to support our empirical observations, one article presented us with the opportunity to put substance to our wonderings, or more accurately flounderings! Atkinson, Thompson, and Grant (1993) were critical of the "counseling profession's" reliance on the "psychotherapy role" when working with ethnic minority clients.

While they acknowledge that there has been an increased awareness in counseling circles of the need for cultural sensitivity and awareness, they suggest that the polarized internal change versus external change ideologies are each incomplete on their own. Their approach is to be multifactorial; their model combines many of the known "bits" of importance to cross-cultural work into a cohesive framework. The crucial factors incorporated into their model are:

- client's level of acculturation
- locus of the problem's etiology
- goals of helping

While some of the roles are beyond those allowed within Western mainstream helping profession training (i.e., advisor), they are more consistent with the range of expectations that our clients have of us than anything else we have otherwise seen conceptualized. The beauty of this model for the practitioners is that it very clearly presents both the range of skills that are required to work with clients from, for example, refugee backgrounds, with the means to assess which role is required with a particular client, at a particular time.

It has also helped us to identify the gaps in our own mix of skills, the need for more styles of support than we can hope to provide within our own agency, and the limited opportunities we have to access more traditional means of support. This latter factor is a specific consequence of immigration policies that result in the ethnic communities lacking sufficient "critical mass" to provide their own infrastructure, as already discussed. From this we have been more easily able to identify what interventions do not work (and why), the areas in which we need more training or cultural advice, and the resources that we need to help clients access services from their own communities.

Advocacy, at local, national, and international levels, has become an integral component of the way in which we work. This has exposed us to some criticism, especially from those referring agencies who must "hold" clients while our waiting list grows. Also, it does not sit squarely with our founder specifications. We have been unable, however, to resist the compelling pressure from our clients that, at least initially, this is what they require of us most. Additionally, as an agency committed to human rights issues and social change, it is a role that we consider integral to our very existence.

CONCLUDING REFLECTIONS

Now as we move into the world of a 5-year-old, having gone beyond immobility, speechlessness, and total dependency, the knowledge that we have gained from our clients and our own staff debates suggests that traditional Western clinical preparations for working cross culturally are deficient in a significant way.

Professional training curriculum commence teaching about the significant theoreticians from, predominantly, European psychology and education. In New Zealand this is then extended to consider issues of biculturalism, which has become a legal (as well as moral) requirement of professional training. Later, and usually as an "add-on" or "optional extra," cross-cultural training may have its place. It is encouraging that this preparation for clinical work with a wider range of clients has seen significant developments in recent decades.

Is it, though, the most effective way? It seems that one of the most significant aspects of training in cross-cultural work is the requirement that trainees must be made aware of, and then challenge, the assumptions that inform their beliefs and understandings. We all must come to the realization that what we base our assumptions on may not be universally relevant. This is central to the ability with which we are able to accommodate the expectations of our culturally diverse clients.

Given that the ability to enter the clients' world devoid of restricting assumptions, prejudices, and predeterminations is crucial to the success with which effective support can be provided, does it not make more sense that this be provided earlier in the training experience? Rather than commencing training with models that "fit" (and confirm) our belief systems, and are, thus, more easily integrated, if we were to start with cross-cultural training perhaps this would assist all workers in the "helping" professions to work more sensitively with clients from *any* cultural background. The emphasis then becomes one of engaging with the clients in ways that allow an understanding of their world rather than the inevitable "shortcuts" that result when we assume that we "know." The benefits for all clients could be quite profound!

REFERENCES

Abbott, M. (Ed). (1989), *Refugee resettlement and well being.* Auckland: Mental Health Foundation of New Zealand.

Adams, C., & Gilbert, J. (1998). Providing effective counselling services to Australia's ethnic minority groups. *Australian Social Work, 51*(2), 33–39.

Aristotle, P. (2001a, April), *Health issues for resettled refugees.* Paper presented at the International Conference on the Reception and Integration of Resettled Refugees, Stockholm, Sweden.

Aristotle, P. (2001b, April), *Responding to the needs of survivors of torture and trauma among resettled refugees.* Paper presented at the International Conference on the Reception and Integration of Resettled Refugees, Stockholm, Sweden.

Atkinson, D., Thompson, C., & Grant, S. (1993). A Three-Dimensional Model for Counseling Racial/Ethnic Minorities. *The Counseling Psychologist, 21*(2), 257–277.

Bemak, F., Chung, R.C.-Y. & Bornemann, T. (1996). Counseling and psychotherapy with refugees. In P. Pederson, J. Draguns, W. Lomers, & J. Trimble (Eds.), *Counseling across cultures* (pp. 243–265). London: Sage.

Blackwell, R. (1989) *The disruption and reconstitution of family, network and community systems following torture, organised violence and exile.* Paper presented at The Second International Conference of Centres, Institutions and Individuals Concerned with the Care of Victims of Organised Violence, Costa Rica.

Bracken, P., Giller, J., & Summerfield, D. (1997). Rethinking mental health work with survivors of wartime violence and refugees. *Journal of Refugee Studies, 10*(4), 431–442.

Cariceo, C.M. (1998). Challenges in cross-cultural assessment: Counselling refugee survivors of torture and trauma. *Australian Social Work, 51*(2), 49–53.

Cotton, P. (2001, June). *Family reunion: An examination of family reunion issues, viewed from the perspective of RMS New Zealand.* Paper distributed at the UNHCR Global Tripartite Consultations, Geneva, Switzerland.

Maslow, A. (1954). *Motivation and personality*, New York: Harper.

Mollica, R. (1989). Developing effective mental health policies and service for traumatised refugee patients. In D. Koslow & E. Salett (Eds.). *Crossing Cultures in Mental Health* (pp. 101–115), Washington, DC: International Counseling Centre.

NZAW (New Zealand Association of Social Workers). (1993). *Code of ethics.* Auckland: NZASW.

NZIS (New Zealand Immigration Service). (2001, April). *Refugee resettlement to New Zealand.* Paper presented at the International Conference on the Reception and Integration of Resettled Refugees, Stockholm, Sweden.

Sinclair, K. (1959). *A history of New Zealand.* London: Penguin.

Sue, S., & Zane, N. (1987). The role of culture and cultural techniques in psychotherapy, a critique and reformulation. *American Psychologist, 42*(1), 37–45.

Tribe, R. (1999). Therapeutic work with refugees living in exile: Observations on clinical practice. *Counselling Psychology Quarterly, 12*(3), 233–243.

Chapter 30

The Afghanistan Situation: Refugees in War and in Flight

Fred Bemak and Rita Chi-Ying Chung

INTRODUCTION

Given the recent events of September 11, 2001, in mid-October 2001 the United Nations High Commission for Refugees (UNHCR, 2001a) estimated that the largest growing group of refugees in the world during the past 12 months has been Afghan refugees. The rapid increase of Afghan refugees is a result of the war and a devastating drought, with estimates that the number of Afghan refugees in Pakistan alone has increased by approximately 800,000 people. This does not include the large numbers of people who fled to the Pakistan and Tajikistan borders (as of mid-October 2001 UNHCR estimated this number at 180,000 and rapidly growing) and became stranded there when the borders were shut down.

The estimates of projected refugees continue to climb dramatically, making the total numbers of refugees difficult to ascertain. In the third week of October 2001 the UN Population Fund estimated that 2 million would flee into surrounding countries (Mann, 2001). Simultaneously the director for the U.S. Agency for International Development's task force on Central Asia reported that there were 3 million Afghan refugees inside Pakistan, with projections that another million would arrive during the next 3 months. He further indicated that 400,000 more people were expected to flee to Iran and more than 100,000 could eventually go to the northern borders (Ricks & DeYoung, 2001). UNHCR (2001b) estimates reported that the 3.6 million Afghan refugees who had already relocated to Iran and Pakistan constitute the largest refugee population worldwide, which causes concern to the organization.

The number of refugees from Afghanistan is not only based on the current war. Afghanistan has been at war for many years, and since 1979 when the Soviet Union invaded Afghanistan more than 6 million refugees (prior to the more immediate mass migration of hundreds of thousands of refugees) fled the country (Lipson & Onidian, 1992). The consequences of the long-standing conflict with the Soviet Union that ended in 1989 resulted in devastation for Afghanistan. As of 3 years ago, not counting the current war, more than 1 million people were killed (Rasekh, Bauer, Manos, & Iacopino, 1998), leaving behind 5 to 20 million landmines. The pre-1979 strong bonds of kinship, lineage, and tribe affiliations were no longer in place to maintain social and psychological stability. Thus, after 1989 government control frequently shifted. Therefore, long before the Taliban came to power "order" in Afghanistan was unrecognizable (Schulz & Schulz, 1999).

CURRENT STATUS

The Taliban are now the ruling group in Afghanistan, although there are remaining factions that resist its rule. Their strong leanings toward fundamental religious Islamic order has resulted in strict laws that prohibit women from receiving an education, mandate men to grow beards, require regular daily prayer, and the adoption of strict religious practices. An overarching theme of the Taliban is to maintain religious and spiritual "purity" in life, adhering to a stern interpretation of the Koran. At the time of this writing, the Taliban is under severe and continuous attack by a coalition of allied countries after the September 11, 2001, destruction of the World Trade Center and the attack on the Pentagon.[1]

Despite the strong religious emphasis and governance, Afghanistan is the greatest producer of heroin in the world. Schulz and Schulz (1999) report that Afghanistan controls 96% of worldwide opium with production rising 25% in1997. Profits have been estimated to be $37 billion a year (Appleby, 2001), money that supports the Taliban government. Even with heroin profits, Afghanistan remains one of the poorest countries in the world. Statistics reveal that life expectancy is 45 years, infant mortality rates are extremely high (165 of 1000), and child mortality rates remain among the highest in the world (257 of 1000) (End of the Line, 2001). Safe drinking water is available in only 39% of the urban areas and only a miniscule 5% of rural areas. Malnutrition is a large problem with 35% of children under 5 being affected. The country falls far short of being able to produce its own food, having the capacity to make only 2 million tons of grain, or half a percentage of the 400 million tons needed.

The overwhelming majority of Afghans are Muslims with most coming from the Sunni branch, although there are 19 ethnic groups in the country. Two major languages used are *Dari* (Afghanistan Farsi) and *Pashto*. The population is heterogeneous and divided based on ethnicity, political views, social class, and place of origin (urban or rural). Prayer in Afghanistan is similar to other Islamic countries and is conducted five times a day facing Mecca either privately, in a mosque, or in a *jumat (*congregation). Allah's command, as written in the *Qur'an*, delineates rules of conduct and behavior. It is expected that one who follows the laws of Allah will maintain cleanliness and keep a diet that avoids pork and alcohol.

THE RULING TALIBAN

The Taliban came to power toward the end of 1994. Generally, the Taliban leaders and members were raised in the camps during the Soviet regime and many of them were soldiers in the war against the Soviets. Since they come from a generally younger age group, they have virtually never experienced a time of peace in Afghanistan, being raised in a war-torn country and witnessing daily occurrences of violence and national disarray. With this as their foundation, there are many reports of governance by terror by the Taliban for violations of Taliban law. It has been reported that punishment ceremonies were a regular Friday occurrence that took place in a filled Kabul stadium of 30,000, including children who are sometimes forced to attend (Amnesty International, 2000). Morning mosque prayers were followed with beheadings, floggings, and amputations for those who have violated religious laws (Schulz & Schulz, 1999). Incidents of destroying property, fields, irrigation systems, and homes were also reported as a form of punishment (Amnesty International, 2000).

The Taliban now control two-thirds of the country, with the strongest holdouts concentrated in northern Afghanistan (Rasekh et al., 1998). Prior to Taliban rule life was very different. Women were permitted to go to coeducational schools and constituted 70% of the teaching workforce; women represented 50% of civil servants having equal representation as men, and 40% of urban physicians were women (Rasekh et al., 1998; Mulrine, 2001). In fact, women were able to move about independently in public, pursue self-selected career choices, and could choose their own style of dress (Rasekh et al., 1998).

There has been a growing list of restrictions by the Taliban government in their attempt to retain "purity." Music and movies have been banned. Parties, telephones and audio and video equipment are no longer allowed. In an attempt to more effectively mandate that men grow long beards, electric razors have also been disallowed. Some children's goods have also been outlawed so that toys, dolls, card games, and board games are illegal under the Taliban. Cameras and photographs have also been prohibited as well as pictures of people or animals. In an attempt to restrict information that is not religiously or spiritually pure, newspapers, magazines, and many books have also been banned. Finally, cigarettes and alcohol have been determined to be against the law (Schulz & Schulz, 1999).

TRADITIONAL CUSTOMS

There are many traditional customs and practices in Afghanistan. Marriages are arranged, ideally between first cousins, which maintains family linkages and bonds. Women typically marry between 14 and 16 years of age and have an average of 5 to 6 children. The extended family is the cornerstone of Afghan family life, averaging 50 to 75 people within tribal units of 1000 or more people (Lipson & Onidian, 1992). Obligation and responsibility to the family is critical to the Afghan social life and psychological well-being. Obedience to elders or one's husband is essential and expected so that children are raised to respect and obey those who older than them. Afghanistan is a strong patriarchal society where men are clearly the heads of family. Polygamy (as many as four wives) is acceptable but depends on affordability. Generally, women are less educated than men and establish almost exclusive social networks with female relatives.

WOMEN AND CHILDREN

Women and children have been the most affected by the Taliban government. Prior to the imposed rules of the Taliban regime, western doctors reported that a vast majority of women showed psychiatric disorders caused by isolation, loss, and trauma (Schulz & Schulz, 1999). In early 1998 the Physicians for Human Rights of the American Medical Association conducted a study of 160 Afghan women who were either living in Kabul or had recently immigrated to Pakistan (Rasekh et al., 1998). Over one-fifth reported incidents of abuse, with 84% subjected to public beatings and 2% were tortured. Violations that resulted in being charged with an offense included not completely covering their face, hands or feet, not wearing a *burqa* (robe covering entire body and face), wearing stylish clothes, wearing white socks or shoes, and wearing shoes that made noise when they walked. Findings showed that 52% of the women reported to be in fair or poor physical health, with over one-third of those reporting that their poor health interfered with daily functioning. Almost one-fifth reported chronic headaches, while 81% indicated mental health problems. Forty-two percent had posttraumatic stress disorder (PTSD) symptoms, 97% had major depression, 86% reported high levels of anxiety, and 84% claimed to have lost at least one family member during the war.

Schulz and Schulz (1999) have summarized hundreds of reports of women being flogged and beaten, sometimes almost to the point of death. There are also reported cases of punishment that included feet amputation, faces and bodies sprayed with acid, being shot, and being subjected to stoning. It was reported that when the Taliban took over in Herat the women marched in protest. The Taliban quickly surrounded them, doused the leader of the group with kerosene, and burned her alive.

AFGHAN PERSPECTIVES ON HEALTH

The translation for the word "health" in *Dari* is "whole" or "wholeness" (Shorish-Shamley, 1991). The Afghan culture emphasizes the interrelationships between the concept of purity and impurity with good health. Important in the culture is regular exercise, preparing and eating fresh food, maintaining a balanced diet, getting proper rest, and staying warm (Lipson & Onidian, 1992) by having adequate clothing and shelter. Maintaining a clean home and keeping children clean are fundamental to the culture. In line with maintaining cleanliness it is important to subscribe to certain rituals such as washing one's hands, feet, face, nose, and inside of the throat before prayer and washing thoroughly after urinating, passing gas, bowel movements, sleeping, vomiting, or bleeding. After sexual intercourse one must thoroughly wash before praying (Lipson & Onidian, 1992).

Although prayer is considered useful in healing illness, one must seek advice of religious leaders and spiritual healers to know the specific verses of the Qur'an that can effectively help a specific illness. Ritual prayer may vary according to the need and most effective way to promote healing. For example, *ta'wiz* requires that special verses are written down and then wrapped in clean cloth and worn as a necklace, *shuist* is where the written verse is soaked in water and followed by a ritual drinking of the water, or *dudi* is when the written verse is burned with incense that is inhaled by the ill person. Each of these practices are used according to what would be regarded as the most appropriate way to treat a particular illness.

The Afghans' conceptualization of illness and health is based on the will of Allah. When one is not adhering to the principles of Islam, there is illness, making it important to be patient with the process of healing, which is truly a course of action that results in repurification. Illness may be caused by the natural elements such as germs, dirt, cold, or wind, although it can be derived from impurities or improper care of the body. Healing may also occur using traditional humoral concepts of Arabic-Persian medicine that emphasizes the balance of "hot" and "cold." This balance may be achieved through the regulation of food and drink and medicinal herbs. Typically herbs are prepared by an older woman who is usually a family member (Lipson & Onidian, 1992).

In addition to impurities and the lack of balance, *Jinns*, or supernatural beings, as well as the *nazar* (evil eye), or punishment from God, may cause illness. *Jinns* may be good or bad and are described in the Qur'an as ghosts or spirits. The belief is that *nazar* is caused by someone looking at another person. Caution is especially important when people are "green-eyed" individuals (impure people) who are more likely to induce *nazar* or individuals who are already ill. *Nazar* can also be unintentionally caused by expressing excessive admiration or love for someone else without remembering to say "In the name of Allah." It is easy to distinguish *nazar* from other illnesses since it is brought on rapidly without apparent cause but can generally be traced back to a precipitating occurrence. Certain people may be particularly susceptible such as beautiful women, children, and fortunate people, although they may take precautions and be protected by charms or amulets, such as blue stones or beads, or protective marks on the forehead. Religious leaders or spiritual healers may introduce special healing rituals using white powders, eggs, prayers, or saying special verses (Shorish-Shamley, 1991).

REFUGEE MENTAL HEALTH ISSUES

Afghan refugees, regardless of the reason that led to being a refugee, face many issues. They have experienced severe loss due to years of war and recent drought. For example, they have lost their homes, relatives (many of whom were killed), their social networks, communities, and country. A 1991 study reported that the Afghan refugee community in San Francisco was found to be experiencing high incidents of depression and psychosomatic illnesses (Lipson, 1991). Although no recent studies have been conducted investigating the fall 2001 Afghan refugee migration following declared war and attacks by the United States and the United Kingdom, we would suggest that similar to other refugees from war-torn countries the prevalence of mental health problems for this population is rapidly increasing. We would also suggest that given the war situation in Afghanistan and the closed borders, there would also be high incidents of PTSD.

It is suggested that the further destruction of social networks and losses as a result of the war would create significant difficulties for the Afghan refugees, especially given the importance of strong extended family units and tribes. The difficult situation of being without food or shelter further exacerbates the mental health issues. In addition, the inability to maintain important rituals such as cleanliness, eating and preparing fresh food, and maintaining a good diet will likely cause an imbalance that will have the potential to perpetuate disharmony and subsequent psychological problems. These increasing mental health concerns are juxtaposed to the devaluation with traditional Western mental health practices in the Afghan culture. For example, in the San Francisco Afghan refugee community, even though there is a majority consensus that mental health is a prevalent issue in the community, there is concurrence that the utilization of Western counseling is a last resort (Lipson & Onidian, 1992) given skepticism about confidentiality within their communities, concern over showing weakness, reluctance to disclose personal information to a stranger, and personal embarrassment and shame to express and expose oneself. Thus it will be critical for Western trained psychotherapists to be sensitive to these issues and be able to align with traditionally based healers who practice culturally bound healing rituals within the Afghan community.

It is also important to maintain an understanding of the traditional role of women and their more recent history within Afghan society. Being subjected to strict laws and punishment by the Taliban, women are likely to be hesitant to trust someone in a position of authority such as a psychotherapist. Furthermore, it would be culturally awkward for them to work with male therapists, especially at the earlier stages of migration and acculturation. This presents issues that must be fully understood and carefully addressed as psychotherapists work with female refugees from Afghanistan.

It is also important to recognize the importance of certain valued cultural characteristics in the Afghan culture. One example is the importance and meaning of status whereby Afghans will be overly courteous to mental health professionals who by virtue of their position as professionals have status (Lipson & Meleis, 1989). It is important to recognize this behavior as deference because of role, rather than compliance or agreement with intervention strategies. Another example is the difficulty in determining events and backgrounds of Afghan refugees. Since it is culturally appropriate to communicate through storytelling (Lipson & Meleis, 1983), there must be an acknowledgment of communication style without expectations for simple and direct answers. In addition, given the collectivistic nature of the Afghan society, it is important to address entire family systems and family needs and issues, rather than individual problems. Based on the strong patriarchal foundation in the Afghan society, addressing men first is necessary in order to honor the family structure and the role of the man as head of the household. Where this may be particularly sensitive is when working with children. Frequently children pick up language faster than their parents or elders and acquire better language skills. This places them in an awkward position of being able to translate for their parents and elders and causes an abrupt and uncomfortable role reversal in traditionally bound patriarchal families. It is helpful in these situations to acknowledge the authority of the elders first, asking if they will allow the younger members of the family to translate for them rather than just assuming that the child will be the cultural liaison and hence speaking directly with the child rather than the older family members.

Finally, of equal importance are the thoughts, feelings, reactions, and political beliefs of the psychotherapist. The events of the previous war with the Soviet Union and more recent war with the United States and United Kingdom affected individuals worldwide. The countries that more recent Afghan refugees are fleeing to such as Pakistan or Iran, as well as other countries where Afghan refugees live, have strong and varied reactions to the Taliban and the current war. The views and reactions to these highly volatile wars will generate feelings and reactions by mental health professionals that will impact the reception and treatment of refugees. Despite these powerful situations and events, psychotherapists must remain neutral and objective to provide the best treatment possible for the Afghan refugees.

SUMMARY

Due to the global threat of terrorism and the worldwide efforts to eradicate terrorism an unfortunate result of this will be an influx of refugees. The recent Afghan refugees are an example of the joint United States and United Kingdom's efforts to eliminate terrorist residing in Afghanistan due to the events of the September 11, 2001, attacks on the United States. It is therefore critical for mental health professionals in resettlement countries to understand the refugee population from a historical, religious, sociopolitical, cultural, and gender viewpoint. Furthermore, therapists must also be aware, acknowledge, understand, and accept refugees' cultural perspectives on mental health and healing.

The events of September 11, 2001, have affected people worldwide. Therefore, it is importance for therapists to acknowledge their own biases, political viewpoints, and negative reactions to clients who come from the same countries or have the same religious backgrounds as the perpetrators. Working with this population, requires therapists to have heighten awareness of their countertransference issues.

NOTE

1. To date the United States and its allies have declared the war in Afghanistan a success. However, the fighting continues even though a new government has been established in Afghanistan. This has impacted other regions and fueled ongoing conflicts, such as, the situation with Israel and the Palestinians. Recently, the conflict between these 2 groups has escalated to the point of being more violent than in the past 10 years with daily shootings, bombings, attacks, and killings by Palestinian terrorists and Israeli troop invasions of Palestinian communities and refugee camps. Simultaneously, fighting has broken out between Muslim and Hindu factions in India. The post-September 11 war on terrorism has led to the capture and detainment of terrorists worldwide who are currently being imprisoned, detained, and interrogated. As the global search for terrorists continues international bank accounts suspected of being related to terrorist groups have been frozen. International discussions and reevaluation regarding cooperation against the war on terrorism continues to determine national policies and global relationships. A major result of these ongoing conflicts is continued displacement of individuals and families as their communities are destroyed, contributing to increased in-country and out-of-country refugee migration.

REFERENCES

Appleby, S. (2001). Reaping the whirlwind. *Insight in the News, 17*(139), 226–228.

Amnesty International. (2000). Annual Report 2000: Afghanistan. Available at http://web.amnesty.org. Accessed 10/1/01.

End of Line. (2001, Feb. 26). End of the line: Afghanistan's three-year drought is scorching the earth and killing its children. Now millions of refugees are pouring into camps that offer little food, water or medical aid. Will the world help? *Time International, 157*(8), 18–23.

Lipson, J.G. (1991). Afghan refugee health: Some findings and suggestions. *Qualitative Health Research, 1,* 349–369.

Lipson, J.G., & Meleis, A.I. (1983). Issues in health care of Middle Eastern patients. *Western Journal of Medicine, 139,* 854–861.

Lipson, J.G., & Meleis, A.I. (1989). Methodological issues in research with immigrants. *Medical Anthropology, 11,* 325–337.

Lipson, J., & Onidian, P. (1992). Health issues of Afghan refugees in California. *The Western Journal of Medicine, 157*(3), 271–286.

Mann, J. (2001, October 26). Facing facts of life in refugee camps. *The Washington Post,* p. C7.

Murline, A. (2001). Unveiled threat. *U.S. News and World Report.* Available at http://www.usnews.com/usnews/issue/011015.ideas/women.htm. Accessed on 10/18/01.

Pomfret, J. (2001 Oct. 18). Afghans now questions U.S. strikes. *Washington Post:* A22.

Rasekh, Z., Bauer, H., Manos, M., & Iacopino, V. (1998). Women's health and human rights in Afghanistan. *Journal of the American Medical Association, 280*(5), 449–455.

Ricks, T.E., & DeYoung, K. (2001, October 27). A week of setbacks tests U.S. patience and its plan of attack. *Washington Post*, pp. A1, A16.

Schulz, J., & Schulz, L. (1999). The darkest of ages: Afghan women under the Taliban. *Peace and Conflict: Journal of Peace Psychology, 5*(3), 237–254.

Shorish-Shamley, Z. (1991). *The self and other in Afghan cosmology: Concepts of health and illness among Afghan refugees*. Unpublished doctoral dissertation. University of Wisconsin-Madison.

UNHCR. (United Nations High Commission on Refugees). (2001a). Refugees by numbers. Available at http://www.unhcr.ch. Accessed 10/18/01.

UNHCR. (United Nations High Commission on Refugees). (2001b). Afghans facing "unimaginable hardships." Available at http://www/unhcr.ch. Accessed on 10/18/01.

Chapter 31

Conclusion

This book presents a comprehensive overview of psychotherapy and counseling with the refugee population. To fully understand, appreciate, and be aware of the refugee situation that will lead to effective mental health training, treatment, and services, this book provides an extensive discussion on the state of the refugee. It examines the history of refugee services that provides a context for modern-day global policy, reviews current international and governmental debates on the status of refugees, and gives a detailed discussion on the premigration history and trauma and postmigration adjustment issues.

It is clear that working with refugees' psychosocial adjustment in the resettlement country is a highly complex process, necessitating a consideration of multiple factors that go far beyond traditional training. It requires that mental health professionals reexamine their training and practice and adjust strategies, techniques, and even their theoretical orientation to serve this unique population. Practitioners must acquire different skills and abilities that oftentimes go far beyond Western-based counseling, developing far greater awareness, understanding, knowledge, and skills to effectively work with refugee populations.

Given the current large numbers of refugees who are living throughout the world and the growing population of refugees, it is overwhelming to think about their psychosocial needs. The population is immense and steadily expanding with situations such as the recent developments in Afghanistan. It is our prediction that given ongoing world conflict and disasters this population of displaced persons will continue to grow. Even with current statistics and large numbers of refugees, very few trainees study refugee mental health and very few professionals have had direct exposure to working or understanding this population.

Traditional training and practice in psychology, counseling, social work, and psychiatry do not account nor prepare professionals to work with the unique needs of this population.

Although psychology, counseling, social work, and psychiatry have made great strides in better addressing cross-cultural mental health, the cross-cultural issues facing refugees are rarely attended to, leaving professionals largely untrained in this area. We would maintain that it is essential in working with refugees to have a thorough knowledge and understanding of cross-cultural perspectives as they directly apply to the refugee population, which includes a knowledge and awareness of the cultural roots and backgrounds of specific refugee populations as well as the interplay and dynamics of working across cultures. It is also important to be aware of cultural belief systems that provide a framework for interventions with refugees as well as the importance of human rights and social justice with this population.

In addition to the cross-cultural issues in working with refugees, it is important to fully understand the refugee experience. Forced migration and movement have significant psychological ramifications for individuals, extended families, and collective communities. The presence of trauma and violence to varying degrees may be generalized to refugees and linked closely to mental health problems. Displacement uniformly causes loss and separation, which is an underpinning to the refugee experience. It is critical that mental health professionals have a full understanding of the experience itself and the aftermath of that experience as a foundation for working with refugees. Fundamental to this understanding is an ability to work with trauma, posttraumatic stress disorder, and depression, diagnoses that are higher among refugees. This is particularly important, since the characteristics and experiences of refugees are generally atypical to working in developed countries and absent from standardized training and supervision.

There are a number of fundamental issues that are basic to understanding and effectively providing counseling for refugees. Issues relevant to acculturation, including theories that describe stages and processes within new cultures, provide valuable information for professionals. It is also important to recognize one's goals and values as a professional so that there are not impositions or demands for adaptation at the expense of cultural and personal identity and psychological well-being. Psychosocial and cultural adjustment has a significant relationship to mental health, requiring an acute awareness by mental health professionals. In addition, an understanding and acceptance of survivor's guilt is important to understand and patiently work with as refugees go through a process of healing. Language barriers present another issue and have been closely linked with cultural adaptation and mental health. To add to this already extensive list, mental health professionals must also understand the relationship of education, employment, and welfare on mental health, and the very complicated situation facing refugees with regards to these three areas.

In combination with the issues discussed above, there are several other highly important issues that are unique to refugees and have serious impact on their psychological well-being. One of these is the shift in family relationships including authority, responsibility, and role, given the new sets of pressures and demands of survival. Particularly in countries that are collectivistic in nature, the changes in family dynamics may play a major part in mental health. Another issue is the institutionalized and personalized experience of racism and discrimination encountered by refugees. Resettlement policies may create unwelcoming and highly pressured demands for acculturation that is reflected in personal and societal communications such as the sign posted on a lawn that the first author saw in a small community. The sign was visible on a main street in town in front of a house and read, "Keep off Hmongs." This type of very direct response frequently mirrors attitudes and values held in the larger society.

To effectively work with refugees and address these complicated and difficult issues, Bemak and Chung have proposed the Multilevel Model (MLM) of counseling and psychotherapy, a four-level cross-cultural intervention approach that integrates traditional Western psychotherapy with indigenous healing methods, cultural empowerment, and psychoeducational training. The MLM takes into account the various aspects that are particular to the refugee experience. Given our belief that it is essential to integrate the past, present, and future at different developmental points in the process of furthering psychological well-being, the model incorporates premigration and past trauma, current experiences of acculturation and psychosocial adaptation, and future perspectives and goals. Inherent in this multitiered model is the inclusion of cultural belief systems, worldviews, acculturation, the need to effectively address racism, discrimination and oppression in the resettlement country, which underscore issues in social justice, and the influence of resettlement policy on mental health. The confluence of these issues provides a holistic framework that conceptualizes a fluid and integrated strategy to meet the multifaceted needs of the refugee population. Furthermore, for mental health professionals to be effective with this population it is necessary for the professional to "step outside the box," and go beyond the traditional boundaries of professional Western training and practice. Successful mental health work within the varied and complex world of refugees necessitates an openness and willingness to truly be open to differences in culture, worldviews, and healing practices, to become practitioners who are well versed and trained in Western mental health, yet open to creative forms of intervention from perspectives that are rooted in family and community traditions, and to become advocates and supporters for social justice and equity for refugee clients.

Index

About the Authors
and Contributors

FRED BEMAK is a Professor and the Program Coordinator for the Counseling and Development Program, Graduate School of Education at George Mason University. His work has focused on cross-cultural psychology and at-risk populations including refugee and immigrant mental health and psychosocial adjustment. Bemak has provided consultation and training and given seminars and presentations in over 30 countries and throughout the United States. He is a former Fulbright Scholar, a Kellogg International Fellow, and a recipient of the International Exchange of Experts and Research Fellowship through the World Rehabilitation Fund. He has been working nationally and internationally in the area of refugee adjustment and acculturation for the past 20 years as a researcher, clinician and clinical consultant and has published extensively in this area.

RITA CHI-YING CHUNG is an Associate Professor in the Counseling and Development Program, Graduate School of Education, George Mason University. Her research focuses on the psychosocial adjustment of refugees and immigrants, interethnic group relations and racial stereotypes, coping strategies in dealing with racism and its impact of psychological well-being, and cross-cultural and multicultural issues in mental health, achievement motivation and aspirations. Chung has lived and worked in the Pacific Rim, Asia, and Latin America, been a consultant for the World Bank, and conducted research and published extensively in the area of immigrant and refugee mental health and cross-cultural mental health.

PAUL PEDERSEN is a Visiting Professor in the Department of Psychology at the University of Hawaii. He has taught at the University of Minnesota, Syracuse

University, University of Alabama at Birmingham, and for six years at universities in Taiwan, Malaysia and Indonesia. He has authored, co-authored, or edited 40 books, 99 articles and 72 chapters on aspects of multicultural counseling. He is a Fellow in Divisions 9, 17, 45, and 52 of the American Psychological Association.

LEWIS APTEKAR is a Professor of Counselor Education at San Jose State University in San Jose, California. He is currently on leave from this position to do research on the mental health of refugees and the displaced under the auspices of the World Health Organization, the Free University of the Netherlands, and Addis Ababa University in Ethiopia. His academic awards include two Fulbright scholarships (Colombia and Swaziland), and the Kellogg/Partners of the Americas Fellowship in International Development. His books include *Street Children of Cali* (1988) and *Environmental Disasters in Global Perspective* (1994), and he has published over 50 chapters and articles in scientific journals.

NANCY BARON is the Co-Director of Global Psychiatric and Psycho-Social Initiatives (GPSI) and provides consultation, training, program design, development and evaluation for UN organizations and international and local NGOs in community and family focused psycho-social and mental health programming in conflict and post-conflict countries. For the past 13 years, Baron has lived and worked in countries during and after war including Uganda, Southern Sudan, Burundi, Sri Lanka, Cambodia, Kosovo, Albania, Guinea Conakry, Sierra Leone, and Indonesia. She is presently based in Africa.

ALAN CHAPMAN is currently the Director of the Wellington Refugees as Survivors Centre working with refugees who have immigrated to New Zealand. Chapman has had a 30-year career in health social work. During that time he has worked as a clinician, a manager of a mental health service, a senior policy analyst for the Ministry of Health before becoming manager of Wellington Refugees as Survivors (RAS) Centre in 1997.

EDVARD HAUFF is a Consultant Psychiatrist at Ullevaal University Hospital in Oslo where he is Director of Psychiatric Education. He is also Professor of Transcultural Psychiatry at the University of Oslo and has a part-time private practice in psychotherapy as well as being an advisor to the Cambodian Mental Health Development Programme. Hauff is the Deputy Secretary General for the World Association for Psychosocial Rehabilitation (WAPR).

SOLVIG EKBLAD is an Associate Professor in Transcultural Psychology in the Division of Psychiatry at the Karolinska Institute in Stockholm. She has extensive experience working in the mental health field and has had major research grants investigating the psychosocial needs of displaced refugees from various parts of the world. She is the author of numerous articles and publications on immigrant and refugee adjustment, has presented at major conferences around the world, and is one of Sweden's most visible refugee scholars and clinicians.

SUNY BROCKPORT

3 2815 00853 0050

RC 451 .5 .A2 B37 2003

Bemak, Fred.

Counseling refugees